T0197186

Zenful: the art of feeling at 'point zero' within the self. An integrated mind and body that is happy, focused, calm and still; able to make confident decisions that are aligned with meaning and purpose.

Zenful Business: mastering the above state in your working life to enjoy a successful and meaningful career that brings you bliss.

Zenful Business

11 Models for Flow and Peak Performance at Work

DEBBIE PASK

BALBOA.
PRESS
A DIVISION OF HAY HOUSE

Balboa Press books may be ordered through booksellers or by contacting:

Balboa Press
A Division of Hay House
1663 Liberty Drive
Bloomington, IN 47403
www.balboapress.com.au
1 (877) 407-4847

Print information available on the last page.

ISBN: 978-1-5043-0163-3 (sc)
ISBN: 978-1-5043-0164-0 (e)

Balboa Press rev. date: 04/06/2016

Contents

Dedicated to the amazing people who have helped both my journey in life, and my working life;

James Pask
Susan Pine
Fiona Santangelo
Claudia Chambers
John Rehn
Michelle Sullivan

AND – the lovely Manly Business Masterminds group...thank you, thank you for being such rock stars. The chapter on Soul Colleagues was inspired by you!

Glossary

Alpha Wave: increased state of awareness and ability to think more creatively, visually and intuitively (a slowing/ smoothing of brainwaves). Our brain patterns slow to a pace where our cognitive functions increase and different parts of the brain light up. In other words, we get smarter and can manifest better when in alpha.

Base Chakra: The core energy point located in the groin of our body based on the Indian system of 'Chakras' energy points. Each chakra point governs a different aspect of your life force and the Base Chakra specifically relates to money, business/money, career, community and tribe. For more information on the 'Chakras' see Anodea Judith's book *Wheels of Life*

Bright Shiny Object (BSO): An opportunity or idea presented that distracts one from their job at hand by offering the promise of excitement and success. Most BSO's are impulsive ideas that are not underpinned by logic or data.

Clairaudient: the power or faculty of hearing something not present to the ear but regarded as having objective reality.

Clairsentient: is a form of intuition through sensing or feeling through the body. The prefix 'clair', means 'clear', and the suffix 'sentience' means feeling.

Clairvoyant: having or claiming to have the power of seeing objects or actions beyond the range of natural vision.

Conscious Mind: is the state or quality of awareness, or, of being aware of an external object or something within oneself. It has been **defined** as: sentience, awareness, subjectivity, the ability to experience or to feel, wakefulness, having a sense of selfhood, and the executive control system of the **mind**. (Wikipedia)

Cytophylactic: process of letting things in via the skin.

Debbie Pask

Dadirri: The art of deep listening to create a healing state.

Electro-magnetic: relating to the interrelation of electric currents and magnetic fields around the body.

Empath: A person who is capable of feeling the emotions of others despite the fact that they themselves are not going through the same situation. Urbandictionary.com

Energy healing: is an umbrella term for any therapy that manipulates the energy circuits in our physical or subtle bodies to regain balance and facilitate our body's innate healing mechanisms.

Entrained: When two or more energies meet and form a vibrational match, creating a flow with one other. The Merriam Webster dictionary defines Entrain as 'to draw along with or after oneself'.

Epigenetics: the study of changes in organisms caused by modification of gene expression (cellular memories) rather than alteration of the genetic code itself.

EQ: Emotional Intelligence adapted from the concept of IQ (academic intelligence, Intelligence Quotient)

Esoteric: intended for or likely to be understood by only a small number of people with a specialised knowledge or interest in that topic.

Fibonacci: The Fibonacci sequence is named after Italian mathematician Fibonacci. His 1202 book *Liber Abaci* introduced the sequence to Western European mathematics.

Gen Y: Today's teenagers or kids in their 20s. Growing up with too much information being pushed upon them, as well as seeing their parents get lost in the 'system' and wind up retrenched or burnt out. these guys have a different and less loyal work ethic to anyone above them and they constantly ask 'WHY?' as their addiction to information becomes stronger. They usually think they can change the world overnight; maybe they can?

Great Red Road / Great Blue Road: A Native American Indian concept describing life and death. The great red road is all about earth, body and your physical life. It is where you incarnate from Spirit into a body. The great blue road is the world of Spirit and is where you return after you leave your body – back up to the Spirit world to be reincarnated once again, having learned your life lessons.

Heart entrainment: When the wave frequencies of your heart meet and match the vibrational frequency of a third party heart wave frequency.

Heart Rhythm Coherence: Coherence, in any system, from the human body to social affairs, refers to a logical, orderly and harmonious connectedness between parts of a system or between people. When we speak of heart-rhythm coherence or physiological coherence, we are referring to a specific assessment of the heart's rhythms that appears as smooth, ordered and sine-wave like patterns. From a physics perspective, when we are in a coherent state, virtually no energy is wasted because our systems are performing optimally and there is synchronization between heart rhythms, the respiratory system, blood-pressure rhythms, etc. https://www.heartmath.org/support/faqs/research

Hologram: in reference to the earth, a three-dimensional image formed by the interference of light beams from a laser or other coherent light source.

Holographic Universe: the entire whole (universal) world or matrix as it appears to us with all of its code, information and structure; ultimately a 3D projection of data and frequencies.

I Ching: an ancient Chinese manual of divination based on eight symbolic trigrams and sixty-four hexagrams, interpreted in terms of the principles of Yin and Yang. Referred to as the Book Of Changes, it is designed as a guidance or prophetic tool to navigate one through life.

Karma: (in Hinduism and Buddhism) the sum of a person's actions in this and previous states of existence, viewed as deciding their fate in future existences.

Kinaesthetic: feeling emotions and discerning situations on a deep physical level through the reactions of the body.

Medicine Wheel: In some Native American cultures, the **medicine wheel** is a metaphor for a variety of spiritual concepts. A **medicine wheel** may also be a stone monument that illustrates this metaphor. https://en.wikipedia.org/wiki/**Medicine wheel**

Mindfulness: The state of being aware and present of your thoughts, feelings, self, identity and sensations going on around you.

Neuroplasticity: The *brain's* ability to reorganize itself by forming new neural connections throughout life. http://www.medicinenet.com/script/main/art.asp?articlekey=40362

NLP: Neuro-linguistic-programming, is an approach to communication, personal development, and psychotherapy created by Richard Bandler and John Grinder in California, United States in the 1970s. Its creators claim a connection between the neurological processes ('neuro'), language ('linguistic') and behavioural patterns learned through experience ('programming') and that these can be changed to achieve specific goals in life.

Personality A type: People who have a tendency to hurry, control things and want to swallow life in bulk quantities in case they miss out on their share. Usually over-achievers and dominant personalities.

Point Zero: The art of staying centred and balanced and calm (knowing exactly who and what you are) whilst the events of the external world play out. Point Zero is a deep concept which has many layers of mastery, but ultimately it requires one to be so deeply rooted and confident in your sense of self (beyond the physical) that anything could happen and you feel in control and peaceful.

Quantum Science: means scientific study of the smallest possible discrete unit of any physical property, such as energy or matter. RNA: ribonucleic acid, a nucleic acid present in all living cells. Its principal role is to act as a messenger carrying instructions from DNA for controlling the synthesis of proteins, although in some viruses RNA rather than DNA carries the genetic information. https://en.wikipedia.org/wiki/**RNA**

Self-actualisation: the realization or fulfilment of one's talents and potentialities especially considered as a drive or need present in everyone.

SEO (search engine optimisation): An online strategy designed to capture and funnel traffic (customers) to your desired web page URL for a specific purpose.

Shadow: Parts of your identity or ego that you do not like, are unconscious of or try to hide due to shame or judgement. Can also refer to an event or incident in life that you cannot move on from, therefore creating a 'shadowy' or unresolved part of your personality. This experience has adverse effects on your psyche, creating a shadow or darker aspect of self that remains unconscious or suppressed in some way. In Jungian psychology, the shadow or "shadow aspect" may refer to an unconscious aspect of the personality which the conscious ego does not identify in itself. www.wikipedia.org

Shaman: Usually revered in indigenous tribes as a type of metaphysical medicine person who acts as an intermediary between the natural and supernatural worlds; life and death and using energy and the forces of nature to cure illness, foretell the future and control spiritual forces. A shaman is known to be able to face the 'death' or 'shadow' for someone and assist them to renew and heal.

Source Field: The energetic matrix that holds all of life together, the invisible layer of energy and frequency that holds time and space together to create what we see and feel in the world around us. All of life is connected to this matrix and hence there is a group consciousness that can be accessed.

Sovereign Self: The idea that there is no power or authority outside of you required to live your own independent life. You take full responsibility for your own actions.

Spirit: The invisible spark of life or energy that generates electricity and flow in your body. This energy is also referred to as higher self or soul, but fundamentally it is agreed that it holds wisdom and a higher level of consciousness than our brain. You don't need to be religious to believe that you have a Spirit.

Sub-Conscious Mind: The word **'subconscious'** represents an anglicized version of the French *subconscient* as coined by the psychologist Pierre Janet (1859-1947), who argued that underneath the layers of critical-thought functions of the conscious **mind** lay a powerful awareness that he called the **subconscious mind**. This mind is responsible for all of our memory recall and autopilot behaviours and habits that keep us safe and alive every day (also called unconscious mind).

Superconscious: the intuitive or 'Spirit' part of us that is non-rational, non-physical and connected to everything.

Torus Field: A torus field is an energy pattern that can sustain itself. In relation to the heart Torus field, it relates to the electro-magnetic energy that arcs out from the heart and back in again, sustaining an energy vibration and flow within itself.

Transcendence: the overcoming of the limits of the individual self and its desires in spiritual contemplation and realization.

Void: A place of the unknown. Womb of all potential. A black space of nothingness. It is also where we find brilliant intuitive answers as it is not limited by the programmed brain. Void: A non-logical, creative and empty space full of all possibilities to emerge. Also a place of not knowing and surrender whereby you wait patiently for the relevant solutions or information to present itself.

X Factor: a noteworthy special talent or quality; an indescribable quality or something about a person that you cannot put your finger on. (Urbandictionary.com)

My Story

I was 27 years old when I experienced my first major career burnout.

I started part time work at 11 years old, bought myself a double water-bed at 14 years old (they were very 'in' back then) and was running a small magazine division within a publishing company at 20 years of age. I was studying a full time philosophy degree whilst working full time in a busy (and highly creative) advertising agency called Saatchi and Saatchi in my early 20s. Working long hours - 8am start and finishing anywhere between 8pm and 10pm at night. Most nights I would do my university studies at work (or home) and finally have dinner later on. I remember having dinner sometimes at mid-night and I can recall throughout my advertising career not going home at all that day if we had a big new business pitch on and needed to work all through the night to get it done. This work late and get up early cycle meant that my working weeks were somewhere between 60 – 80 hours.

I do not resent this time, but can see now how out of whack and unhealthy it was. I clearly remember myself and a colleague in a pickle one afternoon in 2002. We were working on a huge new business pitch to retain our large telco client that was worth a lot of money to the agency. If we lost it, lots of jobs would be on the line and a serious revenue issue for our agency. It was a stupidly tight deadline and of course the art directors and account guys had dragged their feet with changes and additions to the document that needed to be printed as a hard copy book. We had a deadline of 3 pm to get to the client offices and get the stamp of 'delivered' on our book (credentials) otherwise we were disqualified from pitching. Considering 20 million was on the line, we rushed in a taxi over to the digital printing bureau at around 2.30 pm, who then proceeded to create (under extreme pressure from their number one client... us) the beautifully bound book. At 2.45 pm we madly searched for a taxi that would take us to the client offices ten minutes down the road to make the 3 pm deadline. And yes, the client was STAMPING the time of delivery at their mailroom, so we couldn't be one minute late. Of course, in Sydney there is often a lag at 3 pm as taxi drivers turn over shifts and it can be tricky to locate one. We stood on a main road waiting for one to go by but as every minute ticked over, and we started to sweat it out, we knew we weren't going to make it. So, we did what any crazy agency person would do. We stood in the middle of the road and madly waved down a car. Any car would do. Serial killer or not! Two young girls in their early 20s with a credentials book in tow, managed to convince a mother of two to stop for us – jump in her 4WD back boot without seatbelts, go off her school route to collect her kids and drive us to North Sydney in a crazed frenzy of busy traffic – to deliver our book at exactly 2.59 pm. Thank you to that lady out there...

I was earning well over six figures by the time I was 25 and had been elected to the board of directors at the largest advertising agency in Australia (at that time) at age 26. Back then I was apparently the youngest person to achieve board level status and certainly the youngest female. I made employee of the year in 2002 which was a big honour to me then as the Sydney office was 300+ people and they were all pretty committed and ambitious.

How had I done this? Sheer strength of character and will. My greatest gift and also my greatest downfall.

So what went wrong at 27 years old? I was pretty switched on, confident and enjoyed my career success. I enjoyed (and still very much do) the world of business and how it challenged my mind. I could handle pressure and was in control of my world. I certainly didn't feel unhappy on an intellectual level. I felt happy to get out of bed most days.

But somehow my body and my inner self did not seem to agree. I was putting on weight. I had IBS (irritable bowel syndrome) and serious adrenal fatigue. Little things would get on my nerves and if everything didn't run to schedule, I would lose my cool!

Waiting in queues did my head in. One day my automatic garage door failed to work and tears welled up inside of me, which frustrated me even more since I didn't consider myself a helpless and whinging princess. I was operating at such a pace of high out-put that I didn't realise how on edge I was. Nothing could go wrong. Any kind of wastefulness or inefficiency was not allowed on my watch. My outer appearance was pretty strong and charged up. But I didn't have the time to stay in the moment and be mindful. I was always chasing the next thing and achieving more and more. I was a working machine unaware there was a massive piece of life (and spiritual peace) I was missing out on.

I had been programmed to work hard and to over-achieve and my personality type was able to run with that script very, very easily. I was a good consumer and thought that was what life was about. Work, buy, work, buy. I didn't realise that there was a whole other connected world out there that I needed to keep me healthy, loving and creative.

A world where 'me' was not required to be performing, outputting or switched 'on' all of the time. A world where my wellbeing and self-love came before everything else. A world where rejuvenation is intrinsic. I didn't know about this world and how important it was/is to my health and creativity. As far as meaning and life purpose went, that didn't register one little bit. Nobody at school, that includes career guidance counsellors, ever really asked me that single and most fundamental question; 'What are you naturally great at? And what do you really love doing?'

I am not suggesting that you are as stressed out as I was back then. Or burnt out, or chasing success and money. Or allowing work problems to follow you back to your home life at the end of the day. Or have money dominating your career choices or lifestyle choices. Or feeling like you need to perform or 'output' something to be useful or good. Or that you need a 'big hotshot' career to be considered a man or a competent mother who can juggle both children and full time work. Sound familiar?

No matter where you are at with your working life, I think you will benefit from some of the concepts in this book, as your modern fast paced business life always infiltrates some part of you, to some degree. It is a part of being human. I have gathered some serious wisdom from my burnout at 27 years old (and the years of recovery since) and condensed this into 11 core models that I believe every western working person needs to experience the BEST and most Zenful working life we can have. If you don't care about energy, happiness, balance and flow, then don't read on...

I don't regret any of my career choices and experiences as they have led me to today. Some of the ideas presented in the book are a little left of field, because that is the new me – the post burnout me. She has a high performing western business background with an eastern bent of mindfulness and spirituality (really just a word for being conscious and intuitive). Some of my clients have me listed in their phone as 'Debbie Woo' because I am a little 'woo' ('woo'; the art of being a little spiritual and 'seeing' or knowing things that others cannot see with their physical senses). Other people call me the 'Oracle'. People are not used to others using intuition and their senses to find solutions. Other ideas presented may not necessarily be new to you, but hopefully you will see them in a new light which will be enough for you to give them some renewed focus and commitment.

This is not just another 'recovery from burnout' story either. Of course, it all started with that, but learning the things I did along the way made me realise there is so much missing from our business world that is life-changing to your success and happiness. This book describes how I used this opportunity to get into flow with my purpose, my health, abundance and balance. After selling two companies before 40 years old and making a 360 degree change to my career (from advertising to healing and coaching work), I want to share the models I embraced to do this.

The aim here is to enrich, declutter or simplify your working life and paradigms, not add another ten activities to your checklist per day.

My hope is that by altering and adjusting some of your frameworks, you can reach a simple and uncluttered place in your mind. Why? To feel better. To think better and quicker. To be happier in the moment. To be Zenful. To have a career that has meaning, love and allows you to perform at your peak and in flow.

Opening Concepts

Before reading the 11 models ahead, there are a couple of concepts to define as they underpin the entire book.

A. Working with Energy.

Science has proven that human bodies are pure energy (electrical charge), vibrating in a particular pattern to create the appearance of solid form. It can also be called vitality (vital life force), electricity and stamina. The fact is we are not plugged into a wall to get our bodily energy/electricity and yet we walk around animated and alive. We are full of energy meridians and energy channels and even our finest, smallest cell vibrates on pure energy. So it is pretty obvious that you need to look after the energetic side of things when it comes to business. If your energy is low or weak or scattered – so will your business life be low or weak or scattered.

'Get over it, and accept the inarguable conclusion. The universe is immaterial-mental and spiritual'. (Quote taken from "the mental universe") – Richard Conn Henry, Professor of Physics and Astronomy at Johns Hopkins University[1]

For any business owner, executive or entrepreneur, your energy is the number one priority as this is your ultimate IP (intellectual property). It's what gets you out of bed every day. It's what people connect to. It's what draws opportunities to you and it is what keeps you charged up and firing so that you can perform at your best.

So when we say we want more energy, what we really mean is that we want more free flowing and lighter energy (in our body). Our job is to master this flow of our own energy, to understand it better and to know how to turn on the energy tap to ensure our internal electricity is functioning optimally.

Learn how to stay connected to your work passion, make intuitive decisions, be well and to always 'feel the love' with your business life. You are so intricately connected to your business life it often surprises me when people allow themselves to get so rundown yet continue to strive in business as if it is something outside of them. I did this to myself when I worked as a board director at a multi-national advertising agency in Sydney. I was so burnt out that my ability to perform in the end was pathetic. I could hardly drag myself into morning management meetings and my tolerance for challenges finally went out of the window. I put the business role ahead of my energetic health. Bad decision. I wish I had known back then that if I just kept myself charged up and the flow of energy open, the success would follow in business.

I will provide you examples of the science behind energy so that you can seriously tune in to the value and importance of it. But for now, be at ease with knowing you are going to learn how to have the finest romance with your energy and form a deep, deep respect for it. Your business success depends on it.

B. The Mindfulness Revolution

There is a lot of buzz going on in business today about mindfulness*, wellness, focus, authenticity and the list goes on. Big companies are hiring global wellness managers. It seems in our busy world we are trying to fit more and more concepts in for our success. To be better. To do better. To achieve more. You probably picked up this book because you thought it might give you the edge in business. Or maybe you have had enough of the daily grind and are seeking more peace.

Let me revisit quickly that comment above about the modern business world. I don't need to throw mountains of statistics at you showing the seriousness of stress, consumerism and workaholism. A few books I have read recently cover all the stats and yet no real advice on really HOW to change. But why do you think it is that so many people are taking anti-depressants these days and seeking counsellors, healers, coaches and a host of other therapists to feel okay? Some people are aware of it and are suffering; others such as Personality A types* (Personality A type; a tendency to hurry, control things and want to swallow life in bulk quantities in case they miss out on their share) are just driving fast through it hoping they can avoid it like peak hour traffic. Then there are others who have worked it out a bit and are making changes to their lives in an attempt to maintain balance and mindfulness. The fact is, it does exist and you are either conscious of it or not.

It doesn't matter where you fit here, but it does matter what the outcome is. Everyone I know (without fail) is aiming for the same thing. To be the best version of themselves they can be. To experience a happy life with abundance (whatever that means for you) and success.

Being mindful (present and aware of your thoughts) is going to be the key to unlocking your thinking so you can take your energy to a new level.

The Next 11 Chapters

It's probably now very obvious where the next 11 chapters are heading. Yes - they aim to help you to get your energy flowing beautifully with a mindful and thoughtful approach. Everything you learn will either:

a) Enhance your energy flow – the speed, the quality, the life force;

b) Unblock your energy flow – remove obstacles, open up and restore.

We will explore your own personal energy. The energy you get from others. The energy your heart generates. The energy from creative activity. The energy behind ceremony. The energy in food. And more.

When you master the flow of this energy – you can find that inner Zenfulness; that place of centre where all that you do is easy and fluid. I call it flow. This is the key behind being the best that you can be. It's also the key behind success and wealth.

Here are the 11 models I present to you for energy and flow in business:

1. **Master the Flow of Yin & Yang**
2. **Become Conscious**
3. **Your Blueprint**
4. **Leverage**
5. **Soul Colleagues**
6. **Get in Touch with Naughty**

7. **Mindful Moments**
8. **Intuitive Problem Solving**
9. **The Art of Manifestation**
10. **Shadow Work**
11. **HEART Entrainment**

Each chapter will deliver you an idea or model and how that applies in business. There will be some questions you can answer along the way and at the end you have the opportunity to self-assess; to figure out how well (or not) you have integrated that concept into your working life.

Are you a Student, Graduate or Master of this topic? The idea is to understand (across the 11 models) where you sit and how you can make change (if you want to) and implement some of this wisdom into your day-to-day life.

For those that fall into Student or Graduate – try the exercises in chapter 14 to get yourself to Mastery level. If you have mastered any of them already – well done! Your mission is to teach the benefits to other people around you. After all, contribution (to others) is the highest level of happiness according to some of the world's greatest mindfulness gurus like The Dalai Lama and Deepak Chopra.

In addition I have marked several words that are explained in greater detail in the glossary section at the front of this book. I imagine you may not have heard some of these words so look out for a symbol like this * when you come to an unusual word or phrase. I have also included a bibliography of my sources and suggested reading in case you would like to further your knowledge in a particular area.

Enjoy finding your flow in the pages ahead.

With light,

Debbie Pask

References Intro

1.Quantum physicists discovered that physical atoms are made up of vortices of energy that are constantly spinning and vibrating, each one radiating its own unique energy signature. Therefore, if we really want to observe ourselves and find out what we are, we are really beings of energy and vibration, radiating our own unique energy signature - this is fact and is what quantum physics has shown us time and time again. If you observed the composition of an atom with a microscope you would see a small, invisible tornado-like vortex, with a number of infinitely small energy vortices called quarks and photons. These are what make up the structure of the atom. As you focused in closer and closer on the structure of the atom, you would see nothing, you would observe a physical void. The atom has no physical structure, we have no physical structure, physical things really don't have any physical structure. Atoms are made out of invisible energy, not tangible matterhttp://www.collective-evolution.com/2014/09/27/this-is-the-world-of-quantum-physics-nothing-is-solid-and-everything-is-energy/

Master the Flow of Yin & Yang

Quote: 'Vision without action is a daydream. Action without vision is a nightmare.' Japanese Proverb

Key learning: Understanding of ebb and flow, cycles and seasons within your business life and your personal life.

Key words: Yin and Yang. Night and Day. Feminine and Masculine. Reflection and Action. Inner and Outer. Shadow and Light. Intuition and Logic.

The key to mastering your business life is to find that intricate oscillation between Yin and Yang, reflection and action.

In business if you are too 'Yin' – you are the cruisy, creative artist who is brilliant but never gets her exhibition up and running and slowly shrivels from hopelessness. Yet if you are too 'Yang' you are the ruthless executive running on that ridiculous little rat wheel in a tiny cage and cannot make a heartfelt and right decision to save his life. Life becomes wonky. An overload of either is imbalanced, yet I am guessing that if you are reading this book, you probably have the 'doing' or Yang bit cultivated (at least somewhat) and it's the Yin or 'X Factor'# bit you need to give you the leading edge.

The Yin is truly where brilliant innovation and life changing actions stem from. But without the Yang, it's useless.

How do we best explain Yin and Yang outside of the Chinese medicine association? After all, most people think Yin and Yang relate to the body and health, which they do of course, but there is so much more to this ancient concept.

What is the definition of Yin and Yang?

YIN

The moon relates to Yin energy as it is reflective and soothing, appearing in the dark of the night sky and it goes through cycles, just like the emotions. As a result, the moon does affect the emotions and moods of mankind.

Yin is more about sitting within and finding your inner sanctuary. Yin energy reflects inwardly to the body and senses emotions and feelings. It is sensitive and intuitive. Yin is very nurturing and is closely associated with feminine energy. Women who are very Yin-oriented can sometimes find Yang energy too dominant. On the other hand, men can find it difficult to approach someone with high Yin energy – as it feels 'weaker' or shadowy (challenging) to them and harder to interpret. Bold outward action is more comfortable for high Yang energy people. Yin energy does not feel practical or tangible or purposeful. Yin energy is highly creative and utilised best in problem-solving, design and culture. In a business world, however, both approaches are necessary and if you can understand and lead with both, you are way ahead of the game.

YANG

The sun relates to Yang energy as it is charged up, bright and outwardly reflective. A daytime event, the sun holds life force and active energy, illuminating all that it touches. The strength of the sun relates to outer expression and power.

Yang is masculine; it's more logical and rational and projects energy outwards. It is about extending outside of the body and it likes to Act/Do. This can feel dominating at times for someone with strong Yin energy. Men often project themselves in a Yang style as it feels natural. It's a driving, forceful and action-oriented energy. People with high Yang energy (and that can be either sex by the way) can sometimes fail to properly interpret more subtle or emotive messages that are expressed from high Yin people. They are not used to looking beneath the surface of any communication and body language. These high Yang people usually project their energy and body outwards, sometimes totally bypassing the deeper softer messages being conveyed. A typical (and very obvious) example is a strong and dominant male boss 'physically' standing too close to a gentle and more unconfident female co-worker in a conversation, who is obviously cringing underneath the force.

As a result of being outwards, the energy is always turned up and giving or projecting forward. Yang people always have a 'to do' list or a set of goals to achieve and can often crush people in their way.

Let's have a look at the key aspects of Yin and Yang in a simple comparative table, so that you truly understand the difference. Don't make the mistake of thinking men are all Yang and women are Yin. I know many Yang-oriented women who suppress their feminine instincts by trying to exist in the masculine world of business. I also know Yin-oriented men who cannot finish any projects to save their life! If both sexes can understand how positive and powerful it is to have both qualities in balance, business would be so much easier.

Read this list below from left to right so you can see the corresponding and opposite quality of Yin and Yang.

YIN divine feminine aspects (silver)	Yang divine masculine aspects (gold)
Night	Day
Moon	Sun
Receiving energy	Giving energy
Inner	Outer
Reflective	Active
Creativity	Logic
Intuitive	Rational
Spirit	Mind
Shadow	Light
Death (of old)	Rebirth (of new)
Subconscious	Conscious
Quiet	Busy
Being	Doing
Dreams	Goals/Project plans
Internal	External
Back	Front
Water	Fire
Soft/moist	Hard/dry
Venus	Mars
Earth	Heaven

Spending time in 'Yin' mode is the key to filling up with energy and finding that deep place of Zenfulness. When you are Zenful, business and life flows, creativity and vision manifest and your time is more productive and effective. Whilst Yang can feel energising, it ultimately will take energy from you if you over-drive it. Most work burnouts can be pinned back to over-spinning Yang activities and failing to give value to mindfulness. That is absolutely what happened to me at the young age of 27 years when I was sitting on the board of directors in one of the largest advertising agencies in the world.

I have a much better balance between these two states now, but the Yang in me (the practical part) would like to directly apply these principles to business activity. Here goes:

Yin Activities in Business – listening to your intuition/spirit*

1. Downtime – creative planning;
2. Silence – inward reflections and thoughts;
3. Problem-solving – thought and navigation;
4. Usually a quiet cycle in business to reflect (if you don't get one – make one!);
5. Intuition – what feels right in myself and tunes in to what makes me feel excited;
6. Less client meeting times – more alone time;
7. Taking time to nourish the mind, body and spirit to revitalise;
8. Understanding lessons/gifts – working out repeating patterns and blocks;
9. Slow movement and touch – completing tasks mindfully and with presence; and
10. Dreaming up new products and setting vision.

How many of these would you say you do regularly? Note down your answer...

Yang Activities in Business – letting your body & brain execute plans and actions

1. Activity – meetings, presentations and executing creative thoughts;
2. Outwards actions – busy-ness and execution of plans (task-oriented & logical);

3. Meeting people, networking and taking your ideas out to the world;
4. Communication in many forms - marketing, PR, conversations, new business;
5. Juggling many tasks – making noise and broadcasting;
6. Picking up the phone – connecting outwardly;
7. Delivering work and projects – driving milestones and practical planning;
8. Product Launches/Events – meeting an end goal;
9. Accounting – tax, P&L, logical financial tasks; and
10. Pitching – new business.

How many of these would you say you do regularly? Note down your answer...

What was your Yin result /10 ...... versus your Yang result /10...?

So, you can see that Yin and Yang energies both have a place in business and every business category (marketing, networking, logistics etc.) needs to consider both aspects to remain balanced and healthy. Any extreme of one or the other will be detrimental.

I like to call the delicate balance between Yin and Yang in business – 'intu-logic'. Yes, a made up word by me which means 'the practice of combining intuitive heart-led decisions with commercially savvy actions'. We use Yin to dream and Yang to bring the dream into physical reality.

Let's look at some examples of how Yin and Yang can go haywire if out of balance. I am going to start with 'Yang' examples as they are much more common in business.

YANG: Out of balance example - intense

Meet Jill Smith. She is too Yang in business and as a result she has major burnout going on. She has a low stress threshold now and she has dark circles under her eyes and aching calf muscles from adrenal fatigue. She's only just hit 40, but the long working hours and stress have taken its toll on her physically. Coffee has the ability to pick her up (just) and the tiring effort that she makes day in and day out means nothing much is left in the tank for added creativity and strategy, let alone a social life. She performs well at work and keeps it together, but the inner satisfaction she has is waning. Life feels hard and the Yang excess is rife. However, if she were to stop, all of the burden would just catch up and strangle her so she stays working at it, thinking that if she just works a bit harder and jumps a few more hurdles, life can become easier. Sorry Jill, it doesn't and you might get pretty sick.

Key words: Workaholism / Over-drive

I can actually identify with some of Jill's challenges above. I remember staying at home 16 Saturday nights (that's 4 months) in a row when I was too tired to make a fun Saturday night out – and I was only 27 years old.

What does serious stress (massive Yang spin) do to the body?[1]

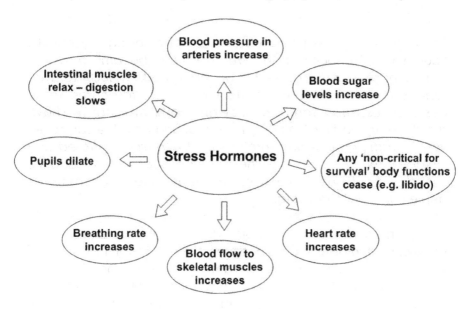

Pretty unpleasant hey?

Further to that, adrenal stress turns on the 'fight, flight or freeze' response in the body, which is fine in short doses, but in the case above, chronic long-term burnout means that your adrenals keep over-firing and then your body starts to break down in different ways as it does not feel safe to just 'be'. The only way to stop this?

Sort out your 'Yin' balance. Later on I refer to an article written by Harvard Business Review on peak performance and recovery and the value of rest.

If you want to really understand how stress (Yang spin) can affect you long-term, an interesting study was done several years back by Jost Sauer.

In his booked titled *Higher & Higher; From Drugs and Destruction to Health and Happiness*, Sauer compares two people with serious health problems. One has a seriously nasty drug (all sorts) addiction and the other person is a corporate stress junkie who has spent a long time in over-drive and Yang spin. They both wound up feeling suicidal and depressed, both having major organs depleted to a similar level and their energy and life force in serious jeopardy. One took drugs to get there and the other was a corporate stress junkie/over-achiever.

The corporate stress junkie had an over-achieving personality. Sauer says in his book *"In the West, we have become a society that …chases external goals that are often work related. We want faster computers, more information, and quick responses. These desires all result from Yang 'advance and act' stimulus, but we have simultaneously lost the Yin ability to 'retreat and wait'. We can't even wait in traffic queues anymore without becoming frustrated and we are naturally attracted to the stimulant drugs such as cocaine, speed and caffeine – all of which make us go faster but naturally deplete the Yin."*[2] Well said.

When a medical test was completed, they both had a similar level of toxicity in their liver, organs and blood work. It seems that the drug 'heroin' and 'stress' can do the same level of damage internally (physically and mentally) and are both seriously destructive. Whether it is a drug you are using or a mind altering 'mood', it seems that your body will become sick if you cannot learn how to live in balance.

The interesting thing about stress is that you often don't think you are stressed until something knocks you over the edge. If you are a Personality a Type, you probably are in early stages or perhaps full Yang spin.

YANG: Out of balance example - medium

Meet John Smith. He is a smart sales guy that heads up a big team that is really hitting the numbers. Work is high pressure, but hey – he can handle it. There's not much time for health and wellbeing (and meditation doesn't even get a look in) due to having a young family at home. Plus, there is pressure to earn money for the new house and the leased BMW car. As a result of high stress, John can at times be an aggressive, confrontational manager who intimidates his staff if little things go wrong. Weakness is not tolerated and everyone needs to play to the same rules. There's not really much space to slip at work and he needs everyone on their game, regardless of what's going on in their personal life. After all, time is of the essence and time is money. He cannot understand why his sales team turnover so much though and leave the business. His team rapport is suffering and his management style is one dimensional. Plus, these new Generation Y'ers* seem to be more lightweight than the older guys in the biz. Can't they handle a bit of tough love?

Key words: Low EQ (Emotional Intelligence) / Lack of compassion / Mild to medium irritation

YANG: Out of balance example - subtle

Meet Jane Smith. She enjoys her career and works hard as well as plays hard. Her social life and decent working hours means she is always on the go and planning, planning, planning. No time to sit still. There's just enough time for a fast and exhausting kick butt cycle class at the gym and a 10 km run every weekend to keep her body in shape. She looks great and keeps sparky. As a result, she keeps her life efficient and controlled so that she can fit everything in and keep the balls in the air. She is great at multi-tasking and can write a 'to do' list like a pro. Her friends love her because she is a natural troubleshooter and can tackle anything. Give a busy girl something to do and it will get done. Jane is pretty happy day-to-day but cannot figure out why she is still single and not starting a family like her other friends. There is no room, space, relaxation or sheer inner child fun in Jane's life to attract inwards (Yin) a lover or romantic experience because life is so damn full and action oriented... Her Yang is stifling the Yin, which is the energy of connection, love and 'bringing in' people and opportunities. It's not that Jane needs to

9

stay home waiting around for someone; more like she needs to have some 'inner' time to repair and receive. She really is not sure how to do this.

Key words: Control / Busy-ness / Over-achiever

What is True Yang (healthy) and False Yang (unhealthy)?

True Yang means that we utilise the healthy and positive qualities of the masculine energy which include action, strength, stability, life, drive, effort, courage, responsibility, will, generosity, articulation and firmness.

False Yang refers to the unhealthy and negative qualities of the masculine energy which include aggression, stubbornness, impetuosity, speed, domination, ego tripping, demanding, control, overly efficient, euphoria, greed, envy and judgement.

1. **Try circling the Yang qualities above that you see in yourself at work – whether true or false Yang.**
2. **Think about where/when these false Yang qualities might surface?**

Make a note

Low EQ*, control and workaholism are all aspects of 'false' Yang (negative Yang) and they impact on your business life and your personal life. Don't get me wrong, Yang can be positive too - such as being accountable, generous (giving), productive, achieving, courageous and intelligent/logical. But when it's allowed to swallow you up and take you to the dark side, it can really pack a good punch. Ego tripping is probably the least desirable of the false Yang qualities. Giving too much is the noblest, but at the expense of the healthy self.

Time to check out the Yin side of things.

YIN: Out of balance example - intense

Meet Angela Brown. She is a hopeless case of Yin overload. She has worked tirelessly in her garage painting to complete a set of artworks for her exhibition. That started ten years ago. She just needs to finish off the last few pieces but most days she procrastinates and finds other distractions. She can often be distracted by BSOs (bright shiny objects) that pull her over into a dreamy state of contemplation. She starts projects but does not have the action or will to follow through. She's brilliant but cannot make it happen. Her friends and family love her but have given up thinking she will bring about her dream into reality. She's intuitive and artistic but lacks any concrete action. As time goes by, she starts to doubt herself and eventually loses any confidence altogether and creates a negative mind loop whereby nothing eventuates. Without any creative outlet or expression, Angela starts to lose her identity and sense of self.

Key words: Indulgence/ Vacillation/ Procrastination

Side Note: I have noticed that people who are too 'Yin' (like the above example) are prone to depression more than others. We have an energy point or meridian in our body called the Base Chakra* point that relates to tribe, vitality, career, community, friends, projects and the earth. When we don't express ourselves into the world or materialise our creative projects, we can become disconnected from this energy point which helps anchors us to the physical world. When we are not anchored into our body properly, we spend more time up in the head and with that overload of energy; it can bring on depression and other mental challenges.

YIN: Out of balance example - medium

Meet Aaron Brown. Aaron works in retail sales and interacts with loads of customers every day. He's an empath*, which means he 'feels' everything going on around him. He doesn't know this. He regularly sucks up other people's emotions as he is sensitive to energy and this makes him not only feel emotionally drained, but as he tries to protect himself from the world and others, he starts to stack on weight. The body will always try to protect you and weight gain is a typical response to empathy. Considering Aaron now has an energy slump, this makes him less likely to exercise (mostly a Yang thing) and more likely to eat for comfort. As the liver gets more toxic, so does depression and irritation set in. That can make him withdraw from the world and become a bit isolated. He will get by ok, but his connection or bridge to the world will suffer and he will spend more time internally focused and not enough time being with others and generating positive experiences.

Key words: Heaviness/ Isolation

Are you an empath? An empath is someone that is very 'kinaesthetic'* which means they 'feel' much more than they 'see'. Being connected to feelings/emotions is a great skill especially for interpersonal work, as it means you can read situations clearly and really understand or 'empathise' with others. However, if not managed properly it can get out of control and you can regularly be affected by others' negative energy bringing you down. Feeling drained at work all the time? People often experience feeling bad even though they don't have anything going in in their life to elicit such a response. It's most likely not your stuff and who wants to carry around 3rd party burdens? My husband James is a great example of an empath who has taken charge of what he 'collects' from others and has learned to protect his own energy and not get burdened by the gift. I am much more visually oriented in that I 'see' situations play out like a little movie in my head. I get flashes of insights and visions. I don't have any hard and fast statistics but I guess that around 30% of people are empaths – anything from mild to seriously affected.

YIN: Out of balance example - subtle

Meet Andy Brown. He started up a consulting business and is generally a pretty smart and capable guy. He's gutsy and great at taking risks and he has a strong sense of self and confidence. He knows loads of people and is well liked. Andy is however lacking some of the Yang principals in business that would make it a glowing success. Whilst it's humming along ok, it's not really growing and taking off. Andy has tried different tactics but tends not to stick at it long enough to really test and measure. He is lacking the hard, commercial and logical business structures that will 'Yang up' his business, so to speak. So the business runs in ebbs and flows, never quite taking off and never having had a strong and firm hand to drive results. The success is based on the natural gifts, connection and intuition of Andy (very Yin!) but the lack of Yang support means there is no real launching pad to hold it all up long term, nor plan into the future growth.

Key words: Unstructured/ Weak / Loose /Procrastination

Indulgence, heaviness and weakness are all qualities of false Yin and will also impact on your business life and potentially your personal life.

True Yin means that we utilise the healthy and positive qualities of the feminine energy which are creativity, intuition, spirituality, birthing, non-striving, calm, essence, mindful, compassionate, yielding, good listener and flexible.

False Yin refer to the unhealthy or negative qualities of the feminine energy which are weak, dependent, isolated, withdrawn, negative, inability to change, victim, self-obsessed, lost, 'world against me' and procrastinator.

1. **Try circling the Yin qualities you see in yourself at work – whether true or false Yin.**
2. **Think about where/when these false Yin qualities might surface?**

Make a note

You can see the beautiful weaving of both Yin and Yang in our business life by these above examples. We should be using Yin to create and dream, then Yang to carry through our will into material expression. I would suggest to you that the business world of today uses the Yang pretty effectively. Yes, you can always improve and strive to get better, do better and be better which are indeed very Yang goals. However, do we really place enough significance on the Yin aspect? I don't just mean creativity and strategy (albeit some businesses could do with more of that).

I am talking about true intuitive and spiritual skills. To create a Zenful business that holds equal weight to intuitive heart-led decisions alongside commercial structures.

Intuitive and soulful skills bring out the X factor in business and in health. They put the energy back into life and to career. When you reach into the void* (Yin) and pull out insights - that is sheer magic. The spirit within is like a spiral – there is no end to the depths you can reach. As opposed to the mind where it is literally a box shape, it has limits to its knowledge and reach because it's only accessing the individual's experience and past, not the greater consciousness or future.

Yin   **Yang**

See these two diagrams above.

Yin = a spiral; signifying that ideas and solutions are endless. The intuition has no boundaries to brilliance. You can reach a higher level and higher creativity.

Yang = a cross; there is a limit to the logical brain and what is can do. It only knows what has been programmed. Its whole world view is four corners wide and stops at those cross points. It is limited by our experience and conscious mind.

You ask any brilliant strategist (and I know quite a few of them) and they will not talk always about it openly, but their truly great work comes from a deep place beyond their logical mind and is channelled into reality through this spiral mechanism. If you want to master your serious X factor*, you will need to delve into the Yin energy.

Einstein himself says "*I never came across any of my discoveries through the process of rational thinking*".

Which one do you lean to? Obviously these are extremes, so there are several levels in between. I imagine if you are in business and reading this, you probably have more Yang covered and have not reached your full Yin potential. Wonderful, you are operating at 50% - 75% power or so. Imagine doubling your energy and success?

Why do you need this strategy of Yin and Yang balance and Zenfulness in business?

- You NEED to stay balanced and energised, otherwise you will suck the life out of your business/career as you are sucking the life out of your wellbeing. Yang is action and Yin is recovery. (We all know you need to stay super-charged and that is the key to staying on top of your business - otherwise ambitious business people would not try yoga, meditation and a host of other energy-enhancing concepts.)
- You create real leverage and wealth when you start playing the Yin and Yang game (as opposed to endlessly exchanging time for money). The Yin game is building longevity of ideas and injecting real creativity and strategy into business/career, whereas Yang is the drive to make them happen.
- Opportunities flow effortlessly and everything around you becomes abundant when you understand the flow of energy inwards (Yin). Yin is receiving and Yang is giving. Getting into Yin mode brings opportunities to you.
- Yin keeps you connected to the passionate and fun side of business – which is why you probably started it in the first place. This will keep you going well beyond any competitors that aren't connected to a purpose.

Debbie Pask

I am shamelessly obsessed with the Yin and Yang aspect of anything in life. What has a front, also has a back. Exploring both sides is intelligent and fascinating. I have found that my tendency to be Yang so much in the past really limited my ability to stay well, refreshed, mindful and in flow with all around me. Now that I have more Yin energy flowing, I find that my creative and strategic abilities as a coach have magnified and opportunities are endless. In relation to my coaching work, here is part of a testimonial written for me by a client who owns and operates a global business.

"I have never met someone so good at going from right to left brain as the situation or conversation demands". CC 2015

And that sums up what it means to use both skills in harmony.

The earliest reference to Yin and Yang is in the *I Ching*[3] (Book of Changes) in approximately 700 BC China and mankind has been working with the concept for many thousands of years. In Stephen Karcher's book on the 'I Ching', he summarises pretty articulately about how to work with the Yin and Yang.

He says that certain times and situations call on you to be great/ strong (Yang) and to direct your will and act. Great Yang people do this consistently and thus acquire good influence and personal power. Yet other times and situations require that you adapt and let go (Yin) – choosing not to impose your will and to just sit and be with the situation. We cover this later when we discuss problem solving and making decisions, but it is worthwhile to note that flowing between the two – Yin and Yang – is the key to having a fully charged business life that is balanced, successful and harmonious. In fact, latest research on peak performance discusses the importance of oscillating between Yang (driving hard) and Yin (recovery) energy.

Mastery of Yin and Yang occurs when you are so tuned in, that you easily flip between the two spaces within minutes and can consciously be aware of that tipping point of change. At first you will need to spend distinct times (perhaps days) in one or the other so you get familiar with it. When I first dropped out of full-time corporate work, I was so Yang (burned out) that I needed to spend a good chunk of time in recovery and internal repair (Yin). Sleep, limited work, taking things slowly and massage etc. It is what Jost

16

Sauer would call 'retreat and wait'. It took a long time for my health problems to correct but they are so on track now, I can hardly see life without the balance and I can see the stress looming in others who are still in the Yang trap. In addition my finances and abundance have never been better since I stopped my high paying corporate job and got down and dirty with the Yin.

So ask yourself, how connected to the Yin are you? What about the Yang? Do you translate your ideas into actions easily? Do you have a good balance of Yin and Yang? Your answers above should have given you some clues.

Choose the below description that matches you in business and then turn to chapter 12 to plot where you sit on the scale.

(NOTE -You can plot your progress for each chapter of the book and then review the big picture at the end of the book, to see which areas you need the most focus on. There will be activities listed there to help you supercharge the area you want to work on for inner flow and Zenfulness.)

Beginner

You are reasonably light in the 'Yin' department and don't really give it much thought day-to-day. You are aware of the importance of your own inner wellbeing and would like to give it more focus, but work and life is so busy, where is the time? You might even separate out business as the hard working part of life and your own personal time as the fun creative time, not realising that business can also have that fun and repairing energy kick. You plan your career around building wealth which then allows you to do what makes you happy, as opposed to doing what makes you happy first to build the wealth. You probably feel the stress and are seeking ways to reduce it, but have not yet cracked the long-term solution for you. You might (or might not) have a low EQ* (emotional intelligence) when it comes to connecting with people and subconsciously know that this needs to change with the current new world.

Most beginners have not learned the art of meditation or inward reflection to be quiet, mindful and to intuitively solve problems. When an issue arises, the solution is usually just to work harder or assert power/control or logic.

Beginners can range from full-fledged stress heads and some power trippers with an over-spinning mind to those of you who are planting seeds of change and inspired to bring a new level of awareness into their work life.

Most beginners cannot easily slow down mentally on the weekend, unless they have a very physical lifestyle where they smash their bodies with adrenalin-related feats of endurance – which in the long term creates additional strain.

Alternatively, you could be so Yin that your whole life is one big procrastination! I don't need to elaborate here but you might just be drifting through life not getting anything off the ground to make you happy.

If this is you – hello beginner, your journey has just started and you have the most to gain here.

Graduate

You have and are developing skills around how to be more conscious and intuitive in business. You understand some basic concepts of energy and have some level of wellbeing and meditation ritual to fire you up when you need it. You value the health of your mind and body, understanding the obvious connection between the two, but you are still learning how to fully be in your strategic and intuitive power. You practice mindfulness 101 and try to apply this to your business life with some success. You may have attended some spiritual classes – yoga, meditation or Tai Chi.

You have a good level of emotional empathy for co-workers and know a little about how to get best results from others through engagement and basic intuition. You may have a tendency toward being an 'empath' which is draining you or allowing work burdens to stress your wellbeing. Sometimes you forget to breathe and let go. Your work day can get lodged in your mind sometimes making it hard to let go and sleep might be challenging. This stress can come home with you and affect the entire household. Weekends range from being stressful and agitated to being more mindful and okay. It will depend on the week you just had, how many challenges you have faced and what sort of pace you work at. You probably even work on the weekend to catch up.

Graduates range from having a good spiritual practice to having a basic one. It is still a little bit of a challenge to bring the intuitive and spiritual aspect of themselves into their job, still seeing work/business as a serious endeavour of driving and acting. Graduates usually have a good sense of what energy they are putting into their body and mind, but sometimes are not 100% certain of how to feed their spirit at work day-to-day.

Once again, there is a range of graduates, from lightweight (with the will to seek out Zenfulness) to more senior graduates (really practicing mindfulness day to day).

Master

You have really built up your spiritual bank, that being you have prioritised the importance of building resilience and consciousness into your working life. You totally get that business has a spiritual/ intuitive/creative side and you are a gun at practicing that. You spend time in Yin cycles, building and dreaming your vision and taking time to get foot massages or the like in the middle of the day when needed. You value your energy and take time out – whether small chunks (two hours) or a whole week to repair and integrate thinking. You may pop out in the midst of your day to a movie if you need time out and you don't fill your diary stupidly so that you run on empty a lot. Yes – you will have times of big Yang work output where you might burn the candles at both ends on a big creative launch, but you don't drive like this all of the time as you know that's dishonouring to yourself and your personal life.

You value personal development and take time to reflect on decisions and ideas intuitively. You have a natural inbuilt radar or intuitive guidance chip for making decisions and you are not afraid to take a risk. You lead with the heart and you also don't beat up on yourself if something fails as you always understand the lesson and gift from the experience. You take the good and transmute the negative – whether that is through reflecting on the issue or doing a ritual. (I like to write down angst and burn it to purify – that's an indigenous concept of giving away the crap to be transmuted by the great spirit of fire.) Your language is a bit different to most – you talk about energy and elements and take time to plant the seeds of this in others.

You are conscious and aware of others and probably have learned a good deal about compassion. People see you as wise and connected.

No, this does not mean you are perfect! Of course you will trip up in the material plane and have times when you slip back into the matrix and get caught up in the false Yang and Yin. But the beauty of a Master is that they have tools to pull themselves out of it, whether having their own mentor or DIY methods – and can see the gifts and light from falling into the void (being lost) from time to time. In fact, that is the richness of life knowing things will fall away sometimes and the next generation of yourself and work is exciting when you really think about it!

Hello Master – now that you have this inner resilience, why aren't you teaching others? And if you are teaching by example, congratulations as you are sowing the seeds of change in the world.

References Chapter 1

1. www.mayoclinic.org Research on effects of stress on the body.
2. Sauer, Jost *Higher and Higher; from drugs and destruction to health and happiness*, Chapter 6. Australia, Allen and Unwin, 2006
3. *I CHING: Book of Changes*, written in the Zhou Dynasty in China (7-9th century BC)

2

Become Conscious

Quote: Lao Tzu Fell asleep and dreamt he was a butterfly. Upon awakening he said, 'Am I a man who was just dreaming he was a butterfly. Or a sleeping butterfly now dreaming he is a man?' Lao Tzu

Key Learning: To approach life from a higher perspective. To be connected to source energy beyond the limits of our ego. To command the 'witness' within.

Key words: Intuitive. Connected. Plugged in. Witness. Higher Self. Aware. Mindful.

Present. Free.

Do you ever ponder larger world issues and give it some serious attention to how 'you' can contribute to the change needed?

Are you really conscious?

This is a really loaded question ... so be careful before you answer. There are indeed different levels of consciousness in people. The more conscious you are, the bigger your X factor. And, in business, your X factor is what sky rockets your success.

But what exactly does being 'conscious' mean? In very straight terms it means you are awake (and not asleep). On a deeper level, it means that you are tuned into the energy around you; your energy and thoughts, other people's needs and how you and they impact on each other and the world around you. It means that you take responsibility for your own shadows* (parts of yourself you reject) or issues. It includes looking beyond just your immediate needs at the bigger picture and collective consciousness. It means understanding that everything and everyone around you has energy and consciousness. The plants, animals, people, car, your house etc. Everything has some level of consciousness and 'aliveness'. Talk to your house when it feels heavy and clear the negative energy after an argument. Connect to the land of a new country when you get off a flight so that you feel strong and centred in this new place. Read other people's energy and figure out how to handle them and the situation. Pretty amazing skill to have in business I would say. You might consider consciousness being like your 6th sense - the vibrational intuitive field that seems to read everything at a deeper level. And I can tell you from experience that this is a huge advantage in your life and in business.

I have made it my life passion to study consciousness on many levels and have developed a strong sense of intuition and gut instinct. I am a bit like a human lie detector. I can sense what is going on underneath the surface.

The three parts of your awareness

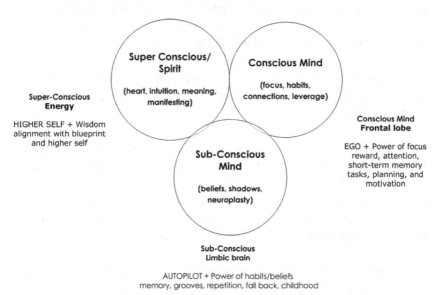

Super-Conscious
Energy

HIGHER SELF + Wisdom
alignment with blueprint
and higher self

Super Conscious/
Spirit

(heart, intuition, meaning,
manifesting)

Conscious Mind

(focus, habits,
connections, leverage)

Conscious Mind
Frontal lobe

EGO + Power of focus
reward, attention,
short-term memory
tasks, planning, and
motivation

Sub-Conscious
Mind

(beliefs, shadows,
neuroplasty)

Sub-Conscious
Limbic brain

AUTOPILOT + Power of habits/beliefs
memory, grooves, repetition, fall back, childhood

In simple terms for this exercise, there are three parts to your awareness:

The Superconscious Mind (Spirit/Energy/Soul) is more strategic, innovative, accurate and X Factor-ish. This is the most powerful mind and is what will give you that intuitive consciousness and competitive advantage that will take you beyond anything your logical mind will ever deliver. If you have not accessed that (and many of you probably have not had the full access), then you are operating at 50% power. Want more? I certainly did.

The Conscious Mind is responsible for your day-to-day thoughts and logic. This mind is the one we are aware of, our thoughts and reactions. It is the brain we use to analyse and make choices. It is always with us, present and thinking. It is the one reading this book right now and deciding how to catalogue this information.

The Subconscious Mind is the hidden mind, the background script and the place where our challenges and blocks live. It is our autopilot, responsible for pumping blood to our heart and other life-saving activities. However, it can be messy in there as it has witnessed all of our life events and feelings, making decisions (or scripts) about who we are and what we are capable of. If there is any trauma or difficulty, the subconscious mind will tuck it away and block it up. Often, these hidden blocks thwart our conscious mind from achieving its goals. We consciously want one thing, yet our subconscious can easily sabotage getting it.

We work a lot in the conscious mind (left brain and logical) – making plans and doing tasks. I don't need to discuss this too much as you already live there …

We sometimes explore the subconscious mind by questioning limiting beliefs and learned behaviours if we are getting stuck on something. In the 80s, Neuro-linguistic Programming (NLP*) gained a lot of momentum as the cutting edge technique to repattern our negative or undesirable patterns and behaviours holding us back. And they are, indeed, deeply buried old scripts that can unravel us.

We rarely work in the superconscious mind* (spirit/soul/6th sense) as it is deemed 'too woo' by many people especially in the business world.

It is not rational or linear, so this kind of mind if not often associated with business. Yet this is truly the most remarkable and intelligent mind we have. More than a mind, it is our gift or finest asset available to us 24/7 ... if we can just work out how to use it properly.

Being conscious does not mean you live in the 'super-conscious' mind permanently. But it does mean that you understand how to use it effectively and can translate creative and intuitive ideas from the super-conscious mind back into your conscious mind for action.

Another way to look at the three minds is to see it as a radiating circle such as the below diagram:

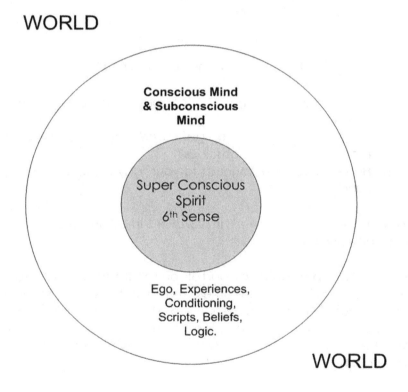

WORLD

Conscious Mind & Subconscious Mind

Super Conscious
Spirit
6th Sense

Ego, Experiences,
Conditioning,
Scripts, Beliefs,
Logic.

WORLD

The outer brain represents the conscious and subconscious mind; a fantastic tool to plan and execute any ideas you may have. It is the bridge between the super-conscious inner self and the outer world - a critical process in your business life - providing us with logical processes, language and more. Most of us live in this world and tap a little into that inner Spirit, but not nearly enough.

Being fully conscious means using both inner and outer brains together in harmony. That is, using the superconscious mind (inner) for blue-sky thinking, with the conscious and subconscious minds (outer) for logic and application. Another way of saying this is to use the left and right brain together in harmony, oscillating from one to the other for super-charged results. As a general statement, indigenous people are often fantastic at right brain stuff (listening, artwork, going with the flow, letting go of time) and westerners are great at logic, time, money management etc. Both have their brilliance and need to be utilised in unison.

Question?

On a scale of 1- 10 (1 being low and 10 being high)

1. How well do you connect with your superconscious or Spirit mind?
2. How well do you investigate and correct any hidden problems in the subconscious?
3. How well do you connect to your 'day-to-day' conscious mind?

Many of us would reach over 8 in Q3, over 5 in Q2 and yet probably sit at 2 or less in Q1.

If you want to tap into that best part of yourself, the most creative and the most peaceful mind; become a master of the superconscious. Make it your purpose to access this part of self as it truly is your greatest tool. Not doing this is like having a personal helicopter available in your backyard ready to fly you to work, yet you choose to ride a bike to work every day.

How do we tap into this superconscious brain?

There are many ways to develop this spiritual or intuitive mind, here are some ideas:

Meditate: this is a powerful tool to gain access to the spirit brain because meditating in alpha* wave means our logical brain stops running the show and gets out of the way long enough to allow inspired messages through. We discuss this mode of thinking later in our manifestation chapter.

Learn: if you aren't engaging in some kind of personal development or self-reflection then you are in danger of being lazy with your own growth. Whether you study with inspiring teachers, read books or articles or use life as your personal lesson book – you do need to be thinking about this stuff to make progress. Evolving your inner being opens up new paradigms of thinking.

Ask Questions: go a bit deeper in your understanding of how the world ticks and your reality around you. Once you start this process, it unfolds beautifully.

These suggestions are a good start, but if you really want to nail your inner conscious you, let's look at it in a deeper and more comprehensive way.

Maslow's hierarchy of needs[1]This next model is my personal adaptation of Maslow's hierarchy of needs. Maslow created the pyramid you can see below and I love this simple and exceptional model of how mankind requires certain conditions to thrive.

First – let's review the original Maslow hierarchy of needs. I have not tampered with this pyramid. This is a well-known psychologically-based tool that analyses our most intrinsic human needs from ground up. You can see in the below diagram that basic human needs start with food and shelter, then safety and then tribal connection right through to confidence and self-awareness followed by self-actualisation and contribution.

Maslow's Hierarchy of Needs

Diagram 1

Maslow's hierarchy of needs (the original as in diagram 1) is a basic assessment of the level of human development as developed by the man Maslow himself. You can see that some third world countries barely have the first layer under their belt, that being basic food and shelter. In the western world, our privileged life means we can attain the top layer, yet many of us rarely do as that superconscious brain is not switched on effectively. It requires intuition and consciousness in good quantity.

Diagram 2 is my interpretation of each layer of Maslow's Hierarchy of Needs and how CONSCIOUS ACTION fits into the human condition on all levels. Obviously it is more concentrated in the top few layers, but we need to recognise that it starts at the very bottom of the pyramid and infiltrates EVERY level. As you review this, think about your own level of consciousness in each layer – you may have loads in the first level but then drop off at level three or above. Or maybe you have layer three mastered but struggle with layer one – basic exercise and a healthy diet. There is no right or wrong here – just awareness of how developed your consciousness is.

Once you measure where you are at, you can piece together any gaps or next steps you might take for your own growth to move up the pyramid. Please note that as you move up the layers of the pyramid, the concepts become more esoteric* (less physically concrete) and spiritual (not religious). You may find these concepts more difficult to understand if you have not heard them before or read much about it.

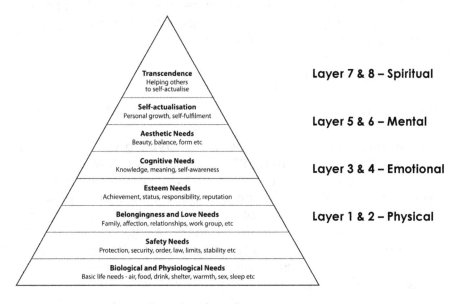

Maslow's Hierarchy of Needs

PHYSICAL: Layer 1 & 2 – Physical and Safety needs

Understanding the mind /body loop. Every ache, pain and illness is related to your mental/emotional health. Fix the issue, fix the body. Where does your food come from? Do you dumb down your body with genetically modified foods, fluoride, sugar etc? Are you using pharmaceutical drugs or mainstream chemical-based skincare or personal hygiene products? Are you placing yourself in unsafe conditions whether that is a bullying scenario at work or with an abusive partner?

Key: Your body is your temple.

Debbie Pask

EMOTIONAL: Layer 3 & 4 – Belonging and Esteem needs

Are you connecting in a healthy way with others? Ability to collaborate and harmonise. Not competing. Being in flow with your emotional health. Creative hobbies, working in your life purpose, and giving yourself joyful and nurturing experiences. Working through your emotional baggage such as shadows and fears. Listening to others, a healthy balance of giving and receiving. Ability to cultivate supportive friendships and colleagues. Are your friends supportive or do they drain you?

Key: Do you have Emotional Intelligence (EQ)*?

MENTAL: Layer 5 & 6 – Cognitive and Aesthetic needs

Do you question authority or believe everything you read in the media or from the government? Do you blindly follow the trends? Ability to investigate your own truth and way of living to meet your own values. Developing a stronger sense of self through study, personal development or creative pursuits to sharpen the mind and senses. Ability to keep your ego in check. Ability to avoid serious work burnout and fatigue. Ability to stay at Point Zero* – which means calm and centred when challenged. Ability to express oneself authentically.

Key: Self responsibility and freedom.

SPIRITUAL: Layer 7 & 8 – Self actualisation* and Transcendence* needs

Ability to enter alpha wave meditation state easily and on command. Making decisions with intuition and 6th sense. Ability to discern deep inner messages vs brain chatter/fear. Following your heart. Having a deep respect for your inner voice and listening to it seriously to make decisions. Deep connection to nature and the universe all around you. Noticing that everything is alive and can be communicated with. Feeling connected. Contribution to a cause outside of self. Steering yourself and others to find their freedom. Recognition of your own internal god/goddess. Realising how powerful you are and the buck stops with you.

Key: Collective contribution

Where do you sit?

As you look at this diagram, how far up the scale do you think you are across the four areas? I know that's a big question. Perhaps you have some of those qualities developed in two categories and not in others. The physical layer has become a little more mainstream and on the humanity 'radar' in the last ten years or so. How many films are there at the moment that talk about juicing, the dangers of sugar and raw food diets? There are cancer documentaries talking about stress creating illness in the body. Our western focus is certainly much more conscious than it was ten years ago. What those films miss is the fact that you should listen to your inner voice. What specific foods does your body need? How do I tap into my hungry self and eat to live – as opposed to live to eat. No one diet fits all.

How developed you are has nothing to do with how 'good or bad' you are. It is about how open and connected and "conscious" to your Spirit (that superconscious mind) you are. We are rarely taught the value of consciousness in the school curriculum or in our life by our guardians or managers or government. Well, indigenous cultures are, but westerners are often not. (If you have been raised in the West and taught this stuff – you should be miles ahead of the game). In fact, we are often taught the opposite. Use your mind (brain) to make logical and practical decisions. Compete. Drive your own ambitions and fit into the norm of society. Make money. Consume. Don't dream too much or spend time meeting your Spirit! Whilst logic is great, it's only half the picture.

Your consciousness is your greatest tool. Not using it or flexing it is like having a high- performance car with no wheels. Your engine is your consciousness. The more you fire it up, ridiculously amazing things manifest and play out in your life. Sure you might get dirty and greasy along the way learning how to clean the engine, but the bigger the effort, the bigger the evolution. If you give it no wheels to drive your life, then it sits useless in the garage, growing cobwebs.

Based on the Maslow consciousness hierarchy, here are some key examples that show you what it means to be conscious at each level. It doesn't mean you need to have every tick box checked, but trawl through these ideas under the four categories, and see which ones resonate and whether you are or aren't doing them. Making a few changes can leap you forward very quickly. Take note also if there is one particular layer that is completely shut down for you.

All of these areas are designed to increase your energy on many levels, and I feel they impact a lot on your working life. I know they have on mine.

Layer 1 & 2: Physical Consciousness – don't dumb down your body.

"Let thy food be thy medicine and thy medicine be thy food" Hippocrates

Your body affects your mind and your mind affects your body (the mind body loop). It is truly a symbiotic relationship. Physical consciousness is all about fostering your life force, energy, earth connection and caring for the temple that is your body. Your body is alive, made up of light and sound waves, whole, natural, organic and very intelligent. How you care for your body is a reflection of how conscious you are. I am not talking about having a tight regimented vegan diet here, although that choice is fine. It is more about how conscious are you of what exactly are you doing to your body daily.

Your body is not separate to you. Your physical energy will dictate how you think, how you perform and how you feel. Put good quality fuel and energy into the tank, then you get a better performance overall.

My mindset around health is that I simply ask a question to myself "Is that food or activity a high vibrational thing or not?" I focus on that as opposed to having a restrictive regime.

Although I am not a huge fan of tennis player Novak Jokovic, I would encourage you to read his recent book, *Serve to Win*, (written in 2013), which explains how he moved his world ranking from no.5 to no.1 by changing his diet. He made a conscious effort to improve his energy and mindset through caring for his body. I myself have practised the eating style he chose and can tell you from first-hand experience how much it changed my life for the better. But there is no 'one way' either. Being conscious means you tap into what is right for you. We are all different so I don't expect we will all eat the same.

Let me show you how the mind body loop works on the liver (one of our key bodily organs). We know two key things:

1. When you eat toxic food (alcohol, bad fats, sugar etc.) the liver can become overloaded, as it is responsible for processing the waste out of the body. When the liver is toxic, we can have a corresponding emotional response of anger or depression, as the chemical toxins drag on our energy and lifeforce. Therefore, poor quality food can emotionally toxify us, even if nothing emotional is happening in our life. Food holds its own vibration or energy and once inside our body, can affect our emotions.

2. When we are depressed and angry about something in our life on a mental/emotional level, that can also have a corresponding physical effect on our liver, making our physical body toxic. Whilst we may have a healthy diet, the liver can still be toxic through our thoughts and negative emotions.

What does this mean? It means that our mindset can toxify our liver and our liver can toxify our mind. Ouch – the body mind loop has kicked in. Want to do a liver detox to feel better? Well learn to watch your thoughts as they can trip you up also and be responsible for a toxic liver. Become conscious of your body and what 'waste' you put into it – food and feelings.

High vibration thought + high vibration food = high vibration work output.

This might be obvious to you already, but do you really know the full extent of how far food and thoughts can truly affect us?

I have heard people say that sugar is the devil, and can be more addictive than cocaine[11] in its addictive nature. I absolutely agree. It is responsible for so much brain fog that when addicted, I believe you are never at your full power energetically as the body is struggling to deal with this overwhelming drug.

James DiNicolantonio is a cardiovascular research scientist at St. Luke's Mid-America Heart Institute in Kansas City, Mo. He recently published a comprehensive review of dozens of studies in which he contends that refined sugar is similar to cocaine — a white crystal extracted from sugar cane rather than coca leaves — and that studies show it can be even more addictive than the recreational drug. "When you look at animal studies comparing sugar to cocaine," DiNicolantonio said, "even when you get the rats hooked on IV cocaine, once you introduce sugar, almost all of them switch to the sugar."[2] DiNicolantonio is careful to differentiate between **refined** and **intrinsic** (sugars that occur naturally such as in fruit) sugars; while the former (refined) have the potential to cause adverse health effects due to their concentrated nature.

There is a theory that cancer cells have many times more the cell receptors for sugar than normal cells.[3] There are several opinions in the natural health world (including mine) that believe refined sugar and cancer are close friends.

I won't lie to you. I do love a good chocolate bar or a yummy piece of cake (Even better an 'After Dinner Mint' -remember those little treats in their cute maroon packets begging to be eaten?) But ultimately they are dead fuel to the body. They don't assist with energy nor do they make you feel good long term. However, I don't suggest you give them up altogether forever as they form part of the 'inner child' indulgence that needs to be satisfied as we discuss in a later chapter. Just don't make them a regular routine or your body never gets a break from that continual toxic pressure.

I am very much against having 'no' as a hard category in my life or any massive restrictions, but I am extremely conscious of my choices whether they are food, alcohol, addictive tendencies or toxic thoughts. Conscious choices mean that we are aware of the impact on ourselves and on others around us. And when it comes to feeding the body so you can be the 'best you can be' at work or life, there are some major considerations to review around how you can potentially dumb down your body (i.e. lose conscious intention).

As a society we are taught to be good little consumers and often forget to question our choices or habits because they are so ingrained in us all. Who says we have to have the new flat screen TV? Who says we have to drink on Friday night after work? Who says that we need to buy a house to own as 'ours'? The same goes with food and consumption of products into the body. Do you really know what toxicity you are placing in your body each day with what you consume? Do you even know where the food comes from? Try Buycott[13], a new phone app that scans barcodes and tells you where the food comes from, which company makes it and where they invest their money etc.

And what are the effects on your ability to think, strategise, workout, negotiate, react and feel? Mentioned below are some of the key physical traps to watch out for and how they can seriously affect you and how you work. I have slowly taken these things out of my life and feel so much more energised as a result. Doesn't mean I never have them, but they are generally not in the routine.

Here is a summary list that I believe are key things that dumb down your physical body, which in turn impacts on your mental, emotional and energetic body. In my mind, these are not conscious choices. Can I first just premise the below with "I am not a medical doctor, nor am I authorised to give out nutritional advice by the TGA Therapeutic Goods Administration - Australia)."

1. **Fluoride in the city/town water.**
   Unless you have a high quality water filter like a Berkey[4], you are drinking fluoride (a heavy metal). Yes, even those little 'water filters' at work are probably not removing fluoride. Considering this is one of the most toxic of all metals, this is the most obvious one to change. If you are drinking tap water with fluoride in it (that's most countries although some are now changing this) then you are pumping your body full of toxic metal. Most water filters in my opinion don't remove it affectively so I encourage you to do your homework. Considering water is so vital to health and we drink it every day, finding an alternate water supply is so intrinsic to your energy levels. It might be more expensive but really... what's your health worth? I am sure you spend thousands of dollars on your car per year. Would you purposely place the wrong

petrol in your car to see how long it takes before it flatlines on you? Here are some of the statistics and science around what fluoride does to the human body:

There have been over 34 human studies and 100 animal studies linking fluoride to brain damage, including lower IQ in children, and studies[5] have shown that fluoride toxicity can lead to a wide variety of health problems, including:

Increased lead absorption;

Hyperactivity and/or lethargy;
Muscle disorders;
Thyroid disease;
Arthritis;
Dementia;
Bone fractures;
Bone cancer (osteosarcoma);
Genetic damage and cell death;
Increased tumour and cancer rate;
Disrupted immune system;
Damaged sperm and increased infertility.

Are you drinking tap water? Will you reconsider? There is a whole organisation created and devoted to fluoride awareness, check it out.
www.fluoridealert.org

2. **Genetically Modified Foods**
   I will keep this short and sweet. Nature has a perfect divine and intelligent plan for us. Whole foods were created to a special fibonnacci* (mathematical formula in which each number is the sum of the two preceding numbers) sequence and house thousands of specific chemical compounds to benefit mankind. Apparently there are around 13,000+ chemicals in spinach and mankind can only understand around 100 or so of them. So I am unsure how they think we are bright enough to modify, make synthetic changes or derive new versions when we don't completely understand the vegetable in the first place? Many wholefoods in big supermarket chains are how stocking GMO (genetically

modified organisms) foods. Think of super sweet corn. Did corn taste like that as a child? Does it taste stupidly sweet? These foods are going to mess with your organic body and hence your energy frequency[6] as they don't have the full delivery system of mother nature. We really don't know the long term effects this will have on us as they are a new phenomenon.

3. **Eating non-organically grown food or processed foods**
Certain types of foods are okay or better – but fruits that have thin skin like blueberries and strawberries soak up that pesticide so easily that you are literally eating chemicals. Chemicals in your body store up and when your body gets overloaded, it creates little 'waste deposit baskets' (yes lumps!) that house the toxic crud until (in our wisdom) we go get them cut out. Then our body gets pretty confused and can create several more lumps as backups to house the processed crap you are eating. A very wise man called Don Tolman talks about this idea of waste deposits so I suggest you listen to his talks on how what we eat and the products we use can make us sick.[8]

I'm not suggesting you don't eat ANY processed food by the way, although I aim to eat very little. We live in a modern day world where it can be hard to always prepare super fresh food. I just suggest that you try to eat a greater portion of fresh life force-giving foods. Make a game of it – for every processed item you eat (in a wrapper, jar, tin etc.), try to eat two portions of fresh food. And if they are thin skinned whole foods, try to find organic. Thin skinned wholefoods suck up pesticides super efficiently and what you eat is what you become.

4. **Beauty Products made from chemicals**
Sorry ladies, this is probably every mainstream make-up company on the market – yes they are the big brand names that I cannot really mention in case I get in trouble. These products are FILLED with some pretty toxic chemicals and considering your skin is Cytophylactic* (it soaks up potions and delivers them directly into your bloodstream), that means that whenever you apply these products – you are poisoning yourself daily. This includes makeup, skincare, perfume, shampoo and body creams. Includes men's

products too – aftershave and deodorant. If you can't eat it, then it's probably best not to use it. Your skin will often deliver these chemicals more quickly into your blood than your gut. There are loads of great natural beauty and personal care products on the market that look amazing and feel so much more nourishing than the chemical stuff. Think ingredients like avocado, macadamia, goji, berries, honey, cacao butter, coconut oil, jojoba oil, almond oil etc. Don't these things sound beautiful and eatable? They are and your skin loves them.

On a side note, I have been using 100% pure virgin coconut oil daily on my face and I often get people commenting on the quality of my skin. I am literally feeding my skin food that can integrate and synthesize straight from nature.

There is a great little pocket reference guide called the *The Chemical Maze*[9] book and it lists all of those 'hard to read' words on the back of chemical beauty products. It tells you the real deal – how toxic they are and key side effects. Read it only if you plan to give up chemicals as it's pretty dire and 'in your face'. I suggest you pick up those commercial brands, read the ingredients on the back label, then look them up in *The Chemical Maze* book and see what side effects they have.

5. **Artificial sweeteners – especially aspartame found in diet coke.**
    These are seriously insane. Some are known to create serious nerve damage as they wear away your body's nerve sheaths over time – leaving you exposed. I suggest you research what aspartame really does.[10] The information and studies are overwhelming.

6. **MSG** – also named (sneakily) Hydrolyzed Vegetable Protein, Textured Vegetable Protein and Yeast Extract (amongst others).
    We know it can affect the heart and nervous system. When I eat out at a restaurant I will know within about 30 minutes if the food has MSG in it, because my heart starts beating rapidly and I get incredibly thirsty. Watch out for other names it uses that are hidden in foods you might buy. I was really

disappointed to find out that a well-known herb brand in supermarkets was loading up their herb mixes with MSG.

7. **Gluten (yeast etc.)**
   Ooh a hidden trap. Even if you are not coeliac (allergic to gluten generally) it's still getting in there and screwing with your digestive system on some level. It is even hidden in the word – 'glue' and it does seem to bind up your digestive track. I feel so much better not eating gluten, but occasionally I indulge as sourdough bread is my big weakness.

8. **Refined Sugar**
   Ouch. Swap it over for organic and natural sugar sources. Sure, have the traditional birthday cake occasionally but best to generally avoid it or make your own with natural sugars. Natural sources include honey, maple syrup, stevia, xylitol, tapioca, coconut nectar and more. If you want a really interesting view on the outrageous levels of sugar in milk, I suggest you read a book called *Have you got the guts to be really healthy?* by Don Chisholm and he will explain not only the sugar crisis, but also some of the other concepts I have covered here. This book is simple and seriously useful.

9. **Anti-depressants/pharma drugs.**
   Ok, let me give you the legal spiel again here. "I am not a qualified doctor or medical physician or psychiatrist or drug pusher so please don't take anything I say seriously. I am not authorised to tell you anything. I am a nobody." Now that's out of the way, the latest research on drugs like antidepressants[11] are creating worse symptoms when taken over time. These symptoms can include suicidal thoughts as reported by latest studies or worse, create new problems that didn't exist by blocking or altering the natural neurotransmitters in the brain. www.psychologytoday.com addresses these concerns in some of the recent articles. Any pharmaceutical drugs you are taking will have side effects of some type and they *are* foreign to the body. Plus, you don't know which drugs interact poorly with other drugs. There have not been properly long-term tested trials on how antidepressants work with the contraceptive pill or heart medication or steroids or pain medication or any other sort of drug in the market.

There are more to mention but these are my personal biggies. It took me a long time to wean off my beauty products and swap to essential oils for perfume and 100% pure coconut oil for skincare. The hardest for me was shampoo and conditioners as swapping over to natural products takes time to adjust and your hair (mine is super long!) can get quite battered around until it adjusts to the new natural products.

Air quality is obviously a big one too. Not much you can do if you live in a big city and the air quality is not great. One of the largest problems with toxic pollution is the burning tyres from cars hitting the roads. The fumes are quite poisonous so try to wind up windows on busy roads and change your air to internal vents. Once out of busy areas, feel free to wind the windows down and hang your head out.

Your physical energy can get bogged down with lots of different toxins – food, chemicals, stress and more. I don't want to promote paranoia. Again I am suggesting taking a conscious approach. Make better decisions over time. Don't live with fear of it, simply practice awareness. Let go of what you cannot change. Change what you can over time.

The cleaner you get, the more energy you have and energy is the King, especially as you age.

Q. What in your environment can you identify that can be changed to reduce your toxic load? What can you control?

Think of it this way. The more toxins I reduce, the smarter and more energised I become. If anyone doesn't want to be more energised and well, then that is a problem in itself.

My top three changes I can make to reduce toxicity in my body and hence help me to become smarter are?

1.

2.

3.

Layer 3 & 4: Emotional Consciousness – your relationship to self and others

I have a few concepts to discuss so let's digest one at a time to keep this brief. Feel free to answer the questions in your head or grab a pencil and scribble yes or no against each statement or question.

a. **Connection and engagement**
Do you listen and ask questions about others and have genuine interest when connecting with or meeting people? Do you listen to your own inner voice and needs?

Listening without judgement to your own emotions and listening without judgement to other people is a critical skill. Judgement congests your energy and lowers your heart vibration. You will see later on how important it is to have a strong heart vibration for success.
As soon as I meet someone that downloads all of their junk on to me in a social situation – and never asks me one question back – I make a little mental note in my mind and classify 'unconscious of others'. This doesn't mean I dislike them or judge them; they just haven't learned the art of conscious conversation and therefore these people conflict deeply with my values of connection.
In business, the skill of engaging with others, both listening and speaking in equal measures, is very energising and useful if you can successfully master this art. This level of true collaboration opens up ideas and opportunity.

b. **Ability to work through and take responsibility for your emotional baggage**
What does it means when your buttons are pushed by someone?
Do you know this relates to an inner block within you that is unresolved?

If someone or something instigates a negative emotional reaction within you, then there is a block within you that has been pushed/rubbed/accessed. Rather than deflecting blame or judgement on that person, the responsibility is 100% yours to resolve. It doesn't mean they are not a total

41

idiot! They may very well be. It also does not mean that you need to be their best buddy if you don't resonate with them, but any adverse reaction is a sign for you to step up and heal an unresolved issue within you. Otherwise you wouldn't react so fiercely. True emotional consciousness places the onus on you to resolve any tension (within you), not other people or outside situations. You are the only person who can control how you feel. And you cannot control how anyone else feels (nor should you want to). When we take time to work through issues, we free ourselves up and the energy wasted on the block starts activating positively elsewhere.

c. Healthy friendships – with yourself and others

Ok, so if you have moved past the 'I want to be friends/work peers with that person' – the next step is to form a healthy relationship that supports both of you emotionally. A peer or friend needs to be a two-way street of giving (Yang) and receiving (Yin). We often fall back into old habits and roles we are used to playing, such as playing the mothering role or the child role. Neither of these are healthy - as the mother role never receives support and the child role never takes true responsibility. Healthy work relationships answer yes to the following statements:

- There is a healthy exchange of giving and receiving support (includes ideas, inspiring one another, listening to challenges, feedback etc.);
- You genuinely look forward to a regular catch up because that person makes you feel good or energises you; and
- You each have a healthy respect for one another and what skills you can share and learn from.

Beyond others, you then need to have a healthy relationship with yourself. You are the greatest friend and lover you will ever have. Answer these questions to see if you truly care for yourself:

Q. When you feel tired and drained, do you stop work and rest or take some time out? Or do you push on anyway ignoring your tiredness?

Q. Are you aware of the negative self-talk and judgements you have about yourself, making efforts to heal these old wounds?

d. Life Purpose / Blueprint

This topic has a whole chapter to itself! However it is worth a brief mention here. When you are aligned with your passion, this is true emotional mastery. To work in a career that feels like it is your creative hobby means that long after everyone else is burning out and fatigued, you are like an Energiser bunny with unlimited drive. Why? Because the heart energy point on your body is the largest and most powerful (read later for the statistics on how much more powerful the heart is compared to the brain). When your heart connects deeply to your career, only then can you be firing on all four cylinders, all of the time.

Are you on purpose? Do you know why?

Does your career feel fun and exciting?

When you are emotionally conscious – you naturally aim to look to fall into sync with the heart's true purpose, as anything else feels inadequate.

e. How do you nurture your creative side?

When you exercise your creativity, you are using your right (Yin/ feminine) brain. This is the brain responsible for flow, fun, freedom and fertility of ideas. This allows you to tap into a whole new level of strategy and vision in your business life that the left (logical/masculine) brain simply cannot reach. Those with personal creative hobbies can visualise better and are exercising and strengthening a part of their creative brain that massively improves your business nous. The right brain pulls magic out of the void, taps into the 'X Factor' brilliance. Whilst the left brain is a fantastic little computer chip that can then execute any magic you pull out.

Q. How often do you dream (creative/right brain) vs do (logical/left brain)?

Q. What creative hobbies or strategies do you have that strengthen your inner spirit and how regularly do you do them?

A summary so far ... Whereas layers 1 & 2 were all about your physical energy and flow and harnessing that; layers 3 & 4 are about connecting to others and the flow in between You and Another at work. We can often run away from a personal friendship that becomes too hard, but in business we often have nowhere to turn. We either work with a person or connect through a business channel so we need to master these relationships and take responsibility.

Layer 5 & 6: Mental Consciousness – your thoughts, habits, mindset and expression

How conscious are you on the mental plane? Do you have a 'Zenful voice'? Do you know how to get into and stay in the zone, i.e. your power centre and place of balance and flow?

Can you communicate, articulate, sell, manage and lead from your inner Zen? Are you truly a free and sovereign being in charge of your own mental clarity and destiny?

Here are some key concepts that help you to gain mental mastery:

1. **Recognise the Sovereign Self* within**
    What does this really mean? It means that you are responsible (can respond with ability) for your health, your beliefs, your habits and your destiny. You are responsible for finding your own truth and cleaning up any messes that you make in life along the way. If you shy away from this concept, it's probably because you have a lot of mess to tidy up!
    So questions to think about are:

    Q. Do you watch the media (negative news) and allow this to drive your reality? If you do, you are tapped into mainstream fear and it will be hard to break out on your own and be a truly free soul. Let's face it – being truly free in business means that you can be unique, exceptional and a leader.

Q. Do you blindly follow trends of those around you? Or do you set your own pace and establish your truth?

Q. Have you taken time to define your personal values (please refer to the final chapters to define values as they are critical) and ensure you live by these within work and personally.

Q. Do you see yourself in competition with others? (you cannot possibly be as you are unique).

Q. Do you question old beliefs systems to ensure they are not holding you back or stagnating efforts in regards to professional goals. A good example here is that old belief that you have to work hard to make money OR you have to do everything yourself to make it happen OR there are no free rides!

You can make money without working too hard. You deserve to get a free ride and if you collaborate, it makes everything easier.

I had a really interesting experience and insight into the Aboriginal culture of personal value systems when I spent three days with an Indigenous Australian elder called Frank Ansell. One of my greatest understandings of the Aboriginal culture and values came about that weekend. It opened my eyes to a whole new way of understanding them and it's worth a mention here. Here is a dialogue (from my memory recall) between Frank and a western person discussing a fairly contentious topic about personal value and Aboriginal (Indigenous Australians) people who don't have jobs.

The Question of Value

The westerner was discussing the issue of how one person in an Aboriginal family will go out and work and make all of the money, only to return home and then give handouts to everyone; mother, father, sister, brother, cousin, uncle etc. At the end of it, all of their valuable hard earned cash would be depleted in moments. The westerner's point was 'isn't that unfair for the worker bees that they are making the money and everyone else skims off their hard work?' Why wouldn't they want to work hard alongside their loved one to help bring in money and even out the load? Don't they value themselves and their Aboriginal relatives working so hard?

Frank: But that's what they do, they share everything they have with their family. Family is life.

Westerner: But how can they watch their family member work so hard and not go out and work alongside him and support him to bring back money? Isn't that lazy and unfair? Making one person do all of the work?

Frank: No. It's every Aboriginal's responsibility to share what they have with their extended family. Family is everything. If you earn money, you share it.

Westerner: But at the expense of him taking on that full burden on his own? He has chosen to work so shouldn't he deserve something for himself? It's more fair if everyone pulls their weight and earns their value together.

Frank: Ah, that's where you don't get it. Everyone has value (intrinsically) whether they work or not. We don't need to feel valued by being successful or going out and earning money. We were born with value. It is part of us no matter what. Family understand that.

Frank's point here is that their whole social fabric relies on the idea that everyone (every life) holds value regardless of whether you work, have children, drink or don't drink. Their social fabric also relies on gatherings and family ties. Although that culture has a multitude of trauma and alcohol/drug problems, the thing that I really understood about Aboriginal culture that day was that EVERYONE has intrinsic value no matter what.

What an interesting idea? I don't need to be a CEO or head honcho to be equally as valuable as anyone else. Making money to feel valued is a very western notion. I am not saying it is wrong, but I do think we are very controlled by money and success which in turn depletes our wellness or personal value.

I often ask my clients, 'Who are you outside of work'? They often cannot answer.

2. **Stress – do you truly know how to be kind to yourself?**
Obviously you can place yourself under stress when you pollute your body, as we have discussed earlier. However, mentally induced stress is so much worse and can switch on the adrenal glands which control your fight or flight functions.

As the term suggests, fight or flight (or freeze) means that your body is preparing to face a conflict, run away from it or become stuck in fear. Either way it's in some type of panic response and when you have heightened levels of stress, these panic levels stay 'switched on' to cope. And that is when the body gets hammered. Physiologically the body releases an adrenalin hormone which turns off most other non-immediate needs, sexual hormones/libido, digestion and more. Who needs to have sex or eat if they are ready to flee? I have been adrenally fatigued and it is very unkind to the body. If you have been in a stressful job or situation for more than six months, you most likely are adrenally fatigued.

A good friend of mine and I often talk about the idea of 'mental gentleness', which is another way of saying that I am not always driving myself to the point of exhaustion. That I allow for times of high performance followed by recovery periods. Apart from the fact that science is now backing this up, we have known for a long time the value of mental rest and switching off that busy 'monkey mind'. You can be a busy bee for a short period but you must learn how to calm the mind, stop the overdrive and re-focus on a gentler, creative and nurturing activity to break up the pace. Olympic swimmers don't race every day! Being conscious on the mental plane means not only recognising when you are in overspin but pulling yourself out before so you can remain in balance.

feel I have mastered that now – and did so after my extreme burnout at the age of 27. Questions for you are:

Q. How do you incorporate rest and recovery periods into your working life?

Q. What technique do you use after you finish work each day to clear your mind and let go?

Q. How often do you practice mindfulness or meditation?

If you cannot answer these questions easily and off the top of your head, you need some support here.

3. **Ego/Prince vs King archetype**
    I won't elaborate too much here as this borders into the personal realm more than business but as it affects your business life, it is worth a mention.

    Keeping your ego in check is important to master your mental plane. Your ego is a beautiful tool but should always be a servant to your **S**pirit (inner voice) that intuitively guides you. When the ego gets out of control, we can liken it to the prince vs king analogy.

What qualities does the KING have?

The King is the healthy 'true masculine' aspect.

The Prince is unhealthy and is the 'false masculine' aspect.

Let's see how they are different.

KING – true Yang	Prince – false Yang
The King is powerful and courageous and goes to battle when his kingdom needs it.	The Prince power trips and can create conflicts just to exercise his big ego – he doesn't always treat his staff very well.

The King is generous and benevolent to all people and connections to gain respect.	The Prince is generous to those people who can help further his status and career in life.
The King is accountable and responsible and uses his position to create a better kingdom.	The Prince has lots of power but has no responsibility therefore no true accountability – he can act recklessly.
The King cleans up his messes – with people, challenges and conflicts.	The Prince creates messes and then leaves a trail of destruction in his wake.
The King understands karma and seeks to bring balance into life and the kingdom.	The Prince is unconscious and does not take time to create a better future and a balanced karmic journey.
The King communicates honestly – not hiding his feelings or his agenda.	The Prince can be secretive or dishonest in communications for fear of being vulnerable or losing ground.
The King will always think about the group or tribe to ensure the future – but values his own identity too.	The Prince is self-absorbed and does not take the time to think about others. His identity is shaky and this can cause tantrums or inner conflicts.

Q. Which do you play? The King or the Prince? Perhaps you oscillate, depending on what comes up. You might be courageous like the King but communicate like the Prince. Have a think about where you can master your ego by employing the tactics of the King. All of us (men and women) have the Prince and King within us or the Queen and Princess which is another story …

You ego can be very draining on your energy if you continually feed it.

4. **Personal Development**
   Nothing is more important than investing in your own wealth - knowing how you think and operate or how

others operate. Entrepreneurs on a quest to master their working life ultimately know they are really studying the ART OF THEMSELVES and how they can get the best out of themselves. We all work and act in our own customised way. We all understand the concept of becoming the best we can be. So that ultimately means we are invested in deeply understanding ourselves. If we nail that – then we know where our challenges are and how to move beyond them. We know where our gifts are and how to authentically express them. We know how to get the best out of others and to collaborate in a way that works fluidly for all involved.

If you don't undertake some type of personal development every year or two, then you are seriously cutting yourself short. I don't mean just a business seminar or technical skill either, although they are great too. I mean a focused effort on understanding you; because when you do this, you make leaps in your working life.

You can read up on it, do courses, get coaching or attend an inspired seminar to log up your PD hours. A mix of all of them is ideal. Types of personal development that I like (and there are loads out there so please don't let me limit you) are listed in the back of this book under the relevant chapter heading.

5. **Point Zero˙ – finding your own point of gravity**
Now this is the serious bit. How good are you at letting go of stuff? How strong is your own sense of self to remain grounded and centred when life throws a wobbly at you? I like to call this state of strength Point Zero, which ultimately means that you are in a conscious, aware and mindful state to respond to life. Whether that is dealing with the day-to-day or a stressful situation. It does not mean you are detached and numb to stuff, but rather you have a deep awareness and observer within that knows:
a) what your values are and identity is, so that any actions are in line with your authentic self (I can be present and authentic with whatever comes up);
b) that when faced with a stress point in life, you can choose to look upon it, rather than be in it, so you remain out of the

battle fire. This takes the bite out of any major drama so it does not consume you. You can certainly have the feelings and feel them (any denial is pointless) but they just don't take over; you allow external events to unfold without them shaking you off centre.

Q. Do you know your Point Zero? Can you get there easily and stay there?
Where is your sweet spot? Find that and you master life.

6. **Authentic Expression**
I won't spend a long time on this one. As discussed above, when we get clear on our values and identity, so should our communication fall into line with that. Our inner world needs to be reflected through our bridge into the world via our brains/mental plane – thinking, actions and language. People that get recurring throat issues or speech issues often have a conflict with what they are doing versus saying. I say I want to leave my job but I am still here. I say I need a pay rise but I don't ask for it. I say my rates need to be increased but I don't do it.
There is a direct conflict between SAY (will) vs DO (act). It is one thing to know yourself and your needs – yet another to communicate those clearly into the world. The best advice I can give you is to find your natural communication style and practice stating what you need until it feels right. If you already do this well, think about whether what you are communicating is truly what you want! If you don't do it so well, start practicing the art of asking for smaller things in line with your true self and see how your grow in your power. If you don't know your true self – then you might want to look into personal development programs such as my 'Conscious Self'[12] online workshop or work on an identity session to really find out what makes you tick.

A summary so far ... Whereas layers 1 & 2 were all about your physical energy and flow and harnessing that, and layers 3 & 4 are about connecting to others and the flow in between You and Another at work... Layers 5 & 6 are all about mental mastery. Taking ownership for your thoughts and your actions. Learning to manage mindfulness, taking time to understand how you tick and your own individual freedom.

Layer 7 & 8: Spiritual Consciousness – contribution and integration

Now for the juicy bit. If you are in any way conscious, you would have nodded a fair bit to the last three layers – physical, emotional and mental. This last layer may be a stretch for some of you. Certainly these concepts may feel unusual or in some cases 'whacked out' (a highly technical term of course!). If you found the last layer a bit of a jump, perhaps save 7 & 8 to another time. Remember Yin and Yang theory. Sometimes it is best just to 'retreat and wait', rather than shove more in.

If you do decide to read the remaining consciousness layers, I believe they are the most powerful of all actions and will 'leap' your efforts significantly, so don't write off these simple ideas of accessing the spiritual consciousness. Let me remind you again that spiritual does NOT mean religious. Unless of course you are of a particular religion and can see the direct path of connection to your chosen religion.

It relates to the unseen, the 6th sense, the intuitive skills we all own but have forgotten to switch on in our age of rational science-based life.

Developing your Spirituality or Superconscious Mind is not like the other layers, it requires you take the time to 'connect in'. We all understand the concept of putting money into the bank. This is kind of like putting energy or deposits into the 'Spiritual Bank'.

There are so many ways to do this, but let me share just a couple of them. I will keep them brief as you may get lost in the meaning if you have not heard them before. Or maybe you are all over this topic and I am not giving you enough credit?

1. **You are your own God**
   You are not plugged into a wall and you have your own powerful Spirit and blueprint flowing within you. Think of yourself like a mini universe and your heart is like the sun, giving you life force. There must be a recognition that nothing

is going to save you, but you. You have full accountability for yourself. Only your energy is behind your physical matter! Self-actualisation occurs when you realise the extent of your talents and powerful spirit with the ability to co-create.

2. **Contribution – service**
   You understand that you need to use your unique talents to contribute your legacy to the world. Contributing positively to others or the world around you becomes a way of life and gives you a feeling of contentment and true engagement. It is beyond needing money.

3. **Freeing others and self-actualisation**
   You realise that there is no race or competition. You honour other people and assist them to find their true power and talents too. You have become awakened to your Spirit and want to share this with others so they too feel the freedom you have found. You are not really separate from others.

4. **Nature and the Source Field***
   You start to realise that everything is connected. You are one part of the whole group (the world around you). You look at the world with new eyes and treat people, animals and nature with compassion and gratitude – feeling as though they are an extension of you. You realise you are in physical form currently and alive (walking the great red road*) but that one day your energy will shift from matter back to Spirit when you pass away (the great blue road*). But this concept seems okay because you accept death and rebirth as part of nature's experience.

5. **Everything is alive: business entity and thought forms**
   As you accept the greater energy around, you understand that everything is indeed alive and has consciousness. That includes a rock, a plant, a business (entity), a home and even your own thoughts are alive. When we get stuck in a repetitive thought pattern it can grow and become a 'thought form' or a 'life form'. You may not be able to physically 'see' energy but you realise the power of it and work in that paradigm to create true change.

6. **Downloading ideas/channelling**

   You accept and appreciate that non logical ways of thinking produce better outcomes in life and business – especially when it comes to creative ideas or problem solving. You learn ways of tapping into the spiritual mind as a daily practice.

7. **Intuitive decision making**

   You hone your spiritual mind so much that you can literally hear 'truth'. You can sense right or wrong when you listen carefully and you become your own human lie detector. You sense the decision that is best for you even if that means a conflict with your rational brain. Gut instincts take over and you are in flow with the universe.

You can see the depth and breadth that covers that question 'Are you conscious?'. Working with Maslow's hierarchy (using these consciousness steps) is such a powerful way of sorting through the layers and reviewing ways to grow this within yourself. As you stand now, how conscious are you really? Review the below ratings.

Beginner

You have dabbled in some healthy physical activity such as yoga, healthy eating, buying organic and supporting your local farmers. You understand on some level the mind-body loop and realise that looking after your body is key to sustaining your business life. Alternatively, you may be one of the few people that haven't even gotten to this stage yet, so if you are not even doing these basics, it's time to get on board.

You hear about companies like Monsanto[13] trying to dominate the global GMO market but have not taken time to really research what is going on in the world around sustainability. You probably take your doctor's advice without questioning anything and you might consider pharmaceutical drugs like antidepressants and reflux pills to stop heartburn before thinking about the reasons why you have those issues in the first place.

You probably haven't dabbled too much in meditation; maybe you tried some of the 'headspace'[14] tracks but you have not mastered mindfulness or a regular meditation practice. You intellectually understand the concepts of mindfulness and being more conscious in your day to day life, but they haven't stuck at that cellular level yet.

You may not even fully know how to take the next step and because you are busy and don't stop much, where would you find the time to squeeze it in?

Graduate

You tend to live a fairly conscious existence. You understand how to talk to your body and ask it what it needs. You have made the connection between food/emotions and know what you need to feel energised and well. You are aware of good and bad vibes around you and can normally sense when something is off-balance, even if you are not sure what that is.

You do some research into ethically responsible food sources or at least pay attention to which companies are doing the right thing by the earth. You respect the earth and what it provides and do your own bit for the longevity of the world – whether that is growing your own food, supporting organic farmers, marching against Monsanto or something similar.

You probably have some kind of meditation practice going and do a fair bit of personal development. You have most likely found a personal coach or natural healing professional to understand your life and body better and have desire for some type of evolvement that is not just about making more money. You are emotionally intelligent and care about other people. You understand your time is valuable though and ensure your free time is spent with interesting and nurturing people.

You may or may not make space for your creative hobbies, depending on whether you have mastered the work/life balance yet. Certainly you know you have to, it's just a matter of time. Life feels pretty good for you and you generally stay connected to yourself and life.

Some graduates are in their life purpose or passion and some are still seeking it. You are however definitely on the upward climb of Maslow and having a romance with your own self as you uncover the layers.

Master

Oooh, you must be in a good place. Masters of consciousness are indeed masters of their own destiny. They take full responsibility for their life path and actions. If you have a sore ankle, that is your body telling you that there are boundary issues or relationship complications. If you have a falling out with a friend or conflict with someone, you ask myself 'What is my lesson?' and what shadow in you needs to be resolved. You see this as great growth lessons. You continually look for ways to learn more about yourself and how to strengthen your Point Zero so that you grow stronger every day. You know this is the key to a successful working life.

Obviously you are human and get stuck in the world of heaviness from time to time, but you know how to climb back out and grow from that experience. You see yourself as the ultimate god/goddess within, not looking outside of yourself for a saviour or higher power.

You have a fair understanding of energy around you and know how to work with the source field. You see yourself as the highest authority and know that you are your own best doctor of care and advice.

You seek natural and non-chemical alternatives where you can and constantly upgrade your life to improve your energy. You are strongly seeking your life purpose and a fulfilling career, or perhaps you are already in it. If you are, you would be quite successful in your field as working on purpose flows many opportunities your way.

You know how to balance the Yin and Yang, taking time to nurture and repair and then going out into the world to kick butt when you need to. You will only accept a life partner, job offer or living space that feeds your Spirit and nourishes your very being.

Congratulations: What's your plan to help other people gain this level in awareness? When you think like a master, you know all of us are connected so you seek a better 'group collective' experience. The more connected in you are, the more the world changes around you.

References Chapter 2

1. Maslow's Hierarchy of needs: is a theory in psychology proposed by Abraham Maslow in his 1943 paper "A Theory of Human Motivation". It has been widely used in the counselling and psychology fields to describe the different levels of human development.
2. http://hereandnow.wbur.org/2015/01/07/sugar-health-research
3. Sugar feeds cancer cells: thetruthaboutcancer.com/
4. www.buycott.com
5. www.berkeywater.com
6. www.fluoridealert.org
7. GMO stands for 'Genetically Modified Organism' and the theory is that it can interfere with our human body as its genetic blueprint has been tampered with making it potentially 'foreign' and dangerous to our body. Our bodies respond to energy frequencies that are either a) in accordance or b) discordance depending on their

energetic match. "Releasing genetically engineered plants, animals and even bacteria into the environment is a form of biological pollution." http://www.earthsave.org/lifestyle/genfood2.htm

8. Cancer lumps: Don Tolman who lectures globally in natural health talks about the process of cutting out cancer lumps, which create more lumps if we ignore the reason why the lumps exist in the first place, that is to bind toxins. www.dontolmaninternational.com/

9. www.chemicalmaze.com/

10. http://articles.mercola.com/sites/articles/archive/2011/11/06/aspartame-most-dangerous-substance-added-to-food.aspx

11. www.psychologytoday.com/blog/mad-in-america/201106/now-antidepressant-induced-chronic-depression-has-name-tardive-dysphoria

12. Conscious Self Program: Debbie's DIY e-learning program with 12 modules, is designed to teach and inspire you to cultivate your own inner strength. www.rezinate.com.au/conscious-self

13. Monsanto: A US based company that creates chemical based products and is currently trying to patent GMO seed versions of fruit and vegetables to attempt to dominate and own the food supply chain. (natural organic seeds of course cannot be patented so they have no use to Monsanto). **California became the first major state in the US to label glyphosate, the key ingredient in Monsanto's Roundup herbicide, as a chemical 'known to cause cancer.' http://ecowatch.com/2015/09/08/california-becomes-first-state-to-label-monsantos-roundup-as-a-carcinogen/**

14. Headspace: an app that supplies different meditation tracks for mindfulness and relaxation

3

Your Blueprint

Quote: "There are many doorways to wealth. Why not walk through the door that excites the hell out of you?" Debbie Pask

Key learning: Know your blueprint or life purpose and align (translate it) to your career. Knowing the 'why' behind your work (your own unique blueprint) and being able to articulate and sell that is the number one priority for an easy and successful working life.

Key words: Blueprint. Soul Purpose. Heart's Passion. Path. Alignment. Clarity. Gifts. Contribution. Mastery.

What is a personal blueprint?

I love this word because it helps me explain a spiritual concept using 'business speak'. Just like all buildings ever created have an engineering blueprint which documents their uniqueness, so do we have our own individual human blueprint. It is more than just DNA or RNA* (helps carry out DNA's blueprint guidelines). Similar to the fact that we have fingerprints that are unique to us, so do we have talents, gifts and innate skills that have been designed to allow us to fulfil our purpose in this life. Plus we are delivered a series of life challenges that shape our character and hone our skills according to this purpose.

A + B = blueprint

A = natural gifts and talents

B = life challenges and blocks

A + B = blueprint

When you merge them, the picture becomes clear.

Whatever your beliefs; Atheist, Naturalist, Buddhist, Muslim, Christian, Catholic or others, this theme is universal and beyond any religion. After so many years of client work and research on this topic, I strongly believe that we all have a purpose here on planet earth. We know at a scientific level that we are pure energy. Yes – when it gets down to our smallest CELLS it is now proven through quantum science that we are not finite solid beings. Check out the work of Bruce Lipton, a leading cellular biologist[1] who says our bodies exist as light and energy vibration and we are part of a bigger connection (source) to the world. We are a hologram* (copy) of the greater universe. So, does that not instinctively make you question "What am I here for"? Do you really think your life experiences are totally random?

Following on from that – isn't the next question 'What are my talents to share with the world?' or 'What do I bring to the table?'. We are often so busy with life: cars, career, house, kids and then bigger houses and more expensive cars that many of us get to 60 years old or more and realise that we never really stopped and asked the question "What am I here to contribute"?

Matching your unique blueprint (your electricity or Spirit) to your career or business is probably one of the most incredible things to witness. It's as though this connection between your purpose and career allows you to come fully alive and work becomes passionate, fun, exciting and emotionally fulfilling. Why create a hard uphill battle when you can flow with ease and grace? This is the first step to real long-lasting success in business and personal happiness. It will take you so much further than just hard work or skill. True alignment of purpose means that you have found your 'calling' and your inner power.

You might already be working in your passion or purpose, as some people gravitate toward that anyway on some level. It might be five degrees off or right on target. But being able to connect the dots specifically and know WHY you are doing what you do, is a whole new energy. It makes decisions and actions so much easier and more effective. It's like you have your own personal light bulb, lighting the way when you lose your way in business or career - you just follow it to get back on track. It's a sure thing.

A very personal experience of this relates to my husband James. He was naturally 'pulled' towards a career in health and wellbeing early on in life. He missed out the stupidly high university marks required to study sports and nutritional science, so he then got convinced by his tribe and support network to pursue economics and finance. Poor guy! What a passion killer. Well, obviously that was a long way off his natural interests so his university life ended after three months of being miserable and disconnected.

James can recall in his early childhood how much healing and health meant to him. His Grandmother speaks of a little child who used to hold her hand (and just know) when she wasn't feeling well. So, James found some work in retail but in his spare time started his journey of alternative health enterprises, marketing the organic food of the likes of Don Tolman[2] and following high profile people supporting herbal supplements and so forth. He had a love for health and healing that couldn't be extinguished.

Throughout his career experiences, whenever that industry of health and wellness became challenging, instead of encouragement to pursue his dreams, many of his support networks would drive him to go back to marketing, or retail or another very ill-fitting career, all of which were considered safe and useful. These careers were passion killers and not within his blueprint. At 30 years old, James was attempting to do a marketing degree to make other people happy. So, guess what? These avenues always wound up in a dead end.

How does this story end? James, at the time of this book publishing, is now one of three people qualified in teaching one of the most cutting-edge healing modalities (a form of Aboriginal Dreamtime healing) in the world. He helps thousands of clients in compromised mental and physical health situations, to come back to health and wellness. He is clearly thriving and passionate about this work and getting well paid. It comes easily to him because it is his purpose. His has clients worldwide and is continuing to expand his work. I recall clearly the day that James sat down and worked out that deep in his heart he wanted to work in the healing and wellness field. He sat down with a vision board and a bunch of coloured marker pens to map out his dream and purpose. He then took a deep breath and decided that this was his life path and calling and not to let anyone else or any failed attempts to prevent the realisation of his dreams.

People take notice when you radiate passion and purpose and they want to do business with someone like that.

Think about someone you know in business who radiates a strong and passionate energy. How does it feel to be around them?

Knowing your blueprint or purpose is the visionary half of the coin. You need to then back up this vision with a clear and practical career strategy to ensure you reflect to the outside world (yang) the power of your inside world (yin). Back to yin and yang again.

You will never have as much clarity, energy, drive and decision-making freedom as when you know your real heart purpose. Sometimes it only takes a five degree adjustment to make a whole load of difference to business success. Some of you may be nodding your head in agreement when you read this and some of you may pooh pooh the idea that we have a heart-led purpose. When you read the statistics and latest research on the electromagnetic[3] energy of the heart (later chapter), you will understand how important it is to have heart and mind connection for full power. Want more energy? Power up the heart with your life purpose and get some serious connection and flow to it because it's your #1 gateway to keep you healthy, super-charged, flowing and on track with work. It is also your #1 sales tool.

I worked with a client who was definitely in the right industry and doing the right work. She was a counsellor who really helped people doing transformational life work. However she had started to move towards more corporate EQ (emotional intelligence) work (by accident) which started to dilute her real blueprint. Whilst it was related to her current work, it was not fully aligned to her true heart's passion so it didn't really generate that strong and passionate energy within her. When we worked out that her real niche purpose was the bigger and more intense personal and trauma work, and that she had permission to really go for that type of client (and charge appropriately), her business went from being okay to thriving. This was only a 5-10% adjustment in heart focus, but a big difference in the success and abundance of her business. She is a total star and is doing amazing work in the world.

We often don't hear the words heart and business in one sentence

I discuss later on some case studies about businesses that have a strong heart alignment and they perform much better in the market. In addition I will look at the organisation called 'HeartMath'[4] as they are doing some pretty incredible experiments and research papers on the power of the heart. It is really very simple but often overlooked in the world of business.

Once you establish your heart purpose, you have the right launching pad. Then you can decide on the creative expression of this purpose into your career. Creative expression is 'how' you plan to deliver it into the world such as teaching, working one-2-one, developing a product people can use, education of a concept, publishing of a book, building group collaboration, inventing and delivering art or cultural concepts, launching radio stations, online TV channels, starting a political party, consulting to an industry, inventing, coaching others, working in a service based industry and the list goes on.

The Two Parts

A. You establish your inner purpose with intuition, creative reflection and a deep review of what makes you tick. This is a 'yin' process. We don't want logic just yet. Your emotions are like a guidance chip that will tell you whether you are cold, warm or hot. You know you have hit the core of your own unique purpose when you get to the 'AHA' (heightened level of realisation) moments and feel an emotional charge in your body

B. Now the logical mind plays a brilliant role by cementing these ideas into a structure or material working role.

Here is a model of how to work on your blueprint from the inside out. Getting these four layers to integrate is like weaving magic and work takes on a whole new meaning once you crack it.

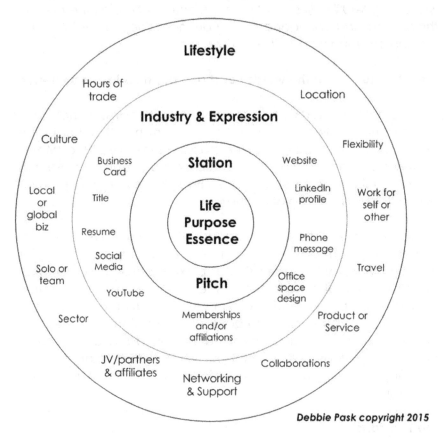

Debbie Pask copyright 2015

1. LIFE PURPOSE/ESSENCE

Personal statement or blueprint of what you are here to do. Often this is an essence or conceptual idea. It is the hardest part to crack as it underpins everything you do (get this part off target and everything else gets muddy). It is a creative and intuitive process.

E.g. *Bringing people together by providing a connected space*

2. STATION/PITCH

Your life purpose translated into a career direction. This becomes your personal identity so people know the 'train station' they arrive at (or get off at) when they meet you. It can also form part of your pitch and personal brand value.

E.g. Building & designing outdoor living spaces for people to connect & celebrate with friends/family

3. INDUSTRY/EXPRESSION

The external expression of *you* into the market place in a particular role or industry

What company, business and role you take that matches your above train station. The industry choice is all about free will; who and what do you want to work with, what is exciting to you on a personal level. This information appears on your CV, LinkedIn profile, your tone, personal brand, phone message, website and any other touch points people would see that tells them WHO you are and what you practically do.

E.g. building and house renovations – specialising in outdoor pergolas and decks etc., working for small, family-owned and fun team.

4. LIFESTYLE

Where do you want to live? What hours do you want to work? How do you want to set up your life so that you feel nourished? What sort of people do you want to connect to on a cultural level? Some of these questions will matter more or less depending on what you need from your working life.

E.g. want to live near the beach in major city in Australia, hence works in building company doing outdoor decks and pergolas on Northern Beaches.

These 4 layers, once pieced together form the backbone of your business blueprint.

How does knowing your life purpose or blueprint energise you at work?

YES and NO Decisions are easy

You easily know what to say 'no' and 'yes' to. Many opportunities come your way and trying to logically work out responses and decisions is clunky and risky. This goes against the rational way society says to make decisions of course! If you get the core of what you are meant to do, it feels so obvious when making a decision. The only question you need to ask is 'does that bring me closer to or further away from my blueprint'? I am not trying to over-simplify this, but simplicity is the universe's intelligence at its best. I love this quote.

"In the beginner's mind there are many possibilities, but in the expert's mind there are few. " Shunryu Suzuki

Your vision grows more powerful

Work does not feel like such a long steep road when you have a clear vision. Usually the western world sees a vision ahead of ourselves - like a little flag sitting on the top of Everest - we are trying to reach and sometimes it moves further way and becomes elusive, and other times it's just within our grasp. The mind will often trick us and move the goal or make it bigger just to keep us entertained! The mind loves to control and move the goal posts to occupy our thoughts and keep us distracted. Read any recent literature on this to understand the ways of the ego/mind. Getting a step ahead of the mind and giving it a clear agenda is very useful.

I like to think of a vision that is not linear or 'ahead' in the distance, but rather one that is deeply within. Not a line, more a circle. You don't go forward on a strange unknown road, you travel within yourself. And the closer you are to your inner vision, the more stable, centred, strong and powerful you are within.

That's real energy. That's real vision.

I feel like this 95% of the time in my business. I am not suggesting I have it all worked out, but I seem to mow down a lot of work easily and still feel energised and healthy. I looked at a picture of myself at 22 years old the other day. I was in my advertising job sitting at a desk and I looked pasty, unhealthy and a little out of sorts. I recently took a photo of myself (now in my perfect career) and at 40 years old, I look fresher, energised and so much more alive than I ever did at 22. This inner goal or journey allows me to become what I am meant to be – the innate blueprint within me. It turns on a magnetic spark within. The more on purpose you are, the stronger your will, your influence and your bridge into the world will become. You will feel vital. You attract the right people, you articulate your message better and you create products and services that seamlessly come into existence because they are from the heart. And most of all, people can sniff out that passion within you and they are very, very excited by it.

Your personal health and wellbeing flourishes

Most people I know who have any level of ambition in business, understand the pitfalls of the modern day working life. People generally accept that 'making it rich' in the world of business has an impact on your health and energy levels. After all, do we really think that working long hours in an office with air conditioning, fluorescent lights and coffee machines are good for our body and mind? If you happen to work for yourself and can avoid the corporate high rises, then there is still the cash flow stress, deadline pressures and challenge of sales – not to mention juggling many balls at once. If you work for yourself you wear many hats.

Working hard takes its toll for sure. However, when you connect with your heart purpose, you will find your energy levels rising and your work becoming easy and fluid. You don't strive to beat competitors because you seriously do not have any. Nobody can quite do what you can do in the way you do it, so the game suddenly becomes all about you and your own pace. But even then it's not as though you can play it slow. The pace will pick up in terms of sales or job offers/promotions even if you are slacking off a bit because you are in flow with purpose and connected to a greater plan.

I won't forget the day I decided to open up my mindfulness training to bigger business. So far, I had worked more with smaller business owners to ensure they were on the right path with their purpose and strategic objectives. I had recently decided to get my programs into a bigger enterprise to make more of an impact. But as I had moved out of Sydney into a smaller town on the East Coast of Australia, I was wondering how this might work? I was not located in a strong business district. And then, somehow, an open-minded person from the local government contacted me to run a stress resilience and mindfulness program across two of the divisional offices. They googled me and must have found my new website. I did not chase this or proactively make this happen. I had not even switched on any search engine strategies on the website so that I could be found. I was more in flow with the universe that I realised and it delivered me an opportunity.

So, back to the point of the personal wellbeing. You don't have the stress of major competition. You feel like you are just embarking on a really exciting and inspired project. You realise you don't have to force or struggle to succeed. In fact, you can relax and still kick major goals. This is an environment where you flourish and repair. There is a theory in many alternative healing therapies that you can pretty much overcome any health problem should you be seriously connected to your heart's purpose. Everything within you resonates to a higher vibration and returns your body to homeostasis (balance and optimal health).

So, find your purpose. It's good for your health!

You MANIFEST faster.... attracting the right clients, partners, collaborations, and support

When you are on purpose, people find you. They want to work with you, collaborate with you and support you. They can sniff out that you have something special because you actually do. Sometimes they are not sure of what it is (about you) and others seem to be aware of the reasons. It depends on how conscious they are. Often these people are a mix of clients, collaborators or staff.

Again I will mention a very synchronistic event that played out in my life in 2012/13. After several years of coaching and energy healing* work, I started to see the need for specific topic-based meditation recordings that would help de-stress the busy cluttered minds of my corporate clients. I had been teaching meditation classes in Sydney for years and was a very experienced meditation teacher focussing on guided visualisations as the technique for focus.

Therefore I came up with the dream to record my own music and meditation tracks. I had no real thought of how I might make this happen, but I put the intention out to the universe that I could meet the right person to make this happen. I knew nothing about music production. That's how it works when you are connected in. You establish what you want and let go of how it manifests. In 2012, I attended a launch of my friend's music teaching website. She asked me to MC the evening because I had helped her to establish the business and we were good friends. Little did I know the universe had big plans for me. At that launch, a small business owner heard me speak and decided that he would be keen to get some coaching from me. I won't bore you with the long story but from that first meeting with him – I met his partner (a music therapist) and her brother (a sound engineer) who became clients of mine and have since collaborated with me to create my first meditation music CD called Zen Business. The universe delivered me the perfect people to make my meditation music dream come alive.

I can honestly say that these three people have seriously enriched my life with their connection and gifts.

Legacy – products fall out that are valuable beyond 'time based' services

When you connect with purpose, you normally extend your thinking beyond just time-oriented services. It's as though you have a sense of contribution and your mind starts thinking creatively and beyond just the day-today working stuff. As I mentioned before, it's not about chasing a flag of fame on Everest, it's more about going within yourself and pulling out the magic from within. It will birth from you naturally once you find your career flow. And this product or research or idea will be the thing that launches you from average to great or from great to brilliant.

So if you are interested in creating an idea that outlives yourself and drive your career to a level beyond the ego/mind, then you need to access your purpose. Again I will suggest you might already be part way or fully in your purpose, but connecting your 'why' clearly into the conscious mind will turn some extra lights on between the left and right brain.

The sales process is easier

Whether you are selling yourself for a job or making a sale to a customer/client, knowing your 'why' or purpose will give you such a powerful platform to close the sale because there is nothing more convincing than truth. People can sniff it out.

There is a famous example that illustrates the power of selling Apple Products. You should check it out for yourself but the premise goes something like this. Many businesses build computers and the customer is not really interested in HOW the gadget is made. Too techie! Somewhere in the laptop is a mother board, a data chip and some RAM. Yawning already... Nor is the customer much interested in price (providing prices are in their budget generally). What the customer is interested in is the THINKING and IDEAS that underpin the making of that computer. Why Apple? And in Apple's case it is their 'Think Different' slogan that captures customers. Apple positions itself as innovative and 'thinking outside the box'. They create mystery and excitement around their launches. People buy into that purpose, not the piece of hardware before their eyes.

Their 'WHY' is clearly on public display and people buy into that message.

What is your 'why'?

How could you apply this concept of life purpose right now in your working life?

It depends on whether you feel like:

    a) I am heading in the right direction and feel passionate about my career/business – but just haven't completely connected the dots as to the 'why'.

       OR

b) I am disconnected to my career and feel either lost or stressed about it.

The a) outcome means that you need to get the creative part of the equation established (your personal blueprint) and then see how it translates into your current career. Look at my shortcut guide below to figuring life purpose, answer a couple of the questions and you will see a pattern forming with your current career if indeed you truly are aligned. Make this connection and you will be pleasantly surprised.

The b) outcome pretty much requires an overhaul of your career. This does not need to be stressful. See the shortcut guide and example below as a starting point and overview. You will need to review all four layers. I also have some online resources (listed in chapter 14) you can use to deepen your enquiry and take it to the next level.

Debbie's shortcut guide to establishing your life Purpose or blueprint

Considering this really is such a significant part of your life and energy, I do suggest you take the careful time to reflect and work through establishing and uncovering your life purpose or blueprint as I call it.

The below questions aim to get you thinking about your individual blueprint. The questions are to be answered personally, but if you get stuck, at the end of the questions I have used myself as an example so you can see how it works practically. Here is a quick summary to start the thinking around your life purpose.

Let's review the diagram again...

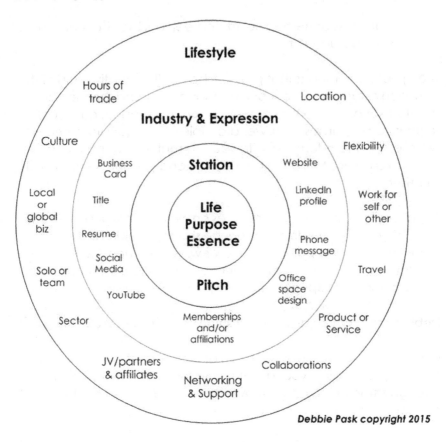

Debbie Pask copyright 2015

Level 1 – Essence (innate blueprint)

Level 2 – Station (translated)

Level 3 – Industry (free will)

Level 4 – Lifestyle (personal needs)

Level 1: What is your Essence? Write some quick notes below each.

1. What are your three biggest gifts? i.e. what do you inspire in others, what do others come to you for? Where do your greatest talents lie naturally? These are not usually developed talents, but ones that you had as a kid or that arose naturally throughout life. If you are unsure, ask someone close to you.

2. What are your two to three greatest challenges in life? i.e. ones that have thwarted you over time; challenges that have made a serious mark in your life and that hold deep significance for you.

If you have answered those questions consciously – you will start to see a pattern emerge as to what makes you tick and what is aligned to your heart.

Your greatest gifts will show 'how' you can contribute.

Your biggest challenges will specify 'what kinds' of contribution you will be drawn to helping with.

So the idea is to have a career using the gifts you already have within you, to resolve challenges that you have faced yourself and hence understand intimately.

You have to make some intuitive leaps as you do this process and you will know it is right when you hit the target because it literally brings a tear to your eye.

Once you see the pattern, you will eventually find the **'seed', the 'essence'** or key concept/idea that underpins your entire existence and this is real power. It is your version of the 'think different' slogan. I share an example later on.

Level 2: What is your (train) Station?

A great way to see this second stage is to think about a train station that you know well. If you catch a train there, you know exactly where you are getting off and what to expect in terms of people, homes, business or culture. Think of yourself like a train station. When people catch a train to your station, what are they getting when they hop off? What problem do you help solve? What do people naturally come to you for? Don't just think business, think about your personal life. What do family, friends and colleagues need from you the most? Write a short answer below.

Level 3: Your Industry Sector

What drives you? What do you like to see happen in the world? What do you get very passionate about? Think in terms of people, projects, the world, the earth. What is it that satisfies you right to the core when it happens?

Then think in rational terms about what industry most excites you. Do you prefer to work for yourself or a larger organisation? What working hours and culture do you seek? Are you working with kids or adults, on products or services?

Level 4: Lifestyle

What sort of life do you need or want? Where are you living? What sort of flexibility is important in your work in relation to hours, location, privacy, availability etc.?

These questions may take time to answer so here is my practical example to make this come to life. I have used my own summary blueprint as a guinea pig, which is sort of like getting naked really!

Debbie's Blueprint and Life Purpose

Level 1 – Debbie's core gifts

- deeply and quickly understanding the needs of others,
- seeing people's pure potential, their inner talents and also their baggage and what they need to let go of to be free,
- confidence and energy – helping people feel powerful and believe in themselves.

I always had people coming to me when I was growing up who needed my strength, confidence in them and my advice. I was helping people with career choices and CV's very early on in life. I could always see a way through a problem of the mind.

Debbie's big challenges

- strong swing toward the yang (masculine and action-oriented) energy,

- letting the mind/logic run the show – control issues,
- work burnout at a very young age – realising I was in the wrong career.

I was a very strong minded child who didn't like being told what to do. I was a natural leader growing up and I played all of the so called 'masculine' sports – soccer, cricket and hockey. I hated the colour pink because it was too girly and was a little powerhouse at 'doing' things. I thought I wanted to be a builder/brick layer at around 6 years old because it looked like a strong person's job! I was good at solving problems and seeing through things very quickly and saying it how it was. I was very committed to equality and wanted everyone (especially underdogs) to have a fair chance. I was very generally calm and happy until I didn't get my way and then I could blow into a towering rage. Control issues were definitely a challenge for me and I burned out badly at a very young age from over-driving and taking on too much responsibility for others.

You can see a pattern forming here. I have a natural problem-solving mind (yin) – alongside a directive and confident personality (yang). Yet, my own life challenge (of burning out and letting the mind dominate) meant that I was forced to learn how to find a healthy balance between heart/creativity and mind/logic for a successful and sustainable life.

Hence my personal essence or blueprint is simple – working with concepts of yin and yang for balance. **My mission is heart and mind coherence (connection) to solve problems (yin) and to cultivate strength (yang).**

Level 2 – Debbie's Station

What do people get when they get off at my train station?

People come to me to **solve their problems** – for a direct, fast and supportive approach that ensures both heart and head are aligned. They have a problem where they need the intuitive intelligence of the heart (a non-rational solution) backed up by the confidence/ action of the mind.

What sort of problems do I solve?

From personal life matters right through to commercial business decisions – I give you focus, clarity and balance - quickly and passionately.

Level 3 – Debbie's Industry Choice

I like to solve problems and cultivate strength in two industry sectors – personal wellbeing and business. I see them as going together, if we are in flow personally so is our career and business.

Overall it's about building strength in people...

- seeing people fulfil their potential (especially life purpose/ career),
- balance of heart and mind (to work at their full creative and mental power),
- identity work (letting the old parts die off and bringing in the new).

Preferences: I like working with adults – coaching, teaching, writing and inspiring people with ideas. I prefer to work for myself as I value freedom and independence for my day-to-day decisions. I like a good mix of services and product creation so that I can interweave the two together. I get bored quickly otherwise.

So how did I translate that all into a career path for me that I can market to the world? Here's what I extracted...

Practical applications/offers for my coaching would be:

Life Purpose Work – helping people transition (death) off their old careers and find a new career, business or passion. Believing in people. Illuminating their purpose.

Confidence Coaching – creating flow, mindfulness and solutions for people going through major life challenges - teaching people how to lead with their heart and follow up with logical intelligent actions. This sometimes means letting go (death) of old out-dated fears or ways of thinking so as to bring in new (birth) powerful energy.

Business & Career Coaching – working with owners or managers on a personal level to succeed. I provide clarity, focus and insight into what is hidden or blocked and help them find a sustainable balance between the yin and yang.

Can you see how my life purpose (life challenges and natural gifts) translate so easily into my business? My core blueprint of yin and yang balance could also translate to other careers such as medical emergency ward (death and birth), obstetrician, psychologist, fertility work (I have done this), weight loss coach, creative art teacher, career guidance counsellor, social worker etc. However, I have chosen (with free will) an industry that *I am most passionate about* – helping people cultivate strength in career and self.

Level 4 – Debbie's Lifestyle

I will keep this brief, but it is important to establish your working life to synchronise with your personal lifestyle needs. These choices may change over time, but my own personal preference is to live in a less populated city and live near the ocean in a rainforest of sorts. As this sort of lifestyle is not a big city with plenty of my client types, I have adapted my coaching business to cater for distance with Skype sessions and also plenty of time in between visits to the city by writing books, creating workshops and content.

So, I live in a rainforest most of the time, working from home and I visit larger cities to see clients and teach when I need or want to. I enjoy the travel and mixing it up. I am a much more relaxed person and grateful every day to work in my passion on my terms.

In my mind there is always a way of aligning your lifestyle needs to the work you do. Even if that means commuting, consulting via distance or negotiating varied hours, the choice is within your grasp. It might mean taking a slight sideways step or fine-tuning exactly what you do. Or if you cannot get that right now in your job, plan for it later on. It starts with intention, so what is yours?

As it currently stands, without having answered those above blueprint questions, rate your current level of mastery in the area of life purpose and blueprint. How well are you really living out your unique blueprint and do you even know what it is?

Beginner

You have not given too much thought to that higher level of purpose and 'why'. You may feel like you are in a job/career suited to your skills but don't have a super clear focus that gives you a strong alignment to your personal purpose. You have not allowed too much creative dreaming as your focus has been on making money to support your lifestyle – whether that is family, retiring early or travel/adventure. You probably plan to retire when you can and enjoy life as you don't see your career carrying you well into your 80s! Work is sometimes great and can also be a drag. If money wasn't an issue you might be doing something different and taking some more risks in life to feel more fulfilled and creative.

OR... maybe this describes you: You are really unhappy in your career. You know on some level it is not right for you but you might feel trapped for reasons such as money, family commitments, confidence issues or others. Thinking about change feels heavy and challenging, especially as life has many other demands on you. You understand the work tasks that you like, but your heart is not really connected to career day-to-day and this is disconcerting for you. Is there really another path you can take to change?

Graduate

You generally know you are in flow with the right industry/career. You are reasonably clear on gifts that you have and feel they are being utilised nicely in your career /working life. You have a natural passion and aptitude for work and it comes easily and pleasurably to you. You don't have a specific end date to your working life as you enjoy what you do and can see it lasting a long time. People tell you they can see a light in your eyes come on when you go about the work you love. You have taken time to understand more about what makes you tick and to ensure that you incorporate that into daily life. Happiness and work satisfaction are high on your list and money comes after that. You also know what aspects of the job you don't like and have made moves to outsource or handover that tiresome work, knowing it takes you off-path from your real joy/skills.

You probably couldn't say in 30 seconds exactly what your intrinsic value is though. You see work as an addition to yourself;

not necessarily part of you and the connection between your life purpose and business role is not 100% mapped out yet.

Master

You know why you do what you do. You are working in a lifelong passion and don't see your career as 'work' per se. In fact sometimes you laugh to yourself due to being paid for something that brings you total pleasure. You probably don't plan on retiring because you see work as a series of creative projects that ebb and flow in life. Sometimes you find yourself working harder and driving and sometimes you are just cruising along taking it easy. You feel you have a place in the world and are here to contribute or leave a legacy. You could do your job with your eyes closed, yet you love learning new things about it. You often do personal research long after everyone else stops for the day because it's your natural hobby or passion. You find things (people, support, resources, and sales) come easily to you around work because you are in flow and in line with purpose. Usually you feel vital and energised and spiritually centred knowing you are fulfilling your life path.

You understand clearly the deeper meaning of your work and can easily communicate this value to people around you. That is why work opportunities flow so easily - people can see the passion and value you offer. Referrals are your number one source of success. People want to collaborate with you as they can sniff out the inner power. You are indeed on your way to becoming (or are) the expert in your field and feel that your work and your inner self are integrated and fluid.

If you are not at Master level and want to get there, I suggest you make the time to get super clear on your individual blueprint so your foundations are strong and inspiring. It will give you a massive edge and boost to whatever you are doing, so why wouldn't you? Whether you are a) generally in the right direction or b) lost in your purpose – getting clarity is only going to boost your business life and help you define your value.

References Chapter 3

1. www.brucelipton.com
2. www.dontolmaninternational.com
3. Electro-magnetic energy of heart; Heartmath.org have proven that the heart has electrical energy and magnetic energy in large doses and when compared against the brain is far more powerful.
4. Hearthmath; www.hearthmath.org

4

Leverage – Leave your legacy

Quote: "There comes a time when you roll up your sleeves and put yourself at the top of your commitment list." Marian Wright Edelman

Key learning: Trading time for money all of the time will eventually tire you out. Conscious entrepreneurs and business people connected to life purpose have a longer term product strategy and a legacy to leave in the world.

Key words: Content. Amplitude. Creation. Longevity. Strategy. Product. Multiples. Legacy. Teaching. Wisdom.

Fishing Story

An American investment banker was at the pier of a small coastal Mexican village when a small boat with just one fisherman docked. Inside the small boat were several large yellowfin tuna. The American complimented the Mexican on the quality of his fish and asked how long it took to catch them.

The Mexican replied, "Only a little while". The American then asked why didn't he stay out longer and catch more fish? The Mexican said he had enough to support his family's immediate needs. The

Debbie Pask

American then asked, "But what do you do with the rest of your time?"

The Mexican fisherman said, 'I sleep late, fish a little, play with my children, take siestas with my wife, Maria, stroll into the village each evening where I sip wine, and play guitar with my amigos. I have a full and busy life." The American scoffed, "I am a Harvard MBA and could help you. You should spend more time fishing and with the proceeds, buy a bigger boat. With the proceeds from the bigger boat, you could buy several boats, eventually you would have a fleet of fishing boats. Instead of selling your catch to a middleman you would sell directly to the processor, eventually opening your own cannery. You would control the product, processing, and distribution. You would need to leave this small coastal fishing village and move to Mexico City, then LA and eventually New York City, where you will run your expanding enterprise."

The Mexican fisherman asked, "But, how long will this all take?"

To which the American replied, "15 – 20 years."

"But what then?" asked the Mexican.

The American laughed and said, "That's the best part. When the time is right you would announce an IPO (initial public offering) and sell your company stock to the public and become very rich, you would make millions!".

"Millions – then what?"

The American said, "Then you would retire. Move to a small coastal fishing village where you would sleep late, fish a little, play with your kids, take siestas with your wife, stroll to the village in the evenings where you could sip wine and play your guitar with your amigos."

"But I already do that now!"

Moral to the story? Find out what it is that you want in life (like the fisherman) and create the leverage in your business that supports that! Don't just try to grow or create something just to make money, but do work in your passion. The fisherman does have an obvious leverage strategy though if you think about it long enough. He loves visiting the bar and playing guitar with his mates every night. So, why not get creative and start recording an album together. He is there each night practicing away. Sell the album to tourists or a music distribution company and contribute to the world by leaving a legacy of local Mexican music. Alternatively, talks on work/life balance to others would work a treat...

What is leverage to you?

If you really get the idea of blueprint, then you will be busting to make your mark in the world. To create something that outlives you or at least delivers to the world a bigger vision. Conscious business people and owners know all about this concept called 'leverage'. Many business owners do not understand the value of leveraging a product or service. It's as simple as this...

Do something ONCE, get rewarded several times over. Or innovate something that has far reaching implications for yourself and the workplace/industry you are in and be known for that (contribution). Or build a network or profile that goes beyond your current job or role. Leverage that profile you create. Examples of leverage for business owners are:-

- Create a CD/DVD. You record it once and sell several copies for not a lot of additional work;
- Online Memberships. You post information ONCE to your subscriber base which reaches many people and hence you create multiple revenues;
- Write a Book. You publish a book and it sells via several channels. Or sells other services that are valuable;
- Teach a class. You share your value with several people and your hourly rate is way higher than normal because you have leveraged the class numbers;
- Launch a Product. If it is popular, word spreads and the value of that idea can keep paying out again and again. Think Arnotts Tim Tams OR iTunes;
- Hire a team of people to expand your offer/volume – leverage a team of people;
- Franchise or license your business ideas or concepts;

- Sell information or research to multiple parties (this works well for non-business owners when/if they want to leave an industry);
- Build a valuable people network or database;
- Repurpose content; create new ways of presenting and delivering products and services
- Magnify your brand attraction – become the expert in your area;
- Leverage 3rd party products that you are absolutely passionate about;
- Create a foundation or charity that is crowd-funded or goes global

---

Recipe for Leverage

Here's what you need...

1 tblsp industry sector

3 tblsp skills

2 tblsp experience (hours clocked up)

1 tblsp blueprint/life purpose

5 tblsp passion and joy

1 tblsp market need/niche opportunity

1 tblsp study/education

Mix it up with some focus and clarity, and out pops your leverage cake.

Now you may think this does not relate to you if you don't own a business and hence work for someone else. If you own your own business, you can set your own agenda.

If you are working for someone else, make sure you choose a company that is aligned to your dreams and you can form part of the team that delivers the legacy. You can still very much build your own expertise and profile so that you become more valuable to your current workplace or more valuable in the market overall. Some of the examples above can be applied regardless of whom you work for.

You might work in a company long enough to become a guru in a product genre or service. Therefore if you decide to leave, you take that brains and knowledge with you to either create your own products OR leverage that in your new job. Keep in mind that (although there is money to be made), the idea is that you leave a legacy out of your passion and blueprint; not just money as per the fisherman story above. If that means you are involved in someone else's vision or business, work within that framework and make it matter.

There are so many ways you can leverage your time, but the key is that you attempt to incorporate this into your working life. Otherwise you will be continually trading time for money (hour by hour) or feeling like you are not making a solid difference longer term. This can feel like a treadmill after a period of time, even if you are super passionate about what you are doing. It's exciting to use your creative powers to build something that goes beyond just the day-to-day work you deliver. In a way, it is like your legacy and a very 'yin' thing to do. It is a creative flexing exercise.

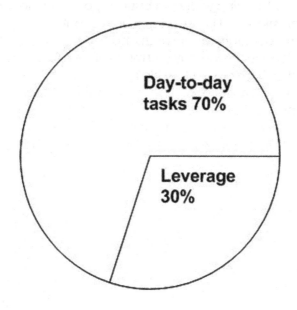

My advice is to allocate between 15 - 30% of your working hours creating 'leverage-able' products and services (if you run your own show). This might seem like a high volume and if you are super cash strapped or unable to do this in your employed role, perhaps work on the lower % scale. My magical formula is 70/30; 70% in the business working and 30% stepping out to create strategies, creative projects and building leverage. For me that is products like my meditation albums, books, online study, workshops (online and offline) and content that I want to share with the world. If you are working within a larger organisation, work out what time you can commit (10% or 15%?) and get that approved. If it is a great idea and your working culture is aligned with your gifts, then getting the support and approval of your manager or employer should be easy. If this is not possible, seek out ways to do this yourself either outside of work or within working hours.

Here's an example of what that 15 - 30% time could entail ...

- Gathering research or data and looking for trends. Does your industry work from trends/analysis of data?
- Is there a clunky process or way of doing things that you could improve or create?
- Could you automate part of your job?
- Can you flex your creative-self outside of working hours (or within if owning your own business) and develop something interesting and in line with your passion?
- Can you share an inspirational story – book, blog, vlog, podcast etc? One day you might have a following of people and charge a membership?
- Can you create a solution to a problem – through software, apps, etc.?
- Could you develop a teaching program (on stuff you currently do) that you could leverage in your industry?

Questions

1. What do you want from life? What excites you and what kind of life do you want to live? Your idea of leverage must work in with this dream. So think passion + lifestyle = leveraged idea.

_____

_____

_____

2. Where can you see opportunities in your current business or job that could be the <u>start</u> of a leverage strategy? What sort of item or solution might it be? Think hard as there is always an opportunity in abundance.

_____

_____

_____

3. How much time and energy do you think it will take to get this going?

_____

_____

_____

Don't see this as a race either, as that can be stressful. Your talents can never be replicated. Finding unique ways to get your value into the market should be exciting and seen as a priority over just 'time for service' charging.

Here are some examples of great leverage models. I have included both smaller and bigger business ideas so that you can see this is not just for bigger businesses.

Power Living – 100 people attending a yoga class (leverage is in numbers/class). Plus they now run training and mentorships for aspiring yogis;

Conscious Club Sydney – large numbers attending an event + building a database of like-minded people to on-sell other services/ events/products;

Zumba DVDs – packaged DIY exercise dance program that can be sold again and again without extra effort after initial production;

Skype – online communication tool that is free at ground level to capture volumes of people – and then additional small cost paid services you can add on for convenience;

Facebook – massive volume of people with collected personal data - with new paid services adding on, such as targeted ads (based on personal data), boosting posts and more;

Michelle Bridges – 12 week online DIY exercise and diet program – high numbers of people joining program;

Rezinate – metaphysical healing based business (mine!) with products created and marketed to captive audience – such as CDs, DIY e-learning, training etc.,

Health Ranger e-books – Mike Adams creates loads of low-cost but super information packed e-books for purchase to get your health where it should be;

Audible.com/Audio books – record the book and sell to mass consumers;

Seriouseats.com/Food blog site – popular food blog site (valuable database);

Media Fire – online cloud software to store your large digital files, and be able to send links to others for easy access; and

Nielson Reports – collects data to create useful statistical reports then sells to several parties.

Building leverage is very energising because there is a greater reward at the end PLUS it gets you to tap into your yin/creative mindset. A double win. I love it.

Summarise your one-page leverage plan using the template below. I have used one of my self-development products (online study) as an example, so you can see how it works.

Industry: Wellbeing	Leverage: Debbie's Product 'The Conscious Self' – a 12 week online study program to evolve your intuitive and spiritual self for more confidence, energy and connection.
Customer base/ target market (e.g. demographic)	People feeling they want more connection, mindfulness and confidence within to face life. Deeper understanding of own self.
Current services/ products offered in your market sector?	To date I have offered client sessions and workshops – but no self-paced study program. There are a few other competitor products in market as online study options so I saw a growth area here to get my program going.
What is popular/ growing?	Online e-learning, Health and Wellbeing industry $750B growing industry. Also life coaching is a growing area so I felt the logic was sound to warrant investment of my time.
How could you leverage your service/time/ product? i.e. think groups/workshops, 3rd parties, online, DIY service package, productisation, systems & processes, content (video/ audio/written), affiliations, memberships etc.	I created an e-learning program from my material collected over 12 years and offered it to current clients and new people looking for mindful self-development. Includes video, audio, and written reflections/questions to give each client a personalised application of all concepts. I uploaded the content into WISHLIST (in back end of my website) and automated the delivery to send the customer one module each week. There is nothing I need to do manually once the client purchases the program.

How can you increase your client numbers, staff engagement, customers, network or database/reach so that you can expose people to your product or idea?	Building database over time of people seeking mindfulness and stronger intuition. Build a good SEO (online search) campaign to capture any people looking for it online. Develop PR to attract customers. Piggyback on other people's e-news.
If you have several ideas, order them in priority of 1st (easiest and most lucrative opportunity) to last.	For me that was marketing to my current client database.
With your Priority #1 – how much $ and time do you require to create it? What support or approvals might you need? What's the timeframe to complete it?	Mine is completed – but here is what it took: Time involved to create content, upload and test – Total timeframe – 6 months Hard Costs – Wishlist e-learning software, assistant/VA, promotional postcards designed and printed
What are the next three actions to take to start your journey of leverage? Suggest you start with scoping the idea and getting some feedback first from people you trust…	

A good tip when working on this project is NOT to do this at your desk. Your desk working space can be heavily administration based and removing yourself from this area can free up your mind to be more creative. This is not always the case though – so get a feeling for where you can be most creative and inspired.

If it's your desk – great! If creativity does not live there, aim to move.

Also – once you start making actions to build your leverage, ensure you break it down into easy to do weekly tasks. There is no race remember. For example, when writing this book I have been giving myself small goals of trying to write a draft chapter each fortnight. These weekly actions build up and soon enough you have a masterpiece.

Rate yourself on how good your leverage strategy is.

Beginner

You have not given the idea of leverage much thought in your business life. You are either not tuned into the idea, too busy to allocate the time or don't believe you have the creative abilities to leave a powerful legacy. You may not be sure where you might start even if you did have an idea to pursue. Your upbringing may not have encouraged this sort of ideation and entrepreneurialism and you might not see this as your role in life. You are happy to just go to work, clock on your time and leave – with the focus being on your outside work life. It would be nice to make a difference though, wouldn't it?

You probably underestimate how much you know and what you can contribute. If you have had zero passion or inspiration to leave any kind of legacy and you are over 30 years old, then you may not have found your ideal career role. Alternatively, the appeal to follow a dream has not been initiated.

Graduate

You have given this quite a bit of thought and have ideas ready to go or may have even started your path to leverage! You are somewhere between starting the legacy and finishing the product/ service but time to work on it can be elusive and life is pretty busy. You may have a few ideas going at once and sometimes BSOs (bright shiny objects) can distract you from finishing something through. The mental intentions are there and relatively clear, but you are not over the line yet and seem to find excuses not to finish.

This may be from lack of confidence in the project, your lack of detail/ability to execute/finish or just that your personal life is really hectic right now and there's not much left in the tank to really nail it. Maybe you are well on your way but cannot get the last 20% finished or over the line. You need to give your projects some more action and physical output, or at least review what they are and cull down or focus on the first big one. If budgets/capital is preventing you from surging forward, then you should look to seek either funding or raise monies to get it over the line.

You have it in yourself to think big, but you just need time to bring it to life.

Alternatively you might be in full swing of making it happen, it's just a longer term plan and other stuff needs to fall into place first.

Master

Ha. You have your first project (leverage) done and completed, if not several. You are aware of the value of allocating time to create longevity of projects/products/ services etc. You are quite proud of the fact that you have created something inspiring that will last the distance. You have a good routine that keeps you aware of the value of leverage and whilst that attention might wane on and off at various times in your life, you are committed to the path. You see it as an intrinsic part of your business life/career and have a healthy attitude toward your own creativity and abilities in your chosen field. You would like to lead your field and positively impact the industry sector you work in.

As a result people wishing to collaborate are drawn to you and opportunities manifest. You can see the value growing in your creations and hence regularly allocate your 30% weekly time to the creation of ideas and a legacy that will hopefully outlive you some day, or at least last your lifetime and contribute something special in the world.

For those of you at this master level, talk about and broadcast your creative projects to get others inspired to start theirs. You know when other people start connecting into it when a light comes on in their eyes. Sharing inspiring stories is a big gift.

5

Soul Colleagues

Quote: "People come into your life for a reason, a season or a lifetime. When you figure out which it is, you know exactly what to do." Michelle Ventor

Key learning: Tap into an authentic community of like-minded business people to supercharge your energy. Surround yourself with inspired souls.

Key words: Connection. Inspiration. Advice. Support. Community. Mentors. Business Sage. Accountability. Transformation. Learning. Sharing. Receiving. Objectivity. Reflection. Dreaming. Inspiration. Propeller. Value.

Where's my tribe?

Happiness catches. This I know to be true. When you connect with inspired business owners or people who have a conscious heart and a sharp mind, you cannot help but be lifted up. It's a real game of give and receive; Yin and Yang. Sometimes they can provide information, advice or even just a patient ear to help you transcend a business challenge. Other times you reciprocate. Don't underestimate the value of connecting with your own group of business peers. Select people or a group that energise you. Don't hang out with energy suckers; rather hang out with people that energise you and where you can give and receive equally. If you are coach or consultant, sometimes your clients will be this ray of sunshine. I am lucky to have several clients like that.

At a basic level, there are two types of people you come across in business:

Energy Suckers – they drain your energy and make you feel tired. It's not about them being negative (although they might be) but rather their vibration is not matched to yours and they rub your 'energy' up the wrong way.

Energy Enhancers – they make you feel like a million bucks. They either spin your good mood into a great mood, or they pick your backside up when you are feeling low. They excite you and inspire you to live a better business life.

If you are empathic (a person who feels things very deeply and can easily take on others emotions) – then someone who is an energy sucker (also called energy vampire) can really adversely affect your energy. We discussed the idea of being an 'empath' in an earlier chapter, but if you watch the world news on television and start to feel sad, overwhelmed or deeply affected by the news, it is likely you are empathic and feel things on a deeper level than others.

Identify who in your peer group at work is an energy sucker or an energy enhancer. Write a list below.

_____

_____

_____

Have a think about ways in which you can connect more with enhancers and less with the suckers. You would be surprised how much this will make a difference in your world and flow of business.

_____

_____

_____

The Power of the Group

Collaboration is a powerful concept. It gives us a joint purpose (intent) and matching values which allows many minds to come together to create something big. Many television shows we watch focus on competition (i.e. MasterChef) which works against the idea of collaboration. This mindset really needs to shift if we are going to grow toward a better future. Don't encourage competition, encourage connection. The big banks compete; we need to group together more to do things differently than these corporate giants.

I came across a great collaboration recently called Oz Harvest. Oz Harvest was founded in November 2004 by Ronni Kahn, who was named Australia's Local Hero of the Year in 2010. Basically it is the only food rescue organisation in Australia collecting surplus food from all types of food providers including fruit and vegetable markets, supermarkets, hotels, wholesalers, farmers and more – and then delivering this food to people in need. I have personally met one of the volunteers called Julie whose life purpose is to help provide for people in a disadvantaged state.

Oz Harvest relies on the food donors and supermarkets, the people delivering the food and also initially the government to pass laws to allow this. The *Civil Liabilities Amendment Act* was passed in NSW Australia in 2005 with ACT, SA and QLD following. This ensured surplus food could be donated to charitable causes without fear of liability.

Oz Harvest is a true collaboration with their joint heart purpose to feed those in need and sharing values of kindness and sustainability.

Tribe is about connecting to a greater social fabric beyond your immediate family. Finding your tribe is like finding your soul family. You connect to something that you feel good about and supported by.

There are many business organisations and groups out there to connect with, some more aligned with your values than others. Personally I have never been interested in a hard line network referral group where the focus is on introductions and sales. That is why I chose to become a part of an organisation called Business Master Minds (BMM) in Sydney Australia. This group is about collaboration and business nous. I describe it as my own round table or management team. The key benefits of BMM are inspiration, connection and education. I have learned loads from these breakfast sessions, made some amazing business friends and have felt a true connection to the group. I found my tribe here in this group and know what a huge value and contribution it made to my working life.

I have heard of other business networks like EO (Entrepreneurs Organisation), EA (Entrepreneurs Australia), BNI (Business Network International) and others. Search around and choose what works for you. Online communities are also useful if you don't mind the virtual world of connection. I personally like face-to-face contact but can see the value in both models depending on how you live your life.

It's also not just a case of having your own conscious group of supportive business networks. Seek partners, supporters, advocates or freelancers that can provide skills and traits that enhance your working world, connect you together for a common purpose and provide inspiration to bring your work projects alive.

I remember coaching a client on his tendency to procrastinate getting the things he needed done to fulfil a huge project/dream of his. A combination of 'too much on his plate' and 'where do I start?' was delaying any kind of traction on the project. I decided that it wasn't the right idea to set him strict deadlines or work through his mental blocks. Forcing through on his own was just not going to work. So I asked him to engage several other third parties to start working on the project with him. To create a tribe. It was a big vision and he just wasn't going to be able to do it by himself. So, with each person doing their part, the momentum of delivering him components kick-started him into doing his actions too. The group energy propelled him to respond to their work.

When he asked for something, they responded with an answer and he couldn't ignore it. Sometimes overcoming procrastination relies on being accountable to a group or person, to engage people and share your vision so you are responsible for something bigger than just us. I don't think humans are designed to work solo for a long period of time.

A great solution of tribal energy, being accountable to an external influence. Action and reaction.

This next sentence is going to be a HUGE relief.

You DON'T have to be a master of everything in business and do it alone, all of the time.

In fact, if you did everything yourself you would be a 'jack of all trades' and master of none. Just like in school, you might have excelled at English or Music but not Maths. That is normal and good and perfectly acceptable. You probably wouldn't know how to build a computer, yet you use one.

You drive a car, but does it really matter that you know how to make one? Don't get caught up in being fantastic at everything – just pick whatever excites you and is your natural skill. Then engage others to do the bits you dislike or cannot do. People who do this seem to climb the career ladder quickly.

It's a bugbear of mine that school advocates a 'normal' benchmark with students. We are all taught to be good at all subjects and when we fall down on something a bit – we are tutored (tortured?) or forced to spend more focus on improving that quality. Imagine if you were just nurtured toward your own unique talents? Everyone would be able to master the expertise that is natural to them. Business is similar in that you need to really consider what it is that you are great at. And then do that! Leave the rest up to people that excel in that area.

What you do need to know is the bigger MAP – so that you can get help, get coached, be supported, delegate or outsource those things you cannot cope with. If you don't know what you don't know, you can get tripped up. I don't expect you to be naturally passionate in every business topic but I do want you to be aware of them. Be a conscious entrepreneur and recognise what you NEED to plan for and what you need to resolve or get supported on.

Here are some of the key support roles I reckon you need in business (some don't apply to people working for a big company or if they do, they are already hired);

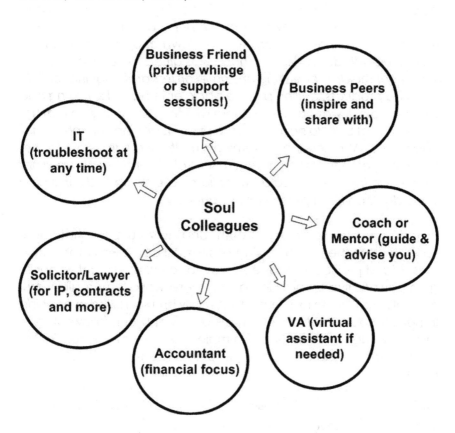

Probably one of the most important roles above is a great friend in business – someone who owns their small business or is at a similar level to your work and with whom you can share your challenges/ burdens and private business matters.

I have a great friend of mine who shares a common challenge that I do in her own small business - that being over-achieving. Whilst she and I both have learned more balance in this area, we occasionally fall back into the burnout trap and over-drive sets in. We are fantastic at, and rely on one another, to pull each other up when we feel the other's work drive is going a bit south and negatively affecting our wellbeing. What an amazing support structure.

I remember a few years ago when she was at the brink of burnout and I had to intervene. We both often reflect and have a laugh together on the method I employed to intervene. So, she was running an online business and a coaching/teaching business of sorts and was juggling many, many projects on her own. The key issue here is that she was finding it hard to shut down and have any kind of downtime outside work. Her iPhone was glued to her fingers every second of the day: checking customer orders and enquiries online, shipping products, calling people back, email checks, texting and social media. It was obsessive. There was so much going on that her mind was not able to switch off. And she was getting very physically hammered. After sensing an imminent meltdown, I drove over to her home office on that day and took control of her diary. I looked her squarely in the eye and said 'No children are going to die in Africa if you don't call that person back right now'.

It kind of just fell out of my mouth, and now I use this statement today if I feel she is over-driving or stressed out. It was probably a messy (and politically incorrect) way to say it, but I wanted her to gain perspective on how important these work items really were. After all, what we think is important, really isn't so. I killed everything in her schedule right back to bare bones and only allowed tasks that, if not done, would signify a major revenue loss for her. Taking this stuff off her plate was a huge relief and she was able to reset her energy. It is so important to have a mirror or work friend out there who understands you and watches out for you. We can get swallowed in the working treadmill very easily, especially if we are intelligent and have any kind of ambition.

I think that most of us are hardwired to crave a challenge, but what we need to remember is that it should not grow bigger than us. When our goal becomes bigger or more important than we are, it becomes unhealthy.

The right people in your tribe

How do you know you have picked the right people?

You will feel something called 'Heart entrainment'#. We discuss this in detail in a later chapter and the science behind it, but the goal is to lock into a deeper level of contact beyond the brain or cognition. We have a thinking mind (brain) and a feeling mind (Heart).

I use a capital H for Heart as I see it like a Spirit – a living and feeling entity and that is where your centre of passion and intuition lives. When people get sad or 'heart-broken' a strange physiological occurrence happens in the body. You can literally get strain and dysfunction happening in this organ, anything from passing out, angina, heart attacks and more.

So, Heart entrainment occurs when you connect with someone on a feeling and emotional level that is beyond just the usual mental intellect. A synergy happens with that person and both of you fall into a similar vibrational pattern when together. Kind of like your heart beat synchronises together. Science has proven this through tests which I will reference in a later chapter.

When Heart entrainment happens within yourself (i.e. your heart and mind connect properly), you become smarter, more visionary and more creative together. When your Heart entrains with another, both of you are more amped up and can collaborate at a much higher level of intelligence. True brilliance I would say. Different people will entrain with you on different levels.

Q. Who have you met in business (or life) that you immediately had this connection with? You will know that feeling because it is kind of like meeting an old friend again that you haven't seen in ages... a switch is turned on.

These people are so valuable in your life, so finding them and connecting with them is a smart way to keep your energy flow strong. So, we know the kind of feeling we need to have around the person, but who are the kinds of people we need?

What are the broad categories your soul colleagues will fall into?

UNPAID

1. Soul Business <u>Colleagues</u>/ <u>Friends</u>
2. Soul Business <u>Peers</u>/ Collaborators

PAID

3. Soul <u>Support</u> People
4. Soul <u>Mentor</u> or Coach

1. Business Colleagues/Friends (time and energy exchange)

These guys are in business or working too and just seem to 'get you'. Normally you swap advice, listen to one another, celebrate wins and counsel any losses! You may have met them through a previous job or working role, a social network (existing friend) or maybe they live next door. You know pretty much straight away when you meet them because your heart entrains soon thereafter. They feel good and they become friends who can share your good and bad times. They will happily hear your whinges and fiercely celebrate your successes.

Have a think about these questions below...

What type of person (qualities, character etc.) inspires you? Why? Sometimes they are similar to you and you just click or sometimes you have different skills and it's a good match to learn from. There is always a high level of respect for each other.

_____

_____

_____

Who in your life right now fits this description? How do they make you feel? i.e. inspired, happy, relaxed, open, child-like, non-judged, supported, smarter etc.?

_____

_____

_____

When do you want to connect with them? How do you currently do this?

_____

_____

_____

2. Business Peers / Collaborators (transacting, sharing or collaborating)

These guys are usually unpaid but it can go either way. You are however transacting in some form or other. Maybe you do business for one another, collaborate, and refer each other or more. Perhaps you are part of a network? They seem to bring a magic to your business and this can be felt straight away or develop over time. They feel like trusted partners of sorts. It is good to be clear with them about what you need when in contact so you know where you both stand: e.g. 'Hey I have an idea for a collaboration...' or 'Can you help me promote my next workshop?' They are sort of like friends but you probably wouldn't hang out personally with them outside of work, it's more of a mutual business connection. Sometimes people cross over between business friends and peers.

Answer these questions below.

What kinds of groups/people do you want in your business peer group? Qualities, values, skills and psychographics (what do they think and feel) that matches to your heart space. May even be an industry or sector that suits you.

_____

_____

_____

Who do you have currently (list names here) as business peers that feel like a good fit, e.g. entrained with you?

_____

_____

_____

If you don't have this, what is your strategy for building it?

_____

_____

_____

Anyone in your circle that is negative or disruptive? How can you let them go?

_____

_____

_____

3. Business Support People (paid)

This is more if you own a business – but can also be for employed people that can afford outsourced help or need to rely on in-house business people. These guys are important for the day-to-day transactional running of your business. I am sure you can imagine the duties – Personal Assistants, IT support, Accounting/Finance, Legal etc. Regardless of whether you see these tasks as more or less important, the same rules apply. How well entrained* or connected are you with these guys because they form the backbone of your working life? They obviously don't need to be as close as the colleagues or friends, but they do need to share similar values.

Self Employed: Have a wonderful recruiting or freelancing process to ensure you hire not just the right skillset, but the right passion, commitment and values that align to those that your business has. Treat this like a serious hiring job. Apart from the skillset you need, check in with these questions:

- Are they in love with their role or work? They need to enjoy what they do or it's all uphill from there...
- What are their three top values and does this match (somewhat) with yours?
- Do you feel good around them? Simple question – do you connect to them?

Q. Who do you have right now supporting you that enhance your business? List names/companies? What ways can you work better with them or get more entrained so life gets even better?

_____

_____

_____

Q. Who do you have supporting you that drain you? Is it time to let them go...?

_____

_____

_____

Q. Is there any support role missing that you need right now? What qualities, skills and values might they have to make life happy and to keep your energy flowing?

_____

_____

_____

Employed: There might not be much you can do here. If you are a senior manager responsible for hiring, please refer to Self Employed above. If you don't have a say, then try these ideas below:

- Is there a choice of support people to draw from and who is your better pick? Again you will feel the specific connection with someone and find it easy to hand work their way.
- If you cannot change who supports you, how can you find ways to entrain more with them to get a better working life? Put your ego aside here as this is a wonderful lesson to learn about 'dealing with shadows' – see my later chapter on shadows*. What values do you share that can form a good connection between you? How can you communicate better with these support people to get the support needed?

Here are two key questions to answer:

1. **What support person/s am I currently entrained with in my workplace? Why or what do we share that makes this a viable 'soul colleague' relationship?**

_____

_____

_____

2. **Who am I currently working with (in terms of support personnel) that feels draining and/or frustrating? What can I do to form a better connection that will a) help me out day-to-day and b) overcome some of my resistance to them?**

_____

_____

_____

4. Business Sage or Mentor (paid trusted advisor)

This is a pretty critical role within your working life, whether employed or running your own business. If running a business, it's probably more important, because you don't have access to a management team or boss than can advise you.

Key Learning: Two minds are better than one. Better yet, two minds that are 'entrained' inspire breakthroughs. Think objectivity, reflection, dreaming, inspiration, propeller and value.

There is nothing more exciting than sharing your business challenges, successes and ideas with another person. Better yet - sharing these ideas with a mentor, sage or someone with a brilliant mind doubles the energy! When I say brilliant mind, that can mean many things. High IQ. High EQ. Evolved consciousness. Super productive. Skilled technician. Industry expert. The list goes on. But we do need energy flow through Heart entrainment*.

Excitement aside - it is intelligent and practical to engage a mentor or coach to increase the value of your business or career. It is somewhat arrogant to think you hold all of the answers within you and that there is no value outside of you. When I use the word arrogant, it is probably not referring to your definition of the word. I believe it is 'arrogant' *not* to deliver YOUR gift into the world that you alone can bring. I think it is everyone's responsibility to hone in on their blueprint and deliver that. It is contribution at the highest level. Whether that is a leader, speaker, technician, mother, counsellor, healer, artist, wealth advisor or stylist.

When you have the right mentor, you gain incredible energy from mentoring sessions. If you are not feeling that way about your sessions – you have the wrong person. You should leave feeling a combination of any of these: commitment, clarity, inspiration, release (having downloaded any blocks), education (new ideas, thoughts, learnings) and drive. Sometimes 'fear', if they are pushing your boundaries. Stretching fear, not limiting fear! Of course there are several types of mentors and they offer different value depending on what you need. There are two ways I see mentoring working:

Question 1. Do I need a Mentor or a Coach?

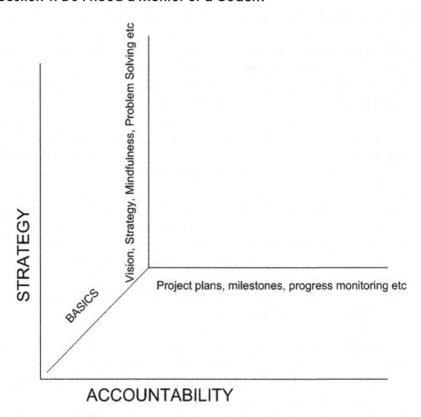

In the above diagram coaches offer more milestone encouragement and mentors are more about strategy and vision. However, most people cross over with both skills, just at varying levels. Whilst their title doesn't matter, what they offer you does.

Mentoring is more about sharing concepts, giving advice, establishing vision, seeing big picture stuff, troubleshooting challenges, sharing expertise, listening and counselling.

Coaching is more about setting outcomes and goals, establishing vision, keeping you accountable to tasks, setting timing plans, brainstorming challenges, listening and keeping you positively connected to your goals.

Obviously these two cross over a lot and if I look at my mentoring style, I would say I am a bit of a hybrid BUT I am much, much better at mentoring. It's not my natural style to check up on people to see if they met their deadline. I expect a certain level of self-drive from a client and I don't naturally think to remember to follow people up. Yet, when I am in a session with a client I am 100% focussed on their business, their challenges and I use my intuitive skills mixed with my commercial background to take ideas to a new level of consciousness. I don't get as excited by just helping someone tick off a project plan, yet I have a good structured mind to help coach their outcomes. Of course, if they don't act to deadlines that is unsatisfying too.

Beyond the mentor v coach categorisation:

Question 2. What kind of skills and value do I need in a coach?

Here are some examples below:

- Strategic and left-field thinking – creative thinking and stretching your ideas – includes intuitive guidance and conscious conversations;
- Technical expertise - such as an online marketing/PR coach, SEO*/web coach or sales expert;
- Counselling/healing role – helping you personally to overcome challenges that hold you back in business (letting you download mental blocks and sorting through inner confidence and shadows;)
- Neuro-plasticity work – employing a modality to help change patterns, improve outlook and deliver tools/processes to achieve goal/desires; and
- Industry coach – someone in your field that has done what you need to do.

Again, mentors can provide a combination of these skills, but it is important to recognise which key value you need. This will change over time. In the past I have had very spiritual based mentors (this took me a long way), left-field thinkers (teaching me value

109

of leverage), technical mentors, counsellors and more. You also won't need a mentor or coach ALL of the time. I am sort of in-between mentors at the moment and realise I need an online SEO and Marketing expert mentor to grow my web skills to a new healthy level.

I also know my patterns and know that monthly sessions are the best cycle for me. I am quite self-driven and can get a long way before needing another session. Although weekly sessions can be good when trying to get some big goals over the line.

A good start would be to identify the top two areas you want to grow in business. For example mine are SEO/online traffic and creative/content writing. Another way of asking this question is to ask 'What challenges you are having in business'? That's where you need to grow.

What are your challenges (#1) and what kind of coach or mentor (#2) do you need? Take time to reflect on this. Think about heart entrainment and what you would be looking for in regards to a values position or way of thinking? Another way of looking at it would be to ask what 'shadows' (personal challenges) do you have that this mentor can help you resolve?

#1.

#2.

As mentioned above, you don't always need a mentor, you will have periods without and that is useful too so that you don't get too 'spoon fed' all of the time. Being independent and trusting your own guidance is key. Having support from another (who is entrained with you) is being smart.

How are you tracking overall with your group of soul colleagues? Rate how successful you are in each area from 1 – 10 (1 being low and 10 being high) for the following areas:-

Business Colleagues/Friends (1-10)

Business Peers/Collaborators (1-10)

Business Support (1-10)

Business Mentor/Coach (1-10)

Perhaps think about the lowest score you got and work on this first if you need to. Now, rate yourself overall as a beginner, graduate and master.

Beginner

You probably have an ad hoc approach to business peers and connections. You may be new in business/career OR you may be more introverted and have not had the momentum to build a strong network around you. Perhaps you have never given much thought to how your colleagues either energise or drain you.

If you are at beginner level you also may not have a wide variety of support in the key areas. For example, maybe you don't have a mentor or a group of soul colleagues, but have a growing group of business peers. Support from other people is one of the fastest ways to boost your business life and you might have a growing instinct to do this but it's certainly not thriving at this stage.

You are probably working with people that drain you and have either not taken the time or energy to sort it out. Likely these guys are taking energy away from you and it's causing leakage in your business. It is probably time to sort it out.

It's unlikely, but you could even be on the extreme scale and hardly connect at all outside your world of business; if this is you its more probable you run your own business and have developed an insular world.

Time to get out there and find your soul people.

Graduate

You have a good network and probably a good set of business peers. You are steadily growing this and you may be a natural at creating good business alliances. Perhaps you have a great mentor but haven't yet found your soul colleagues. Or maybe you have a nicely forming inner group of great inspirational business colleagues but don't yet have your master sage to push you to that next level. You're on the road to a healthy set of soul colleagues but there is definitely more room to move to make your business life not only successful but fun, happy and loved up with a group of inspired people.

You also might have accidentally stumbled across a great group of people and sort of practice Heart entrainment generally, but have not given it a whole lot of conscious attention. It might be the time for you to get more specific and take your soul colleagues to the next level.

Perhaps you even have all of the soul people you need but just don't give these contacts the attention required, due to time pressures, energy, BSO's* (Bright Shiny Objects)or more.

Work out where you are at and choose to jump to the next level of support and collaboration that will truly make you shine.

Master

You are a master at networks and 100% value the people in your working life. In fact, you see it as an intrinsic key to your energy flow and happiness at work. You make it a priority to connect with others and see this as your leading success factor. Collaboration is your middle name and you can see the power behind connecting, sharing and ideation together. Whether you are sharing your wins or losses with your closest soul colleagues or fluidly transacting with a peer, you know you have the emotional, intellectual and physical support there when you need it.

You may go through periods without a business coach but you always have your soul colleagues and business peers on board, ready to support you or inspire you when you need it. You seem to know 'your type' when you come across them and find it easy to connect to them. In fact you are very clear on how this feeds your success, that it becomes blatantly obvious when you don't have this support in life.

You have a great balance of social connection in your career, alongside a driven and logical personality so that your work/life balance is kept healthy. A little in-built radar chip tells you when you have tipped balance too far in one direction and you have a list of strategies you can pull out of the hat to course correct. You also notice when others are lacking these vital ingredients and you encourage them to reconnect to other people for some nourishment and inspiration.

Many people at master level are either senior executives, entrepreneurs or sales (or similar) people. These soul relationships are intrinsic to their role and survival. However, all roles in business will thrive having this master level soul colleague set-up.

If you are not at Master level and want to get there, I suggest you answer the questions in this section and start the search for your soul colleagues. They will indeed change your life. If you are already at Master level, then enjoy being on the sea of soul business love. Float around and congratulate yourself for being open to receiving good energy.

6

Get In Touch With 'Naughty'

Quote: "It is a happy talent to know how to play." Ralph Waldo Emerson

Key learning: You need to feel naughty at least once a week to truly value your business freedom and to turn on your creative power.

Key words: Fun. Inner Child. Ad hoc. Intuitive. Dream. Nourish. Revitalise. Breaks. Power. Creativity. Freedom.

Tortoise and The Hare – a fable

There once was a speedy hare who bragged about how fast he could run. Tired of hearing him boast, Slow and Steady, the tortoise, challenged him to a race. All the animals in the forest gathered to watch.

Hare ran down the road for a while and then paused to rest. He looked back at Slow and Steady and cried out, "How do you expect to win this race when you are walking along at your slow, slow pace?"

Hare stretched himself out alongside the road and fell asleep, thinking, "There is plenty of time to relax."

Slow and Steady walked and walked. He never, ever stopped until he came to the finish line. The animals who were watching cheered so loudly for Tortoise, they woke up Hare.

Hare stretched and yawned and began to run again, but it was too late. Tortoise was over the line. After that, Hare always reminded himself, "Don't brag about your lightning pace, for Slow and Steady won the race!"

This is a great lesson about being slow and steady here... yay for the tortoise. I agree that is sometimes a wonderful strategy. But I would like to turn the attention to the Hare. This rabbit was obviously an over-achiever and in need of a good rest. Good on him for taking that naughty nap even at the expense of losing the race. The fact is there is no race with ANYONE. It is a great example of rest and recovery in between the sprint of life and business.

The western world cultivates and rewards over-driving behaviour. Sometimes we need to sprint, then we really need to rest. It is healthy and useful to do both.

We all go through slumps at work and periods of time throughout the day, or a week or month where we feel less focused, more ratty, stagnant and slow. Perhaps we have just been running too fast and are buggered. We think we need to push through those moments with accelerated action commitment. Whilst that can be a strategy (not a smart one), it is definitely not the most effective nor is it the kindest one to deploy.

Taking time out to be 'naughty' (even for a minute and jump aside for a sleep mid-race) without a doubt, is by far the quickest way to get back on track when you are having one of those challenging, down, stagnant and lost days in business. We all have them but we mostly just try to sit in our office or at a desk and push through it. Force works right? Not a smart strategy! Whilst you can force some things, ultimately it becomes a wasted day. But it does not have to be.

You will need to employ 'downtime', or if you are relaxed enough make it a regular activity in your schedule; time to dream, have fun, muck around, act like a child and generally feel like you are avoiding work. Of course, doing this day after day is procrastination! But if you do it intermittently, it supercharges your energy and drive. Sort of like adding oil to a dry engine. The engine will burn out if it runs empty, but thrive with a top-up. We are not too different to cars.

Why does being naughty rejuvenate us more than just physically?

When you do something you consider decadent or being 'naughty' you short circuit your rational brain and release all that tension and blockage that is causing the stagnation in the first place. It's like an immediate relief strategy. And there is nothing an entrepreneur likes more than immediate problem solving or zigging when everyone else is zagging (a nice little analogy I learned from my business masterminds brekkie meetings).

So, when I get stuck I normally take myself off for a foot massage. That seems to be my poison of choice. Apart from the fact I LOVE having my feet rubbed, it is actually a very grounding (sensory) thing to do as the sensations bring the attention from your logical over-spinning mind back into the body and especially the feet. Your feet are what anchor you to Earth energy[1] and there are electromagnetic pulses that come from the earth into your feet. Standing barefoot on bare earth is even better. You connect back into the earth which is a much calmer place than the mind. If you think about it properly, your feet are what 'walk' you through life and they are the first anchor point to hit the ground and pave your path forward. Look after them. Some amazing studies have been done on the power of 'earthing' your body into the soil. See Clinton Ober's book called Earthing[2] to understand the science behind it and why you need to incorporate it as a health strategy.

It doesn't matter whether you work for yourself or another, this is not an exercise in bludging, it is a motivational reset and a necessary one.

Time to activate your 'funster'

There are loads of things to do to activate the inner child and the 'fun' button. Better if you can do these in your so called 'working hours' which makes you feel decadent. Depending on where you work and how much flexibility you have, I suggest activities that are fun and creative such as:-

Lunchtime cinema;

Swimming in the ocean or pool quickly, a surf?;
Walk in nature or park and focus on a plant, flower or tree (the latest studies on 'nature for attention restoration' is now taught in the positive psychology movement; it's actually an ancient practice, lost and now found again.);
Massage – could be a foot or quick neck massage;
Lying/sitting in the sun reading a 'fun' magazine;
Meditation - please learn a few techniques you can easily do;
A good decent lunch break – maybe even super long with friends and fun;
Spa treatment;
Late breakfast on your own (or one before work and get in 'just on time');
Reading a fiction novel for 20 mins or more;
A yoga class or game of golf.

If working from home, add on these...

Painting;
Have a bath;
Take a dog for a walk;
Gardening if you love it;
Bake some yummy treats if you enjoy to cook.

Frequency and Length?

Make sure you choose what delights you or relaxes you. This is not wasteful, as you will return refreshed and renewed and a better business person/owner. How long to take? It depends on how burnt out you feel or how stagnant you feel. If you're feeling quite low, take at least a day. You can always push a deadline back. And hey, if it makes you twice as productive later in the week, it's a super smart strategy. If you are completely burnt out, then you need to devise time off and have a good break, otherwise it will take you three times as long to fully recover. I speak from personal experience here.

My personal guide is this…

Having a slow day – inject one thing to break it up;

Having a bad week – inject two to three funster activities in to help you feel replenished;

Having a bad month – get naughty several times over a couple weeks;

Having a full meltdown – take minimum of a week off altogether and restore back to health. I have suggested to clients with extreme fatigue to go on extended holidays for weeks at a time if they get to breaking point.

Best Ideas come when you are feeling relaxed – a personal story

For me personally, I find that when I stop work in the middle of the day for a body massage, my best and most creative ideas come to me. My theory is that my head is full of data and information and wisdom from my working life. There's a lot buzzing around in there. What seems to happen (by accident) is when I lie down and my body is massaged, those ideas start to anchor downward and become 'earthed'. In energy healing terms – when you get back into your body and stop drifting off up in the head, you 'earth' yourself. You are more present and focused and able to materialise things. So, these ideas earth themselves in my body properly and become clearer and more tangible when I get a massage. I use massage as a vehicle to both relax and bring ideas to the front of mind with clarity.

I imagine other body type activities also get you into flow like this. Work out what yours are and do them. A swim in the ocean? Playing with a dog? Planting a tree?

When the Harvard Business Review published a paper called 'The Making of a Corporate Athlete'[3] it mentioned a couple of high level executives who I would consider have Type A personalities.

For those that want further clarity – A types are very driven, usually a high 'D' and a high 'I' type on the DISC profile system[4] and are mental, quick-thinking doers who have a high achievement strike rate. They normally find it hard to slow down and stop because they are always on overdrive. In positive mode, they are probably your best team mate as they are quick, agile, smart and solution focused. In negative mode, they can get impatient, a bit volatile and are prone to burnout. Although you would never know it...as they still try to fire away when they are in adrenal meltdown.

I am a Type A personality (sober and recovered) so I know about this intimately. In the Harvard paper, they mention a guy called Jim Connor, CEO and president of FootJoy. Jim would arrive at the office first and be the last to leave and therefore created a very structured and driven working life. Whilst he was successful on a commercial level, it was not sustainable. He became stuck in a rut and found the only way out was to break up his working day. After initiating strategies to break away from the routine (such as a golf lesson), he found his energy, passion and commitment coming back. He has a sustainable working life now. These small deviations in our logical and busy day can have serious and profound awakenings for us and reconnect us back to our inner spirit.

I don't need to spend too long on this point as it is pretty simple. Really intelligent business people understand the value of mixing up activities creatively. If you are not doing it now, try it and see how effective it is. Here are some questions to get you started.

A short note on Type A & Type B Personalities

I have never given too much thought as to where these personality distinctions came from. During the writing of this book, a few people asked me if there is a Type B personality. Certainly there is. If you are interested in knowing a bit more information, please read the brief history and what a Type B person is.

Type A

Type A personality behaviour was first described as a potential risk factor for heart disease in the 1950s by cardiologists Meyer Friedman and Ray Rosenman.[5] After an eight-and-a-half-year-long study of healthy men between the ages of 35 and 59, Friedman and Rosenman estimated that Type A behaviour doubles the risk of coronary heart disease in otherwise healthy individuals.

Type B

"The theory describes Type B individuals as a contrast to those of Type A. Type B personality, by definition, are noted to live at lower stress levels. They typically work steadily, and may enjoy achievement, although they have a greater tendency to disregard physical or mental stress when they do not achieve. When faced with competition, they may focus less on winning or losing than their Type A counterparts, and more on enjoying the game regardless of winning or losing. Unlike the Type A personality's rhythm of multi-tasked careers, Type B individuals are sometimes attracted to careers of creativity: writer, counsellor, therapist, actor or actress. However, network and computer systems managers, professors, and judges are more likely to be Type B individuals as well. Their personal character may enjoy exploring ideas and concepts. They are often reflective, and think of the 'outer and inner world'."[6]

Questions

Reflect on your current working life:

1. What fun/inner child activities do you currently employ into your business hours? How do they (or can they) relax you when you get stressed?

2. If you were to schedule some fun activities for yourself in working hours – what would you choose to do? What is possible? Rate it on a naughty factor of 1 - 10 (10 being really naughty) and don't choose anything under 6.

3. What two naughty things do you commit to doing in the next month ahead? Once written, go and block them out in your diary now.

    A)

    B)

If you struggled thinking about what is fun and exciting or if you need some inspiration about how to get into your personal flow and revitalise yourself, here is a good strategy for having on hand.

Beyond naughty - make your life powerful

This is a longer term strategy and a great inventory to have on hand for when you need to be naughty quickly and you are too stressed to remember how!

When you really know yourself, you know your power practice. I love this quote and it is so relevant to this chapter.

"It's important that people should know what you stand for. It is equally important that they know what you *won't* stand for". Mary H. Waldrip

Same applies to you. That is why your power practice has a 'DON'T DO' list and a 'DO IT' LIST.

Knowing how to get yourself back into your power centre means having a great understanding of what makes you tick. What you love and what you don't love. What energises you and what drains you. Whilst we would all love to stay centred, mindful and happy 100% of the time, the reality is that life and business can knock us off centre.

The trick? Knowing clearly what is on your power list so you can quickly return to a more harmonious state.

You are a creative being, living a life where you choose to express yourself in specific ways. Here are some categories of expression. It is useful to have several outlets so when one is challenged or difficult to express, you have others to nourish you.

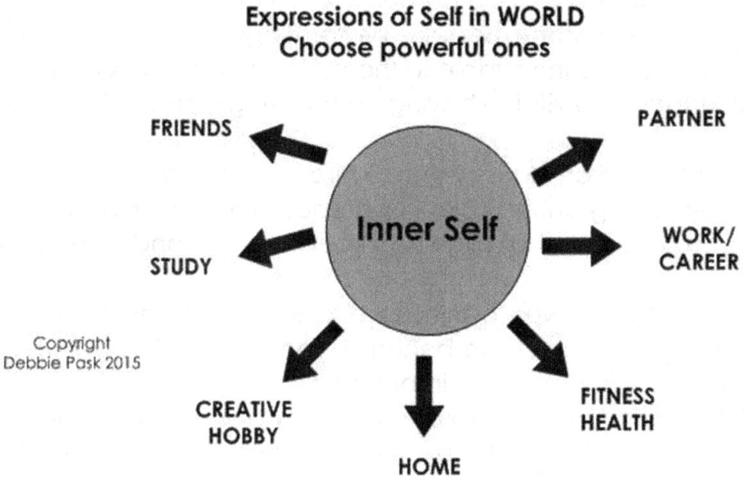

Expressions of Self in WORLD
Choose powerful ones

FRIENDS

PARTNER

Inner Self

STUDY

WORK/ CAREER

Copyright
Debbie Pask 2015

CREATIVE
HOBBY

FITNESS
HEALTH

HOME

The diagram above shows a central circle and this circle represents your inner self and power. Think of that inner circle like a diamond or core power centre. It is super light, precious, perfect and shiny. It reflects many faces into the world depending on how the diamond is cut, but they are all underpinned and integrated into one core strength. The strength of a diamond.

It is your inspiration. It is indeed where you are strongest and most powerful. It just so happens that through our lives, we get run-down and tired out. We tend to forget our inner needs and can start making decisions about life that are dictated by those external influences: friends, work, study and more. In this place the categories outside of the circle such as work, friends, fitness (as shown in the above diagram) can start to influence us from the outside in. Our mind or ego then can dominate our decisions based on pressures from these external places and start making decisions (about what to do or how to think) that are not congruent with our inner authentic self. This can leave us feeling drained and sometimes feeling completely off-centre. Being authentic to our inner self gives us power and energy. Our expression into the outside world needs to align with and strengthen our core inner self.

A simple example of being 'out of your power centre' in the workplace is when you are performing a task or job that is completely boring and un-inspiring to you. If someone placed me in the finance department processing invoices for a large company I would go insane within a few hours. Or if someone asked me to edit and proofread a large complex research document, I would shrivel inside. For some people, performing in a sales role is in-authentic and uncomfortable to them. How you express yourself in the workplace is so vital to having an amazing working life.

Firstly you choose an industry that inspires you, and then you should start to get more granular in your approach until you are performing the day to day tasks that align with your inner self and inner spirit.

It is quite simple - if we do things we love we grow stronger. If we don't do things we love, we become weaker. We all know what it feels like to have those days in business when you are firing on all cylinders. Where you glide through the day and everything feels in balance and aligned and you are doing what you love. Those days happen when you are in your centre of power – in the diamond and aligned with your passions and expressions.

The days where you feel drained, time poor, money lacking etc. happen when you get lost in the mental crap and do things or see people that are NOT aligned to who you are and what you want. This crap can stick to the walls of the diamond (dulling its spark) so it's important to know how to reset, recharge and get back into the light of the diamond by doing your power practice.

So, how do you get back 'in' when you drop out? How do you stay in there permanently? It's all about knowing what takes you **in power** and what takes you **out of power**. If you know this simple equation, then you know how to get back in. I would argue that knowing your power centre means you know your identity more clearly and hence confidence comes a LOT more easily to you. So this next exercise does two things. (I love a double strategy.) It helps you to get back into your centre and flow when you become disconnected and it helps you to know yourself and your identity better which breeds confidence long term. Clarity is confidence. It's when you 'don't know' that fear sets in.

Here are two questions to ask yourself;

Q1. What things do you do, or people do you see, that bring you IN power? i.e. that energise you and makes you feel great. Write a list.

In Power LIST

Things you do   *People you hang with*

_____

_____

_____

Great. When you do these things or see these people, you can slide yourself right back into energy land. They are the things that will help you regain your centre. Of course, if something has knocked you 'off centre' then you need to look at why and integrate that issue.

It seems so simple, but I ask many clients what brings them in power and they scratch their heads as if they have not been asked that question before. Ask it.

Debbie Pask

Debbie's 'in power' list:

(It's not short and neither should yours be...these things help me get my mojo back when I feel drained):

Horse riding – probably my most favourite thing!
Walking on the beach
Hanging out with my cat or any animal in fact
Watching inspired TED talks or any type of business or energy education
Laying in the sun reading a magazine or paper with a coffee
Hiking in nature and bird watching
Swimming – especially in the ocean
Doing jigsaw puzzles
Spending time with my friends and family – be specific here because some friends and family can actually drain you!
Meditation (ahhhh – love it)
Holidays and travel
Meeting new inspiring people
Sunrise and sunset
A fantastic client session
Teaching others to be more conscious
Great yummy and healthy food (dinner out is a favourite of mine)
Foot massages
Comedy shows/skits

Q2. Now, what are the things or people that take you OUT of power. i.e. that drains you, that take you out of flow?

Out of Power LIST

Things   *People*

_____

_____

_____

Debbie's 'out of power' list:

Admin – doing crappy paperwork like insurance, car rego and all of those life things
Tax/BAS and any detailed financial stuff... snooze...
Cleaning the house...arghh
People/acquaintances that don't ask me any questions or take an active interest in my life and just talk about themselves all day
Whinging and moaning about something – whether that's me or listening to someone else
Getting sick and not looking after my health/body
Bad food – especially sugar
When I put on too much weight and feel sluggish
Drinking too much
Racist people or unconscious people who are selfish
Large institutions that hold too much power or greed
Cruelty to animals
Gross consumerism
Watching the nightly news ... ouch – that's a one way ticket to depression
Watching reality TV shows (especially competing ones)
Sitting indoors too much and not getting out in nature

The In and Out of Power question really clarifies what experiences you want in your life. So then the decision becomes as simple as this...

Does that thing or person take me IN power? Say YES to that/them.

Does that thing or person take me OUT of power? Say No to that/ them.

If a person is a 'no', either let them go from your life or if that's too hard (i.e. they are a parent, a boss or a sibling), then you need to work through the reasons why they fall into the 'no' category and learn to stay powerful in their presence. That can be hard but it's such a juicy lesson around power. Obviously you can choose to spend less time with them and that is cool also.

The interesting thing around your personal and business skills or passions is that society has it all backward when trying to train little souls in the world to be happy and well and powerful. At school, they try to round you out so that you are okay or good at all subjects. There is a natural lean to ensure all students are even or similar in skills. I think this is short-sighted. Whilst I definitely see use in making sure kids can read and write, I believe that each person should be encouraged to master their natural strengths.

Each Spirit here has their own journey and their own talents to explore. Master what makes you feel good. Follow what ignites your passion, because that will lead you to an energetic state of being that cannot be matched by ANYTHING. Being soul connected to your career is like being on a drug for life. Whilst I consider myself a work-in-progress, I am generally doing this and I smile every day at my work knowing it's truly what I am designed to do.

So, let's apply this theory now to business.

What Business tasks put you IN power? Name your top 5.

Common ones are training and development, spending time with like-minded work colleagues, coaching other people, product development, strategic plans etc.

1.

2.

3.

4.

5.

Okay, so make sure your Job Description (or future ones) has these 'in power' tasks included so that you thrive.

What Business tasks take you OUT of power? Name your top 5.

Common ones are asking for pay negotiations, political agendas, change management, presentations/public speaking etc.

1.

2.

3.

4.

5.

Now the good bit... If you're drained by it, outsource it! Clever business people know that doing crappy stuff just takes twice as long and sucks energy. Get someone to help with it or hand it over altogether. Remember we spoke about soul colleagues ... find those ones that can support you (as paid help). Now go back to your 5 'out of power' tasks above and write next to them *what your actions will be for reducing their drain on your power*. Once you do this, you will feel like a million dollars. If you happen to be doing all five of those annoying things, then you are probably in the wrong job or need to do some serious delegation.

Now, some people have the opinion that when we dislike something we should overcome our fears and push through to master a weakness.

A good example here is public speaking. I understand and somewhat agree with the philosophy that when we push our fear boundaries, that can be exhilarating and transformational. I think we need to make the distinction between 'don't enjoy' vs fear. I prefer not to try and work on any traits that I simply don't enjoy and focus on what I do love. For example, I am completely drained by doing bookkeeping and detailed financial analysis. Top level is fine, but the nitty gritty is very tiring and annoying for me. I just don't love it but I could do it if I had to. I am not scared of it. However, if I choose to do a job or run a business where that skill is deeply intrinsic (or I

Debbie Pask

fear it but secretly want to master it) then I am open to pushing the boundaries and testing my fear levels in pursuit of it.

A personal example of this is when I travelled to Central Australia and did some journeys into the beautiful natural gorges surrounding Alice Springs. I have taken risks in life emotionally and mentally, but not often physically. So there was an amazing gorge (a narrow valley between hills or mountains, typically with steep rocky walls and a stream running through it) located in a place called Redbank. It had water holes leading all the way to the top of the mountain and the idea was that you swam into each water hole, climbed over the rocks to the next water hole – which were surrounded by steep rock cave walls. The notice at the entrance said to beware of baby python snakes dropping off the steep walls. You couldn't see what was on the bottom of the rock pools all dark and cold due to lack of sunlight and it looked like the cavern was closing in as you climbed higher – to eventually see no sky or land. So, I was super excited to go and explore it but a deep fear surfaced that had me paralysed to go for it. What about the baby python snakes? What about the dead things on the bottom of the water holes in darkness? This is a perfect example of wanting an experience, but afraid of the risks. Needless to say my divine outback adventuring friend dragged me through about 5 water holes halfway up until we swam into a dead dingo and decided to swim back due to hygiene reasons. On the way out I encountered what I thought was a scorpion and several other sludgy things that touched my legs. At the end of it? Pure delight and an extreme emotional high. I had fought through my fear as opposed to sidestepping something I pretended didn't matter to me. It did.

In terms of working life, you just need to be conscious enough NOT to chase what you don't love and only spend time overcoming fears when you deeply want the skills/experiences of what exists on the other side of fear! I wanted to experience the water hole experience? What do you really want but are fearful of doing it?

Having public speaking as a goal when it is not your heart's passion, but you think you need to test your fears, is wasted energy. It would only be useful to nail public speaking if it was a lifelong dream or intrinsic to your career success, and the fear was getting in your way.

Beginner

You probably are not doing anything 'naughty' to balance out the stress of work. Whilst you may dabble in the odd exercise routine at lunchtime, you have a strong logical and driven focus at work which allows little time to include creative or fun tasks. When you feel stuck or stagnant, most likely you try to push on through this feeling, or switch tasks which help somewhat, but they tend to still be work or mind focussed. You might feel like you could not take your full lunch break or if you did, work would still be on your mind. You would take phone calls about work related matters. (Some of you might be saying to yourself here 'what's lunch?')

You have not given much thought to the idea of creative versus logical balance in your working life and you are too busy to take any kind of time out to fulfil these sorts of decadent ideas. Your mindset has usually been to work hard and play hard AFTER work, not during. Work is for work and that's the way it has been for a while now. You would feel quite uncomfortable (lazy) in getting a foot massage in the middle of the working day.

You might understand generally what tasks make you happy, but having an 'in' and 'out' of power list is very unlikely for you, as taking the time to relax, let go and have fun feels like a long way away.

Graduate

You understand the theory of creative breaks during work hours but just don't seem to execute quite regularly enough. You go through stages of being more plugged into it and not. Working life is pretty busy and your focus is strong - you sometimes do the longer lunch or go for a workout with work colleagues, but this has not developed into a consistent routine. You might not plan ahead enough to do the 'naughty' activities in work hours, but you have seen the value of doing this in the past and it's somewhat on the agenda. You know it and feel like you need to do it, and sometimes you do.

When work gets rough, you understand the concept of rejuvenation and make the decisions that you need to ensure you don't meltdown. You happily explore naughty when you need to, which is fantastic and a good inspiration to your friends.

Debbie Pask

You have a power list of sorts and practice it part-time. But you have definitely not mastered the art of living and breathing it to secure a strong and long-lasting power practice. It's not second nature yet, but with a few nudges, some accountability and better diary planning you could really nail this area. Intellectually you are an advocate, but you haven't reached a cellular habit at this stage.

Master

Creativity and fun during work is like a breath of fresh air. You totally get the value of this task and do it automatically now. You may take the time to schedule it regularly as your key strategy OR sometimes it is so ingrained within that you just automatically switch over to this when you feel the pressure mounting. It's nothing for you to take a power nap if you really need it, or to leave work early for a swim or a massage.

In fact, the 'naughty' time suddenly feels normal to your schedule. You do go through those cycles of business where you get busy and have a big project with some big outcomes due. Naughty can fall off the radar. This can fatigue you at times but you know that is part of the Yin/Yang cycle and you can work hard for a short period, knowing you can follow it later with recovery; and recovery includes naughty time activities so you are telling your body that you care for it and that the adrenals can switch off for a bit. You realise that life is about balance and naughty time out, which makes you a better person (at work and at home).

In fact, you don't see it as naughty time anymore. It feels like it is simply a part of your business existence required for you to thrive. Some Masters have their power list pinned up to a wall or created as a vision board of excitement and abundance. Looking at it regularly and practicing it is part of your life.

References Chapter 6

1. Ober, Clinton and Zucker, Martin *Earthing; The Most Important Health Discovery Ever* (US, Basic Health Publications 2010). Earth energy relates to the electro-magnetic energy pulses that the earth gives off when we connect to it with our bare skin. There are many theories that we can recharge from this

energy and feel more present and relaxed in our body, with less inflammation and better circulation.

2. Ober, Clinton and Zucker, Martin, *Earthing; The Most Important Health Discovery Ever* (US, Basic Health Publications 2010). The powerful healing affects our body has when in direct skin contact with the earth's magnetic pulse.

3. Loehr, Jim and Schwartz, Tony, *Harvard Business Review: 'The Making of a Corporate Athlete'*, 2001.

4. DISC Profiling system for personalities, www.thediscpersonalitytest.com

5. *Friedman, M. and Rosenman, R. (1959). "Association of specific overt behaviour pattern with blood and cardiovascular findings". Journal of the American Medical Association 169: 1286–1296.doi:10.1001/jama.1959.03000290012005*

6. https://en.wikipedia.org/wiki/Type A and Type B personality theory

7

Mindful Moments

Quote: "If you are seeking creative ideas, go out walking. Angels whisper to a man when he goes for a walk." Raymond Inmon

Key Learning: Keeping a healthy mind and body requires a mix of consistent emotion and spiritual activity (reliable and easy) blended with dynamic learning.

Key words: Simplicity. Joy. Lightness. Motivation. Meaningful. On track. Healthful. Calming. Mantra. Sacred space. Ritual. Reflection. Ease. Focus. Blend. Variety. Tempo. Magic.

Don't mistake mindfulness for meditation

Meditation is one way to cultivate mindfulness. True mindfulness is all about staying centred and present to whatever you are doing, wherever you are and whomever you are with... and being able to enjoy that moment without judgement. Don't mistake this for being BORING. It is actually quite a blissful place to be and can be as passionate or quiet as you choose that present moment to be. Whether jumping out of a plane or washing the dishes, the objective is to stay connected and present.

The key is not to forward project and let your mind wander to the past or the future. That 'mental' wandering kills the moment and keeps you distracted from your body and the physical beauty of experience.

So, though I believe meditation practice is important in life and work, this chapter will instead focus on the four concepts that underpin what it means to be mindful and present, then we can look for ways of cultivating it in a way that works for you.

CONCEPT 1: Point Zero

Point Zero* is a term I use to describe what it means to stay centred, strong and calm when external influences are attempting to throw you off balance. To be at Point Zero means you stay balanced and in flow with what is going on around you, observing what is happening from a higher level of awareness and hence removed from being compromised or negatively affected. This could be a conflict with someone that affects your emotional state, a lost piece of business that stresses your financial security or colleagues around you creating problems. I have a little saying I use regularly that goes something like this;

"Relax, **nothing** is under control. The way to feel 100% in control is to let go 100% of trying to control anything".

This may sound like a paradox, but what I mean is that we can never truly control our external influences (seasons change, the grass grows, people will act however they want). However we can control how we respond to it and how much energy we give it. We can stop projecting the millions of scenarios that could happen.

Trying to mop up a mess that you cannot fully control or be accountable for is flawed. Responsibility really means 'to respond with ability'. What can you THINK and DO within your control that feels right and calm for you.

Knowing who you are and what 'values' you have (we discuss in a moment) create a much greater sense of flow and energy. You can control how you react, and our only mission is to stay true to ourselves and act in accordance with who we are.

Have a look at the diagram below. This represents what is means to be at Point Zero and explains the various levels of happiness.

The Conscious Self

Unhappy	Happy (bad reason)	Happy (good reason)
X	X	

OR... **Mindfully Happy** at a source level; present/engaged

POINT ZERO

Focus on **space** (not objects) & **creativity in the moment** (not projecting)

Live by your VALUES eg mine are
- Consciousness
- Nature/Connection
- Passion

You can be unhappy – not ideal.

You can be happy for a bad reason – i.e. a fake drug high or hurting someone to get your way.

You can be happy for a good reason – a job promotion, holidays, meeting the love of your life.

OR, you can be happy for no reason; just mindfully happy in that source state which is true 'Point Zero'.

'Money cannot buy you inner peace; it has to be cultivated and it's the ONE thing that everyone is looking for'. *Debbie Pask*

We can see that being truly mindful and present, at Point Zero, is the ultimate target in life. What it means is that external situations (losing staff, client screw ups, work politics, sales, goals and KPIs) don't drive your entire life. When things are working out, fantastic – you will be happy for a good reason. However when things inevitably arise that are difficult, your mind can attempt to spin and you will be thrown off your centre. I am certainly not saying to play down the good stuff when it happens, or deny being human and feeling emotions when things don't work out. Celebrate the good and express disappointment at the bad. But when crappy things do happen – learning the art of true mindfulness and staying at Point Zero will keep you on track and flexible, able to still enjoy your life and world with energy and flow. You cope better and hence you are a better leader, manager, colleague, employee and friend. Our challenges and how we cope define us much more than our wins do.

Mindfulness goes beyond just a daily practice; it needs to weave into our life and work.

When you face a challenge, do you want to be mentally tortured or strong and centred?

I am not saying we should be immune from emotionally reacting. We are human and it is healthy to allow expression of emotions. The word detachment in eastern practices feels like a cold and stoic response to many people. I think we interpret 'detachment' in an incorrect way. We need to make space in our mind for feeling strong emotions, but just don't let them become who you are or let them overtake you. You are bigger than your emotions. They belong to you but don't own you.

Detachment really means to respect your feelings but not become the sum of them. They are actually quite fleeting if you know how they work. That one tiny moment when you experienced a thought or emotion can stick with you, especially if you are not aware and then it becomes your story - a fictional version of who you really are. Our monkey mind should never dominate the warmth of our Spirit or Heart. Allow it a voice but not the lead command. You are bigger than your emotions.

Don't wait for a crisis to try and learn mindfulness techniques, rather become a master of mindful moments and Point Zero, to strengthen your inner self so you have this incredible backup and store of energy ready and available when life or work goes awry.

Q. When was your last big working challenge that riled you up? Did you let it overtake your happiness and balance for a day, a week or longer? Did your emotions 'stick' and dramatise the reality?

Q. How did you recover – come back to Point Zero?

_____

_____

_____

Q. Do you rely on outside events to determine how happy and valuable you are? e.g. new car, promotions, good sales figures etc.

_____

_____

_____

CONCEPT 2: Values versus Goal-oriented life[1]

"Try not to become a man of success but try to become a man of value." Einstein

This idea is very simple and probably quite obvious but I know I have fallen into this trap several times, so maybe you have too? We spoke about mindfulness and not projecting our thoughts into the future or past. Chasing goals (promotion, new business, holidays, new car, buying a house, finding love, having children, moving country) is a normal and human experience. It can also be healthy to set goals - I know I do. However goals ALWAYS project us into the future. They are about a future time and place whereby you will have achieved this particular desire or that outcome.

So, how do we live a life that allows us goals (future projection) but also keeps us mindful and earthed in the present day so we can flow and be contented? That all boils down to establishing whether you live a goal-driven life or a values-driven life.

A values-driven life is having the clarity of what feelings/state of being is important for you day-to-day and MAKING CHOICES that deliver that feeling to you. For example, one of my main values is freedom. Therefore my life choices involve taking actions that move me closer toward freedom, not further away from it. For example, I work for myself as I like the freedom of being my own boss. I chose to live in a rainforest because I like space around my house. I choose not to have children because I want my days and weeks to be fluid and not structured; to work at my passions when and where I want and to have my body as my own.

Of course I still have goals and I work toward them, but my happiness is not contingent on *only* meeting those goals.

A goals-driven life is when my goals are the key driver and focus in life. If only I had this... If only I were this... If my goals were the focus and core strategy of my life, I would forever be unhappy with exactly what I have now. For example: I want to lose 10 kg, I want to own a horse, I want a large property with an animal sanctuary and a healing/training centre on it. I do not have those things right now and if my only focus was to get those goals achieved – I would not be in flow with the current moment. In fact, any setbacks I had would be life shattering and unhappiness would set in once I realise how far away those dreams were.

The beautiful thing about a values-based life is that you can still have goals, but you enjoy the happy and mindful journey along the way, living your values and feeling content that you are experiencing the feelings you want. You don't need to be reliant on outcomes – you just need to create a space where you live in flow with your inner values and appreciate the pursuit of the goal as much as the goal in itself.

Someone who has recently inspired this above idea of values and goal-based life is a guy called Russ Harris. He has written a bunch of books on this topic and has a great little You Tube illustrated clip[2] about two kids going on a trip and the happiness difference between the 'values-based kid' versus the 'goal-based kid'. I highly recommend you watch it. You will want to be that happy values-based kid and not the goal one, I promise.

Q. If you were to adopt a values-driven life, what would be your top three values?

For example, some of my key ones are freedom, purpose (clarity) and passion.

CONCEPT 3: Deep Listening and Contemplation

I think that we have become a culture of distraction. This is not a judgement but more an observation. We don't have a lot of stillness or reflection time. We race through life experiencing both good and bad times, but rarely stop and let the dust settle and integrate our feelings and thoughts. In fact, it is widely known in the psychotherapy field that people who experience trauma, often detach or disconnect their body from the event for the very reason that it is too hard to sit and be still with it. Healing comes from a space of sitting and accepting who we are and what we experience.

In business, we take little time to truly reflect on and celebrate the good stuff; to rest after a big workload and pat ourselves on the back. Then if it is a negative work experience, we are so quick to move on, choosing not to reflect on the reasons why it happened but often hold on to the pain or angst whether that be conscious or unconscious.

When you truly sit in stillness, you are open to messages, insights and your inner voice. Just think about when you walk into a rainforest: you trudge through with your heavy human shoes and you cannot see any wildlife straight away. You are the one making the noise and you are being watched. All of the animals are aware of your presence and remain hidden. Once you stop and be still for a few minutes, the rainforest comes alive. The birds start making their native calls and you see the real picture. You connect to the gift. Being still brings treasures and insight.

An aboriginal Elder called Miriam-Rose Ungunmerr-Baumann, talks about a concept called 'Dadirri'[3]. Dadirri* is a form of deep contemplative listening and it is about finding your peace in this silent awareness. True heart-based listening - whether it be for yourself or to support someone else - gives us the ability to release and let go of negative feelings. It also helps us to tune in to our own needs and learn properly.

In business, we have already spoken of the need to balance Yin (quiet) and Yang (busy) cycles. This stillness is an extension of the Yin, but with the ability to gain deep wisdom about yourself and your work. Next time you experience either a big career high or a big career low, try practicing the art of Dadirri to really soak up and integrate the experience. Don't rush to cover up the bad, and remember to stop and celebrate the good. With the good stuff it will double your energy and energise you. With the crappy stuff it will help to let it go in a loving way that has a much better chance of staying gone.

Slow your pace just a bit to experience the richness that exists underneath your work and life.

CONCEPT 4: Creating Meaning in Life

Creating 'meaning' behind the things you do in life is critical for cultivating mindfulness. We are only truly motivated to change when the activity has a true heartfelt meaning to us, as opposed to a mental 'check it off the list' type activity. Checking something off a list involves WILL POWER, which inevitably runs out. There is a theory that our willpower starts off strong early on in the day and that by the afternoon, it dissolves into a bare thread. I agree, so if you plan to force an action, get it done first up in your work day.

That is why people don't often stick to meditation practice, even though there is overwhelming science that tells us it rejuvenates us on a ridiculous level! We all know we should but yet this simple ten minutes gets dumped to the end of the queue and feels like a forced duty. But when we apply 'meaning' to why we meditate, that is a different story altogether.

Harvard Business Review published an article "The Making of a Corporate Athlete"[4], which talks about the value of meaning or purpose to make serious change. A high level female executive was trying to give up smoking because she felt it impacted on her work productivity. After several attempts, she considered herself a failure. However, when she became pregnant, she quit immediately due to the deeper purpose of the health of her unborn child. She had a true heartfelt meaning that allowed her to easily change her habits.

Prescribing meaning to a project, an idea or a value you wish to cultivate will be way more successful and effective for you. Meaning is not about a goal, it is about having a deeper feeling and emotional connection to why you do something. It will harness your drive and keep you present and mindful about the project at hand. It comes from a deeper place than willpower - it's not about force, it is about freedom.

A colleague of mine talks about the importance of attributing a **dollar value** to a business project you do, so that it sets the intention and drives the strategy to ensure that project makes money. Clever idea. I like the idea of creating a **meaning value** against a project, to ensure you stay connected and mindful (in the moment and emotionally connected) so that it has every chance of success possible. The financial value is the Yang aspect and the inner meaning value is the Yin. Both have vital importance.

Let's apply 'meaning' to the four levels of wellbeing which are:

Physical Body - exercise, nutrition, relaxation;

Mental - work, hobbies, achievements;

Emotional – leisure, joy, creativity; and

Spiritual - connection, mindfulness and contribution.

We need to apply meaning and purpose to stick at anything we attempt. If we know 'why' we want to do it, the way becomes clear. That is why companies need a clear mission statement or vision to truly engage staff. Understand the why and you get people on board. The same logic applies to yourself. Find your meaning.

However the first two, Body and Mind, seem easier in regards to the 'why' so I have grouped them separately. My reasons? I consider the Body and Mind categories more logical and left-brain in their approach. We know we need to fuel our body and keep it running so that we can work. Otherwise we would starve. We also know that we need some sort of work to make money in this world, so we can afford to eat. So, by force, somewhat – we have to exercise, eat and work. The intrinsic meaning is survival. Of course, some people have mastered the work and exercise better than others (through creating leverage) but all of us have this same goal. We find a meaning to do our work and exercise even if it is not super heart-driven, as it serves a practical purpose to survive doesn't it? Perhaps if you are falling down in these two categories (work and health), you need to find a stronger meaning to underpin why you do them so it improves over time.

I am much more interested in the Emotional and Spiritual categories for these are more right-brained ones and less obvious to our day-to-day survival. They are not necessarily mandatory for survival, yet they are so critical in our recovery, flow and rejuvenation, that I feel they are worth a special mention. In our western world, they are not given the importance and focus they should have. They tend to connect more with our values and keep us at Point Zero. Hence I see them as the key to unlocking mindfulness and inner bliss. You really need to find your meaning and purpose behind why you do the activities in the Emotional and Spiritual category – so you have to work a little harder to uncover your motivations, but the payout is tenfold.

Hence they will be my focus when I talk about the 'Daily Mindfulness Practice'. It is important to find meaning across the Emotional and Spiritual categories because, although they are not directly related to our immediate **survival**, they are critical for us to cultivate a healthy and **sustainable** longer-term working life. There are several books around about how to achieve your work goals and also your health goals. But what about the emotional and spiritual categories?

Debbie Pask

Daily Mindfulness Practice – emotional and spiritual rejuvenation

Outside of my theory above, I could give you a million reasons why it is important to include a spiritual or mindful practice into your everyday (working) life to cultivate wellbeing and health. The statistics on stress are enormous, but they actually bore me now. I feel like I have heard a record played over and over again. Yes I get it; what do I do about it?

I am going to refer you again to the article published by the Harvard Business Review titled "The Making of a Corporate Athlete". This will give you a great overview of the importance of having your own sacred mindfulness practice for alignment on all levels for better energy and performance. They mention many case studies on executives and how much richer their lives are for embarking on this mission. I can also refer to indigenous practices that show us the magic and energy we have access to through ritual, dance and creative arts. We can learn a huge deal about indigenous cultures and their ability to stay in the present and be highly creative to the world around them for better flow.

Ready to implement or think about a mindful practice?

Daily Mindfulness practices are designed to set you up for the day ahead. They are not logical, they involve feeling connected to meaning and your own senses so that you grow resilient and stay nourished. Basically they set you up for Point Zero. Remember that Point Zero is not a detached or stoic state, but rather a rich and flowing state, ripe with potential.

The hard part is getting over your chronic busyness to make this part of your life.

Before we start here, let me tell you a hilarious short story from one of my entrepreneur 'A type' clients after a recent coaching session.

So, he had a really stressful week and after me continually prompting him to cultivate his mindfulness resilience so he could cope and develop good habits and not fall into overdrive again, he was forced to succumb to letting go and doing some relaxation activities and practice to rejuvenate and heal. A breakthrough!

This really worked and he got his mojo back pretty quickly – feeling committed to keeping this going.

The next week I asked him whether he had maintained his mindfulness routine, expecting a 'yes' after only one week. His response "I only like to be mindful when I am having a nervous breakdown. Otherwise I don't have time."

Hilarious! And doesn't that just sum up western corporate business thinking? We don't change or allow space for something unless we absolutely have to ... otherwise we keep the wheels in the cage spinning. Sometimes I think that we should place a dollar value on our mindfulness time. How much value does a 30 minute super rejuvenating meditation or break cost? $100, $200 or more? We need to place a commercial value on our wellness and have the courage to back ourselves and place ourselves at the top of our priorities. We are bigger than our work commitments.

The intelligent business person will make time for ritual and mindfulness weekly as this establishes their ENTIRE energy flow for the week. That way, burnouts and breakdowns don't happen... plus creativity, intuition and the 'X Factor' increases.

I believe every clever business person should have their own customised practise that sets up their energy or vibe for the day or week. Doesn't mean it has to be the exact same practice every day, but certainly an *allocated time* taken just for yourself (not your kids or your partner or your work commitments or your parents or any external drain). When you put yourself at the centre of your world and practice your own ritual or ceremony that honours your time and energy, then you are telling your body and brain that you are more valuable than ANYTHING. That you come first always. Apart from feeling great, do you realise the impact it will have on your deep inner confidence?

Now that is what I am referring to when I say that we need the 'meaning' behind our activity. You will never adopt a mindful practice and maintain it if you don't see yourself as the #1 Priority and give your practice meaning.

I have a quote I throw at my clients all of the time. "You are bigger than your job or your business". If you really believe that, then you make time for yourself first.

This is the habit of a God or Goddess. This is the habit of a highly intelligent and benevolent being. This is the habit of an entrepreneur. This needs to be your habit.

This practise should be exercised in a MINDFUL way so that you are bringing your energy and self into the present moment, in harmony with the laws of synchronicity. When you do this, you set up the flow of the universe to flow alongside you, which brings countless energy. When out of flow, damn the world feels harsh and everything gets clunky. You know when you are out of flow as everything feels jagged, out of sync and frustrating.

Maybe the true genius lies in figuring out when you are out of flow and having the wisdom to stop then, be mindful and reset it?

The goal is 'Zenfulness' for flow and peak performance. What's yours? The key is to figure out what mindful activity gives you flow and then do that. Everyone is different, albeit I do have a small flame of hope that everyone can and should master the art of seated meditation to fully awaken the alpha or theta flow (slower brain waves where we are more connected to creative problem solving). We discuss this in a later chapter. But it does not need to be a seated meditation, it can indeed be a moving meditation. Providing it's a moment of mindfulness, anything goes …

Mindful and Meaningful at Source Level

So, being mindfully happy at source level is the ultimate state. Find something that allows you to draw attention to the present moment so that you feel connected to a bigger more 'observing' state of being. Then, no matter what you do during your day, try and come back to that place of peace.

With a growing busy-ness in the modern lifestyle of communications, juggling priorities and such, adding more and more ritual and 'things to fit in' is just going to make the bubble burst for you. There are endless processes to attempt such as gratitude lists, journaling, release lists, affirmations, prayer etc. I am not dishing these wonderful simple habits, but I do think they can feel stressful – especially if we don't get them in and we then feel guilt all day about tripping up on that task. I have NO time (or energy) for guilt, do you?

My advice? Keep it simple and ensure you love these mindfulness rituals. If you don't, they will slip off and end up in the 'things I should have done today' junkyard which can be very depressing and make us feel like we have failed.

Here's my thoughts on how to approach it:

a) First get clear on your **meaning** - why it is important to you.

b) **Time for yourself** – need time to go within, un-interrupted and practice Dadirri – otherwise our own nature gets swamped by the world. This can be simple as sipping your coffee down by the ocean or park, or on your balcony if it's peaceful. I personally suggest you connect with nature as this is truly where you get the best spiritual connection. Nature has been proven to energise our focus, not tire it.

c) **In POWER list** – choose something that lights you up from chapter 6.

d) **Meditative state** – there are so many types of meditation styles – breath, visualisation, transcendental (mantra-based meditation), Kelee (brain and heart-based meditation), moving meditation. Just choose a style that feels right and learn how to get into that zone.

e) **Nature** – as previously discussed, our life matrix disconnects us from nature ... so paying attention to nature means we feel the magnitude, vastness, power and kinetic energy that natural landscapes provide us.

f) **Theming the day is a nice approach.** Take five minutes to think about you and your day. Why not plant some suggestion for the day into your subconscious mind? I need a productive day today. Or a calm one. Or a happy one. Or a communicative one. Support? Rest? Fresh? Fun? Vitality? Choose something that resonates with you for that day. Once that is sorted, you can translate that idea into a specific work theme such as I need to focus on finishing that report this week, or getting systems into place or recruiting for a role. Focus is important to feel you have met the value you need.

g) **Time of day, frequency/when, who with, where and why** is super important. Whilst I suggest your mindfulness happens in the morning first thing, we can get caught up with the idea of 'should'. If you can get connected to and love the why ... you'll stay with it. If an afternoon or lunchtime ritual suits your lifestyle, so be it. Maybe different days have different time slots depending on your schedule.

I personally think that this exercise should be done aside from physical fitness exercise, however practices like yoga encourage a stillness and meditation at the end so that works for me too. Anything hard core like running, boxing, circuits etc. is not going to give you that space and hence you will still require a good alternative practice and 'stillness' balance. Remember the theory of Yin and Yang - Yin receives in and Yang gives out.

Here's what a week in my life looks like based on the Emotional and Spiritual categories ... I don't need to run you through my exercise routine or my work inspirations, as discussed they are sort of intrinsic to survival.

Daily – I get up early and have a coffee (freshly plunged and high quality) on the balcony of my house which overlooks a rainforest. I try to do nothing but watch the birds and reflect on the beauty of nature. Even if I get zero additional time that day to have fun or be mindful, that 30 mins is the most precious time of my day. It is all for me and I prioritise me first.

Then I usually visit the beach for a walk (after exercise or for exercise), check for dolphins in the water and usually sit and meditate on the beach at the end. Sometimes I do stretch, yoga or tai chi on the sand. I allow at least two hours for this. I am not suggesting you get two hours for this, but as I have mentioned my values personally are about freedom, and time is my idea of freedom, so I live by this principle.

In the evening I connect with my partner and our two kittens. I only socialise with people that energise me and feel they are like minded and happy souls.

Weekly – I go horse riding with an experienced group for minimum two hours. This is my personal fun and bliss. I like to see the entire process as a mindful experience. I brush the horse, clean out his shoes, saddle him up and put his bridle on. We walk, trot and canter through a rainforest and I can honestly say that it rejuvenates every cell within me. Afterwards I wash the horse down and ensure he gets fed and thanked before I leave. That gives me fun, nature, connection and freedom.

If life gets busy, I adapt my routine to ensure I still get that sort of theme in. If I find myself falling out of sync, I stop and reflect and then reset myself. Business gets busy and life works in cycles. Sometimes my practice drops off a bit but I always come back to it. I once heard that the secret to breath meditation is that if your mind wanders, don't judge it, just come back to the breath. Learning to do that is mindfulness itself. Same goes with your practice, coming back to your practice is the art.

Just make sure you give it 'meaning'. These practices are meaningful for me because they echo my values directly – freedom (I come first in morning), nature (beach, dolphins, horses, cats), consciousness (meditation, mindfulness, interaction with a bigger world than me) and connection (hanging with like-minded people) etc.

Define your simple mindful practice here for your emotional and spiritual meaning. What are you doing? When? With whom? Why is it meaningful for you? How does it match your values?

Debbie Pask

Beginner

You are unlikely to have a mindfulness practice and may not have even considered it as a critical function to your work/life. Or perhaps you know the theory behind it and want to find your own practice, but have not cracked it as yet.

As for values and mindfulness, you probably know generally what makes you happy and inspired but perhaps you don't give it enough attention. You are likely to still be hanging out with others that are not on the same vibrational pattern as you. Maybe you have the older and harder school of thought going on which tells you just to 'suck it up' and get on with life and work. At the extreme you think that hippy meditation stuff is a bunch of crud and you are doing fine as you are. Either way, there will be something niggling at your inner self – a quiet itch that cannot be scratched. It will grow if you decide to ignore it.

Some beginners are full-fledged Type A personalities that cannot slow down. Although you like speed and power, it is important to stay balanced and be still sometimes so that the speed can be enjoyed, as opposed to burn you out.

Graduate

You are pretty aware of your own needs and development. You may even block out time in your diary to fit in the mindfulness stuff as you realise the importance of it. Some of you will have a daily mindfulness or meditation routine that is building your mental resilience, which is wonderful.

You have a good idea of who you are and what to do to feel sane again after a hard period of work. The idea of self-nourishment registers, however you may still hang out with people that drain you or do things you feel you cannot say 'no' to. You oscillate between being plugged in and aware (practising mindfulness and flow) – to being caught up and pushed back into the rat race where routine and fun drop off the radar.

Perhaps you will have not sorted out some of the dead ends with relationships or family members which can have the ability to pull you under a bit when you feel stretched. Overall though, you are on your way to mastering your power practice and just need to make some further tweaks to feel the full impact. You are a work in progress so enjoy this journey as big insights come up in the pursuit of mindfulness.

Master

You are indeed a wise mindfulness advocate. You understand the ebb and flow of life enough to be playing the 'observer' or Point Zero role most of the time. You practice meditation of some sort or certainly have a daily mindfulness exercise that helps you generate energy, balance and flow. People probably see you as centred and focused, a person that has their life together and questions the bigger universal forces at work, choosing to spend less time getting caught up in the drama of life.

You would have worked out who and what in life energises you, and actively engage with these people and things. You have probably dealt with any draining influences or work people so that you either don't spend a lot of time with them or perhaps you have worked out a way to accept and own your feelings responsibly in their company, so they do not drain you anymore. Masters work on their own shadow regularly and understand that every challenging person is a lesson for growth. They actively manifest and seem to attract good things as they are in command of their energy and presence.

There is a peaceful balance and a healthy sense of meaning to most things you do. Work does not take first place before your own personal wellbeing and hence your life and work flourish for you.

Masters should encourage their co-workers to seek this kind of peaceful balance and to define their own personal ritual for strength and power.

References Chapter 7

1. Values v Goals Life: Russ Harris Work, www.actmindfully. com.au
2. Russ Harris You Tube clip; https://www.youtube.com/ watch?v=T-IRbuy4XtA
3. Dadirri www.upliftconnect.com
4. Loehr, Jim and Schwartz, Tony, *Harvard Business Review:* "The Making of a Corporate Athlete", *2001*

8

Intuitive Problem Solving

Quote: "Your mind/ego should be a servant to your Spirit" Eckhardt Tolle

Key Learning: Logic will deliver you stable results. Gut instincts will deliver you magic. Just learn how to use them both (in the right order) for best results. Use your gift of intuition freely and consistently every day to solve tricky business problems.

Key words: Inbuilt radar. Gut instinct. Gifts and lessons. Body talk. Shadow. Void. Integration. Not knowing. Vision. Indigenous wisdom.

Intuitive Decision Making and Problem Solving

Intuitive problem solving is about reaching beyond what your logical mind knows to find a better way and one more resonant with you. This can be applied both to personal and business life. One of the things we learn growing up is to try and have all of the answers and know as much as we can. That is what school tests are all about. How much do you know and how many questions can you get 'right'?

Whilst that can certainly help us in mastering our business, we also need to leave some room for space, mystery and flexibility. Doing new things and looking for different ways of solving problems allows us to expand and stretch. It is a rich experience and sometimes, we get a far better result with this approach.

It is nourishing and intelligent to be still and listen (Dadirri) and let the answers come to you with force. What an honour to give your mind the space it needs as opposed to rushing to every solution straight away. Of course not everything can be resolved that way. It is smart once again to oscillate between what requires an intuitive (Yin) problem solving technique versus a fast logical one (Yang).

I have three intuitive models here that are useful to know. They are not necessarily more important than each other but I will spend a little more time on the first one as that is more complex but so worth it. One of the models has its origins from a colleague of mine (at least her model explains so clearly the concept) so I will attempt to briefly explain it in a way that will do it/her justice.

So, let's get them on the table now.

1. **Medicine Wheel** – Learning how to navigate stages of a problem and also how you can evolve from the lessons and not repeat them. This is an indigenous tool and relates to emotional intelligence and cycles.
    Business application: Use when you have the same recurring challenges and you need to move on from this old broken record. Also use in times when the situation gets quite intense and emotions run high. It has a distinct process to follow that is very calming and puts your problems into perspective.

2. **Complex and Wicked Problem Solving (Organic Problem Solving)** – Working with a problem that presents itself but has no obvious solution going forward. There is not enough information on the table to really tackle the heart of it. I learned this one from a cool chick and wicked problem solver (Mo Fox[2]) and it is useful for what to do when something is freaking impossible.
    Business application: Use when you have a business block or decision to make that has no obvious starting point or

way through; this organic process will help open up a path so you can progress.

3. **Fork in the Road** – The <u>timing around decisions</u> and why we don't need to be forced into decisions before we are ready. It also pulls us up when we are procrastinating. It will help put things into perspective so decisions are not rushed and poorly executed.

    Business application: Use when you have a major decision to make that has consequences that are far reaching; most of the time you will feel pressure to decide something before you are truly ready and this model will help take the pressure off.

Whilst I totally accept we have intelligent and logical brains that can do amazing things, I accept even more the simple fact that we have an intelligent Spirit that can go far beyond the brilliance of the mind. Ask any inventor and they will say that their greatest discovery was intuitive and divinely guided, as opposed to 100% rational.

We all have this inbuilt radar that knows what we should do far, far in advance, should we simply switch it on. Here's a collection of quotes from one of the world's greatest genius ... and what he says about intuition (heart) over mind (brain). Yes, I am quoting him again because he's a legend.

EINSTEIN

"Logic will get you from A to B. Imagination will take you everywhere."

"Imagination is more important than knowledge."

"The only real valuable thing is intuition."

"You can never solve a problem from the same level of consciousness that created it"

Yep, he is officially my guru ... I am certainly not suggesting we do everything from intuition and use zero logic or zero structure. I am suggesting we start with intuition to guide us and follow up with the logic to execute our grand plans.

First, Some Thoughts

I think on some level, as business owners or managers, you know that getting in flow and using those gut feelings will give you an evolutionary leap rather than progressive steps. The biggest challenge is the 'how'.

How do you get plugged into the energy flow of making conscious, intuitive and hence intelligent decisions and actions? How do you select business partners, employees, projects, Joint Ventures (JVs), products and services that are right for you on a deep level? How do you bypass the mind for a better outcome?

And secondly, when a big business challenge arises, how do we treat it intuitively and resolve it at a deeper and more effective level? A level whereby the issue does not morph into something bigger and nastier. Often practical problem resolution does not fix big issues longer term.

Example:

A company management position seems to have a high staff turnover and the last three hires have not lasted more than 12 months. This is an expensive problem.

Logical resolution – Tighten up the recruiting process with specific questions and skillsets and do exit interviews to ascertain the key problem. Do better reference checks and widen the candidate search. Increase the number of interviews before hiring.

Look for an external 'fix it' solution.

Intuitive resolution – Ask 'why' these people hired have not made it. Look at common patterns between the managers and where culturally they did not fit in. Maybe it's a values clash? Who are they reporting to and is that manager coping? Is the team environment toxic? Look at what these failed positions are telling the company at a much deeper level and resolve the problem in the business first before hiring. Seek some wise counsel from several different roles within the business (with different cognitive qualities) to see what perceptions are out there as to why this is manifesting.

Look for an internal 'fix it' first.

You can then still tighten up the recruiting process but the intuitive process goes deeper into the heart of the matter.

Any business owner or manager needs to switch on their intuitive self, so don't fall into the trap of thinking you are not gifted in some way. Everyone has the ability to tap into their intuitive self. You were born with it and you have either chosen to ignore it (like I did in my advertising career for many years) or enhance this wonderful gift. Some people use it more effectively than others and learn to trust their gut instinct. In fact, I would say that most successful business owners or corporate executives must access this gift on some level otherwise they would probably not have progressed so far in their career. It's good to know what type of intuitive gift is more prevalent in you naturally – although I would say you can grow all of them over time.

What gift is the strongest for you?

1. You are more clairvoyant* (see pictures and images with clarity). This gives you clear vision, ability to seed ideas with people and good gut feelings on how staff or colleagues would perform in their outward communication and energy. You 'see' energy around someone; is it thriving or weakened?
2. You are more clairsentient* (get really strong feelings in the body). This allows you to deeply explore the personal emotional state of someone and get under their skin to see what really makes them tick. Your empathy levels will pick up anything 'offbeat' and your body or senses will warn you in advance if there is a looming issue long before it plays out.
3. You are more clairaudient* (hear clearly the right answers and truth when it's spoken). Dialogue and conversing will give you much more information to make intuitive decisions about someone than would their appearance. You are good on phone calls and tap into the heart of the issue through

voice and sound. The more you speak and converse, the closer you hone your intuition.

I am a mix of all three although I would say my clairvoyance is most dominant. Sometimes I see flashes like a movie reel before me. It's very useful. I can read people's energy pretty quickly and know how to respond. If you use the analogy of the diamond again, you can see that each person has their different reflection or ray of light and they can use that by simply choosing to open up and switch it on. You must be aware you have it and you must be willing to trust in it and work with it. I then use clairaudience to 'hear' truth or what people are saying and feel either strongly connected to it, or not. If I don't feel connected to the idea or dialogue, it's either not right for me (my business) or perhaps they are hiding something?

I find this very useful when I coach people. When they mention starting a project or following a course of action, my alarm bells will immediately trigger when it is an incorrect path to take. Alternatively, I feel amazing warmth around my heart and buzzing in my body when they speak about a project that is right for them. This can be much harder to do for yourself, but pay attention to other people first and start to hone this gift. You need to get your ego out of the way for this to work, so don't practice it on someone who you have a political agenda with or that crazy monkey mind will take over and pretend it is your intuition speaking!

Bring It To Life

So let's use a decision-making example that has probably occurred in your business or career. I like to label this type of business decision or opportunity as a BSO (Bright Shiny Object). We get distracted by them all of the time! We are going about our work day and someone calls or visits with an opportunity. Or perhaps you are reading something and the idea pops into your head. BSOs are great but can be stupidly distracting and draining if you don't keep them in check. These are the perfect examples to use intuitive decision making for. Let's use a real example.

Joe owns a training company where he goes into different businesses and offers negotiation and sales skill training. He is a master at sales training and many of his clients rave about the improvements he makes to the team. Joe is a one-man band and enjoys hands-on training and running the programs himself because he knows his stuff and loves interaction with others.

An opportunity comes up with his current client Nick who says "Joe, I love what you do so much and you are so important to our business that I want to make you our full time General Manager (GM) of sales. I can pay you handsomely, anything you want! I will then have you here onsite training my team 24/7."

Joe "Thanks Nick, but I love what I do in my training business. My days are flexible as I have a young family and I don't have a lot of stress. But I am very flattered to have the offer."

Nick "Well Joe, what are you earning? $150K? I can pay you double that, $300K."

Joe "Really? Wow, OK that's way more money for me. How can I not take that offer? (thinks to himself logically – can pay off mortgage quicker, send my kids to private school blah blah.) When can I start?"

That is a common trap we all fall into. We are served up something flattering or commercially exciting and we say yes (logical money decision) before thinking intuitively about it and whether on a gut instinct it feels right. We don't practice 'Dadirri', that deep listening to ourselves.

On a deep level of personal satisfaction, money often obscures our thinking too. When we get excitable 'adrenal rushing' feelings about something, I question whether it's exciting to the mind on the surface, but setting off negative nerves underneath around the gut instinct.

I have fallen for this rush of excitement so many times! Argh. I have found these projects don't work out and I have learned to interpret that nervous rush for a 'no'.

I think true gut instincts are NOT that nervous rush feeling (rush of adrenal flight, fight or freeze) but rather a YES decision that feels stilling, knowing and calming. Just right at a very deep intrinsic level.

Joe would be taking a stressful GM role with sales targets to meet and he probably won't be doing too much training as he will be sucked up into sales targets, board reporting and a host of other management duties. He will be doing less hands-on training and more administration that may stifle his Spirit if he is not interested in that. He will lose flexibility of his days and more. Late nights, more pressure. $300K does not mean an easy ride in the business world. Probably a bad call. Maybe more money but probably not the right intuitive decision for his lifestyle that obviously provides him flexibility, family time and rest.

Most of us fall into the trap of thinking that we should take a good offer and that we need to respond quickly and say yes. Both of those statements, in my opinion, are false.

So, how do we start integrating our intuitive mind with our logical mind? Here are some great intuitive problem solving tools that I use regularly.

#1 The Medicine Wheel* – navigating tricky problems and understanding repeating patterns so they do not re-occur

The Medicine Wheel has been around for a long time and can be interpreted so many ways; all of them useful. I was shown this way below and it is one of my most powerful problem-cracking resources and I use it for re-occurring business problems, and even more so for personal issues that my clients present with.

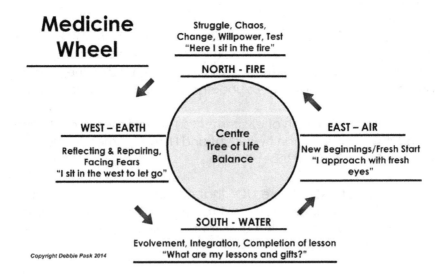

Its origins stem from indigenous cultures that used it to understand cycles and patterns, as well as how to work with change.

The beauty is that it's simple and easy to get. Let's play. The idea is that you follow the wheel around anti-clockwise (starting at east) to represent the cycle of a particular issue, challenge or event. Obviously the east direction symbolises the start of it. The round circle represents completion and the idea is that you can never get 'stuck' on the medicine wheel. You will always move from one stage to the next – it is just how well you integrate your lesson/s that determines whether you cycle endlessly with the same issue around the wheel ... again and again and again.

For example, it is common for people to start again (east), experience chaos (north), fall into a heap (west) and then, **instead of going to south to learn their lessons**, skip straight back to east to start again. Hence the endless cycle of the same annoying issue that repeats in life. Each direction gives us something we need, so the idea is to stop and honour that direction we are in, so that we learn and move on.

Want to resolve some negative patterns or major challenges in life or business? Want to make decisions and next steps from a wiser and more intuitive framework?

Hopefully that is a YES. The Medicine Wheel can teach us how.

What does the Medicine Wheel teach us?

1. Lessons we are being taught currently and how we are evolving internally;
2. Difficult cycles mean we are transcending to the next level of our personal or business development (bigger lessons = bigger evolution – so learn to love it);
3. There are cycles in life and nothing can remain static – you have to move forward even if you don't think you can. The Medicine Wheel helps you understand 'how' to move forward;
4. It is impossible to get stuck and not move to the next cycle – things that are difficult do get easier but you can

cycle around again and again until you shift. You really don't want to do this;

5. It is important to deal with issues – not symptoms – otherwise we will experience the same lessons going around the wheel again and again;

6. Challenges not fully understood will continue to get more intense until you

evolve. This can happen in that the same challenge will repeat and become more serious in nature – whether that is people conflicts, poor relationships, work challenges, health deteriorating etc.

Let's apply it to yourself

Step 1. Write down the main challenge or negative situation that is happening (or keeps happening) at work or in your business. It may be a pattern, a one-off event or situation that you are facing. You may choose to reflect on something recent from your past.

Example: Joe is conflicting aggressively with a colleague at work – it is stressful and competitive and occupying his thoughts constantly. He cannot let it go after leaving work every day. He feels compromised in his role and is not enjoying work.

Step 2. Establish where you think you are placed in the Medicine Wheel:

NORTH (major meltdown and/or right in the middle of the challenge) – for example the conflict has just occurred with Joe and his colleague and it is very raw and stressful.

WEST (the major issue has only just happened and now you have fallen into a heap as the stress has taken over). Joe is now a few weeks into the issues with his colleague and although the immediate stress and conflict has receded, he is mopping up the mess and feeling very drained and unmotivated at work.

You may even be just entering the SOUTH (integrating your lessons and wisdom) but still have not truly understood why this happened and feel confused, stagnant or just aware of the fact your issue is not yet completed/resolved. There are varying levels of stress - from major issues to an annoying block - so don't worry how great or small your challenge is. In Joe's case, he would be trying to figure out what happened to trigger this work conflict and how he can resolve it (practically and emotionally) and understand how to not only let go but also not repeat the same pattern.

You may be in EAST, having just quickly moved on and not really resolving it. Perhaps you need to ensure this new beginning is not just a quick fix, so you need to understand how NOT to make the same mistake again.

In Joe's case it would be in relation to NOT getting into a tricky situation with a colleague again. What were the dynamics involved and what is Joe's part in all of this? If he doesn't look at it, and just blames the other person, then it is likely to play out again with another colleague at work until he makes an adjustment. The person he conflicted with is not the issue here; rather Joe needs to look at his role in this and why he attracted this situation to him.

So, where are you in the wheel i.e. what direction?

Step 3. To really overcome this challenge and move on from repeating events, patterns, negative experiences etc., you need to follow the cycle of the wheel (anti-clockwise) and work with the direction you are in, starting from there and giving that direction (West, North, South etc.) the energy and focus it deserves...

Whether you are starting in East, North, West or South (they follow that exact order!), choose the starting point and use these tools/ questions to move you through the situation. For example, if you are in NORTH – you need to move through the immediate fire (crises) and then cycle into the WEST where you can face your fears, get supported and prepare yourself to rejuvenate.

Then you will be ready to understand your SOUTH lessons and hence evolve. The South part probably requires the most analysis and thought, as that is where you understand the events and can make change. It is also the direction that most of us skip over because really doing the inner work is hard or can be hard.

Please note: the overall outcome you need to get to is to **reach and master the SOUTH DIRECTION** – where you understand the lessons and gifts you have been given from this situation and how it has evolved your working life for the better. It is the direction that asks for you to transform. Remember that the bigger the lesson, the bigger the transformation. When you reach this place, all of the drama falls way and you change your need to experience this same irritating lesson again and again. You will feel renewed and released and ready to start a new cycle in the EAST.

So now that you have chosen the challenge or area you wish to work on - and you have ascertained what direction you think you might be in - it's time to do the work.

Understanding WHERE you are in the wheel in relation to your problem is the first BIG step. Accepting the state of play as it is becomes important. There is no race. Understanding WHAT to do next to get through this business cycle and ensure it does not repeat again is the key outcome.

In my example of Joe and his conflict with a colleague, let's assume he is in the North and feeling the heat big time. He is fired up and his agitation is at the peak of his stress. So I would expect Joe to practice the exercises in the North direction and then the subsequent others. See below for descriptions.

Think about your challenge too, and the direction you feel you are in. Read the below summaries of the direction and apply that intelligence to your specific issue.

NORTH = in the FIRE. Experiencing a tough life lesson and feeling the pain of it all. This could be a simple bad relationship Joe is having at work or it could be quite a serious bullying situation or breakdown of a core colleague relationship or business partnership. On some level it will represent a trauma or loss of some kind.

Chances are Joe is not really in a position to reflect and face the fear. He is caught up in it. It's probably too fresh in his mind (or happening right now) and mentally it has taken over a bit. Joe needs to let go of it all, step away and seek some supportive time out. Trying to resolve now is pointless. Joe needs to admit that he is not okay to just push through and he should step back from the situation to get some space. He needs to LET GO on some level (mental, emotional or physical) so that he can transit to the West, where he will be able to face the shadow/issue/fear and get some much needed insight and restoration.

Suggested action for Joe:

Take some time out from work, seek a massage, a healing or pampering, go swimming to wash out the emotional turbulence, rest, write a release lit of all negative thoughts (then burn it to purify), try scream therapy (yell out in nature to get it off your chest), write a letter to a person affecting you about the issue/s and never send it and generally just be really kind to yourself. It's not a time to push or drive or beat yourself up. The secret here is to recognize that you are in the fire and seek ways to ease the pain. If Joe is in a seriously fearful place where his physical and mental health is dire due to stress – I suggest he contacts his closest friend/family member and ask them to help remove him from this situation ASAP. If it's a job that is 'killing' Joe, then it's time to stand up for himself and just resign. Joe's health is more important than a job. Take action to get out of the crises or difficult time, or find time to rest.

If Joe can just leave the stress of the situation long enough to allow the space – then he will move to the next stage which is the West. The energy of the break from the crises will repair him and provide the energy to move forward. It might be one day or two weeks. This is flowing with energy. This will give him the intuitive space to work through it.

This is NOT a logical solution to the problem. Our western minds want to push through the issue, gloss over it and move on quickly; to confront, to 'man up', to push through and to mentally 'win'. This is not seeking the deeper lesson required and is not useful. This pattern will repeat again and again, until the core issue within Joe is ironed out. I am not suggesting his colleague is not responsible for the issue. We cannot change him or her, but we can work intuitively with ourselves.

So what does Joe seek in the West?

WEST = in the EARTH for healing. This stage can be still pretty intense but much more gentle (no action, more reflection). The element is earth this time and you need deep healing to release the pain of the north. It is very reflective and requires sitting in shadow/darkness to witness what is really happening on an energetic level in your life and asking questions that seek a deeper meaning. Why did this happen? What's it showing me? Why is this business issue occurring again or at all? It is a great time to get counselling, coaching, healing and sessions that do a lot of talking and exploring. Spending time alone is also important – Joe will need to heal independently and from the inside out. He needs to face the situation and any fears head on. It does not mean Joe needs to fully understand and rationalise this fear. It simply means that he admits there is a problem and commits to resolving it.

Suggested action for Joe:

Spend time in nature contemplating. Write down your issues and see where else they have occurred in life and whether this is indeed a pattern with you. Try creating a space for meditation and creative outlets. Lie on the Earth or bond with animals. The idea is to seek a connection with the bigger universe and realize your life is like one big school classroom – each phase is like a different class topic and you are here to learn and master it so you can evolve. It's a great time to allow receiving – friends, family and loved ones to give you support – financial, physical, and emotional. In the case of Joe, he really needs to think about why this is happening and if it has happened before. Why is he attracting this situation? There will be a buried shadow (inner conflict) somewhere that is creating this scenario (as annoying as it is) to force him to change. The desired outcome is to truly let go and release this issue so you are lighter, more aware and ready to master your lesson and evolve in the next stage ... the South.

SOUTH = in the WATER. This is my favourite stage as it means completion, unity and moving on ... truly. The best way to work with the South is to ask yourself several questions until a breakthrough happens. The breakthrough is that you finally understand what these challenges have been teaching you – to the point where you accept it and love it. Why? Because it means you have mastered that class in the school room and your evolvement means getting to a great space for new things. I always call the South the place for gifts and lessons. What 'good' did I get out of this situation? Another way to ask this is – what did I learn about myself, my energy and my personal needs and values from this situation? What am I prepared to put up with? Or not?

In the case of Joe, he might need to do some repair around his energy, the way he communicates and the way he handles other people. It might even be a case of him mastering his own personal space so that colleagues don't get under his skin. People are going to clash with you in business, you need a way of not buying into the drama or it can take over your life and affect your health. Perhaps there is something in that work colleague that reflected back to Joe a part of himself that he did not like. That's very common. What we hate in others is often what we secretly fear we have in ourselves. Hence we reject it.

Suggested action:

Write down the key question to ask yourself? What did I learn from X situation? X being the issue in the North (conflict, trauma, event, pattern, pain, issue). You should list *at least 20 things* that you learned about yourself and the gift/s you got out of it.

A failed relationship at work may just be defining for you what values and culture you want to work in. Maybe it's telling you to find your own voice and be confident within your skin? Perhaps that work burnout is a reminder about your health and wellbeing and how hard you are on yourself. A major life event may help you find a new power you didn't know you had in you or make you feel grateful for the life you have. Out of those 20 things, you will find that 3 or 4 of them are real gems. They are big emotive triggers and will evolve your identity and purpose in this lifetime. The desired outcome for the South is to integrate these lessons, thank the person/ situation for helping your evolving karmic journey and decide what changes you plan to take with the 'new' enlightened you.

If you place a lot of time and energy into your working life, please remember that MANY of your lessons to evolve will unfold at work, as that is where you spend loads of your time. So, don't write this off as a personal tool that is more emotionally based. Your biggest lessons will play out at work and having a way of navigating the cycles is a huge advantage in business and life.

In Joe's case, his lesson might by any or all of these gifts:

- learning not to engage in competition at work;
- that he is the only person who can control his wellbeing and stress levels;
- that his colleague was reflecting something back in himself that he didn't like and that was triggering him(that's the most common one!);
- that his current job was not honouring him and it's time to move on;
- that he has some buried issues about winning that need to be let go;
- helping him to understand what is really valuable in life; and
- learning about what it means to be a good supportive colleague (by example of what is not a good colleague).

The list goes on.

Once you understand the gift, the stress seems to diminish and you truly can move on. Understanding lessons truly does take the bite out of the problem. Please remember though that if your situation involves another person, you will need to ensure once you thank them for the shift you have – you let THEM and YOURSELF off the hook. Staying in judgement of that person means that you bind yourself energetically to them. They have been a catalyst for your change – so allow them to continue their journey (with you in their life or not) without a big energetic chord linking the both of you. That is not good for either party. If you cannot let it go, then you're not yet done with the South!

Unresolved conflicts with others become dead energetic weight you carry around with you.

There is not a real need to troubleshoot EAST as it stands for new beginnings. If you arrive at the start of something new and shiny in your life, love the adventure, wonder and mystery. If anything, review your last experiences and have a clear intention of what you want next time around. Go with your intuition and enjoy. If you are fearful of a pattern repeating in your life to take the joy out of your new venture, try skipping back to the south and exploring your past issues around a specific topic – relationships, work etc. Start the East with a clean slate and magic will happen.

That is the medicine wheel in a nutshell.

#2 Organic Problem Solving / Complex Vs Wicked Problem Solving – useful for when you have no real solution on the table available

A great friend and business colleague of mine, Mo Fox, talks about complex and wicked problems. I am only going to discuss the idea briefly and I suggest you visit her online to find out more because, between you and me, she's a bit of a problem solving genius! www.mofox.com.au

I always understood this process as a 'let go of the outcome' process and surrender to the answers that come forth. Follow your intuition and so forth, but Mo's structure and explanation of it allows a deeper integration of the process.

This model is all about 'not knowing' and organic business decisions. We have an interesting dilemma in our western world, in that we feel that success is about control and having a plan. Our society is based on 'coming up with the answers' so I present this model as a different perspective. I love this 'not knowing' passage that I have quoted below. It was passed down to me from a counsellor, who had it given to her years earlier. None of us can remember where it comes from so sorry to plagiarise the words whoever you are wise soul, but don't you think it is hilarious that all of us not knowing where the 'not knowing' passage comes from and being okay with that is quite fitting to this argument?

"Connecting with our soul can take us beyond the ego's experience. And we do this by being willing to just be in NOT KNOWING. This is very scary for the personality. But if we can genuinely feel what it's like to NOT KNOW, we find it's a very spacious place to be. It's ripe with potential. Doing this, we take ourselves out of the box of our old thinking. And if we can sit there quietly, not giving in to the ego's pressure to do something, we'll support the changes we're looking for." *Unknown source*

I see the idea of 'not knowing' and accepting that, to be quite a fantastic solution to some tricky business problems. Creative and brilliant ideas arise when the mind is shut down from control. After all, our mind only knows what is programed and cannot reach outside of that unless given free license to be imaginative and intuitive.

So, some business decisions require an intuitive approach that says 'Let's just do one organic step at a time, which will then lead us to the next step. Allow the information to come to light when it's ready after the previous step is complete.'

We always feel like we need to KNOW all of the time... it is truly relieving to move to a different view or vantage point.

Now here is a much more eloquent way of describing, as was passed on to me by Mo Fox.

It is about 'Complex vs Wicked Problem' solving.

What is a complex problem?

A complex problem is when you need to sort out a whole lot of operational crap and roadblocks. You basically run a think tank session – where yourself (and others if you need them) throw all of the mess on to the table and sort through the data. You start piecing together a clever plan of how to move from Point A to Point B. There might be ten steps you can take in linear order to fix the problem and achieve an awesome outcome. It's normally a little strategic but generally fairly analytical. There might be some course correction in there – but it's 80% right. If I just follow these ten steps, I will be successful in solving my problem. Complex problems are solved logically once the time taken to think through the process is complete.

What is a wicked problem?

A wicked problem is unsolvable by logic or strategy alone. The 10th step and many others are ultimately hidden and cannot reveal themselves in the current environment. The data available at the time cannot produce the outcome. The roadblock is either too big, there is too much emotion or just a plain good old- fashioned pickle of a situation.

The only way out is to take ONE intuitive step at a time which - once completed -then leads you on to the next correct intuitive step and so forth. Wicked problems mean that you couldn't even begin to set a plan in place for the future because each step requires the one before to occur before it can come to light. It's truly organic and works off a flow of energy and movement.

Now that is pure INTUITION at its best. It requires patience and trust. Setting step one is not even logical – it is what feels intuitively (instinctually) best for you at the time based on the facts and situation you feel/know. Because it's wicked, you don't know what will work so you try what FEELS best and prune from there. Once that step works, and you are ready to do Step 2, follow the same formula and feel what fits best.

This can be a huge relief for people when they understand that they don't have to have all the answers upfront or decide on things they are not ready to (or cannot) decide upon. Often the outcome is better because it's not pre-determined or boxed. It evolves to what it should be with freedom and authenticity. There is no outcome, no final step and no linear movement.

This works for both business and life. I work with many clients going through quite a big divorce or separation and this often involves children, which complicates the situation even more. Practicing this type of intuitive problem solving is a huge relief and works so effectively. In business it works well when creating products and testing marketing.

Every single step is intuitive due to the nature of the problem. The key here is that you don't need to 'know'. We are a culture obsessed by needing to know and being in control. It's such a relief when you are let off the hook and given permission to 'not know'.

Q. Where in your life do you have (or have had) a wicked problem arise? Where there is no clear way out and you just needed to go

with the flow at the time and take a first step? Were you able to let go? If yes, did it work out?

_____

_____

_____

Think about that situation and how this might have shaped your life more dramatically than other smaller life challenges. What did it lead you to do, think, be or feel that really changed you for the better? We can learn to intuitively make choices even when we are not challenged with something wicked. In fact, the more tuned in we become, the better the road we travel.

Reflect on this for a bit and really get the sense of how intuitive you can be. Perhaps if you have a wicked problem right now, write down the first intuitive step you might need to do?

_____

_____

_____

#3 The Fork in the Road – get your timing right

Intuition is not just about WHAT to do, but WHEN to do something. Many of us make decisions and solve problems either:

a) Too early for when the decision or outcome is available to us (control), or
b) Too late and the timing has been lost or past its 'due by' date (procrastination).

Many people I work with feel a deep pressure to make a decision about a life or work challenge. To decide. To choose. To change! This pressure can feel overwhelming and stressful and we are the only ones placing pressure on ourselves. Some decisions just haven't been cooked yet. Similar to the not knowing, we also have that same pressure around 'not acting'. Speed can be awesome when well placed, but it can also be destructive when poorly thought through.

Although it is important to flow in life and take new paths, it is really important to do it in a pacing that is right - not forced or rushed or hurried. We often feel the need to make a decision as soon as an option is on the table. If you are confused or unsure or hesitant, that is probably (not always) your intuition telling you not to move just yet. Of course it can be fear too, and the intelligence is deciding which one it is - **fear or wrong timing**. Usually we know when it is fear holding us back.

I have a saying I use regularly that goes something like this...

'Let your decision meet you.'

And this really does form the basis for this model being presented.

There is a fork in the road when a decision becomes clear and exciting and you get the inner knowing and urgency to act because you are 100% ready. This is a fantastic time to make decisions as you will accept the outcome regardless of consequences. Regret usually happens when you don't feel clear in your decision making regardless of the outcome. It is not about getting it 'right' as much as about having a clear and meaningful choice. We are then happy to face the outcome no matter what.

Getting the timing right in your business decisions has far reaching consequences. I started writing this book three years before it was published and I knew there was something missing until I reached a point in my life to finish it. I was missing some key information that needed to present itself in 2015. I could have forced the deadline earlier but at the expense of delivering a less than great product.

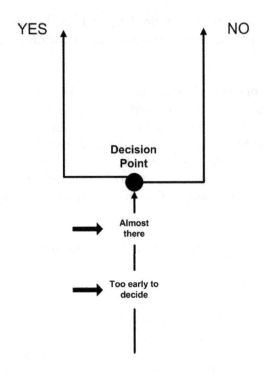

See the above model. There is a clear decision point and several stages before you arrive there. When making a big decision, take your time and allow the pieces to fall into place naturally – without your logical 'solve it all quickly' left brain taking over and hurrying an outcome or decision point. Your deep inner self knows what to do if you step out of the way.

If you don't know, it's not yet time to act. Don't play to anyone else's timing either. I have clients say to me 'but it's not fair to keep someone hanging for a decision when I am in the way'. I disagree. It's worse to deliver a decision that is not the right one for both of you. Don't rush, you will feel like you want to if you are a Personality A Type. Don't procrastinate either, you might do this if that's your personality type. Remember those words 'let your decision meet you' and once you have the knowing and gut feeling of clarity, take the courage to act on it.

As the 'fork in the road' model relates to a decision (yes or no) or a course of action to take, it is obvious when that arises in your working life. Some examples include;

- Knowing when to resign or leave a role;
- Decisions about when to start or end a business partnership, venture etc.;
- When to launch a product to market;
- Major announcements of news – internal and to public;
- Staff movements, re-structures, redundancies, hiring, firing;
- Take legal action or serious conversations in business to address an issue;
- Appointing suppliers or contracts;
- Investment in business – people, equipment; and
- Expansion or contraction.

I have found the most difficult issues arise in relation to people – partnerships, hiring, firing etc. In regards to personal life, when to actually leave a partner is the most intense. The main thing to remember with any fork in the road is not to cave under pressure from others. Everyone will have an opinion. The other idea to keep in mind is when you are:

a) **Not ready to decide.** Information has not yet come to light or you are still considering what it is you really want. This is where you wait and honour yourself with some time and space. I like to give myself time blocks as we tend to put a huge amount of pressure on ourselves to decide ASAP. For example, you might set an agreement with yourself that you are not going to think again about your decision to move work office space for another two weeks or another four weeks. Then you must honour your commitment and not consider the decision again until that time. Tell your brain to let go of that pressure. You know you are not ready when you are conflicted about both paths to take – yes or no to that move.

b) **Procrastinating on a decision.** You know you are procrastinating when you have a deep gut feeling about the course you must follow but fear comes up to freeze you from moving. Fear feels like a mental vice. Not knowing yet feels like confusion, so allow the fog to clear. But fear feels like more of an edgy emotional state whereby you constantly go back over a decision you have come to and cannot seem to face it. You start projecting forward with scenarios. That is the mind creating imaginary stories that are fear based, but probably have no reality. When this happens, the best idea is to act on the decision by asking others to support you and being accountable to them. My theory is that even if you make a so called 'wrong decision', you need this for your growth so don't judge it or resent it.

Start practicing following your gut instincts and solving problems from a more intuitive state; your life will change remarkably as a result. Whether you have a wicked problem to solve, a decision that you cannot rush or a repeating pattern you need to unravel - all of the above tools are simple and easy to work with. Try them out and see your working life change for the better.

Answer these questions below to start you thinking ...

Q. Name a situation where you rushed a decision due to logic and should have waited to feel clear and knowing?

_____

_____

_____

Q. How do you make business/career decisions – more logically or intuitively?

_____

_____

_____

Q. How good are you at following your gut feelings? Do you have a good tool/model to help with this?

_____

_____

_____

Q. Do you reflect on your big career challenges and attempt to learn the lessons you need and ensure you don't repeat them again?

_____

_____

_____

Debbie Pask

Beginner

You probably make all of your decisions logically and in a somewhat linear fashion. You might use your creativity a little here and there to find solutions, but it is structured and has a process behind it. When a major event happens in your working life, you don't really stop and think about the inner lessons you are being given, nor how you might have played a role in attracting that incident. When you are faced with a problem or business crisis, you have a tendency to either push right through it and batten down the hatches until it resolves or avoid it in some way.

That might be delegating it, glossing over the issue or focusing on something else. Perhaps you put it down to blaming others and their incompetence. It is likely that you feel the need to always be in control, to have the answers or at least drive and strive until you can work things out and make sense of it all. The focus is more on the outer action (Yang) then on the inner reflection (Yin), which means that your creative brilliance and 'X Factor' is probably not 100% accessed.

You probably put a lot of pressure on yourself to get things right and to forge ahead with decisions. Some of the time that works for you, other times it bites you in the rear end. Your motto might be 'you win some, you lose some'.

Graduate

You appreciate the intuitive and strategic approach to problem solving and have the ability to let go of that typical linear approach to resolving challenges. You rely equally on gut instinct to guide your actions and also see the value in others assisting the process of resolution. You may even try a meditative or quiet approach to problem solving, whereby accepting it and letting it go returns you positive solutions.

You may approach outside parties such as coaches or energy practitioners to help you reflect on the challenge from a different perspective and from a higher guiding level. That higher level represents that wiser fractal aspect of your own self that is removed from the day-to-day pressure of work. Intuition is respected and has earned its place at your dinner table.

You take responsibility for the role you play in your own life challenges and are interested in working this through to heal. You may not know all of the different ways to access your intuition but your library is growing steadily and you are more tuned into your gut feelings these days. Work seems to flow better the more tuned in you are and your energy is a lot more relaxed and accepting about business challenges. You have faith in the process.

Master

You have truly mastered your intuitive approach to business. Decisions come from the heart and then you vet those decisions with logical thought and practical strategies. Your working issues are enjoyed as a wonderful insight into where your own personal energy is at and a chance to evolve or change.

You have developed your own set of useful diagnostic tools to work out your actions and steps based on good vibes or feelings. You have found a good flow and have clearly established your 'yes and no' (gut instinct) responses in the body, alongside an uncanny sense of 'lie detecting' whereby you can literally hear the truth. When someone speaks without authenticity it is like they are a beacon flashing out at sea. You are happy sitting in the 'void' (deep and confusing place where there is no answer) when you need to, accepting and trusting that the resolution will come forth when the timing is right. Doesn't mean you love it but you certainly respect it. Your view on your working life is broader and you have the ability to see the bigger picture so you can stay relaxed knowing that it is working as it should. Sometimes you know and sometimes you don't know - that is cool too.

As a result of this behaviour, you find that the universe flows easily and in sync with you, delivering you insights and ideas that have an 'X Factor' feeling to them. That is what happens when we let go of outcomes - better opportunities arise and present themselves. Happy days.

References Chapter 8

1. www.mofox.com.au

9

The Art of Manifestation

Phrenology of an Entrepreneur

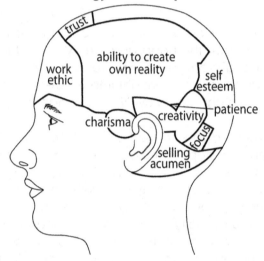

Quote: "What you seek is seeking you" Rumi

Key Learning: Working with the source field and using creative visualisation is one of the most powerful tools for attaining your dreams, goals or business vision. If you want to get serious in business, get serious in your ability to visualise and connect in.

Key words: Meditation. Visualisation. Manifestation. Channel. Source field. Universal lore. Energy magnet. Lucid dreaming. Repetition. Vibration. Ripple effect.

Work with the Energy of Universal 'Lore'(Law) to Manifest

Look at the image above of the brain and see what is located in the core centre of the image; the part of the brain responsible for *creating your own reality*. This has more weight to it than you might realise.

This is not just a chapter on meditation and creating a vision board to manifest your goals, although that is/can certainly be a component of it. Rather, this chapter on manifestation has been the most difficult to write for me as it's actually quite complex to explain. How do you communicate to someone what has taken me years to learn and integrate? People who edited these chapters for me pretty much asked me to explain every word or term along the way, so I hope I do this justice. It is actually an incredible and mind blowing concept to understand, especially in terms of succeeding in your business goals and truly learning the art of manifesting.

I have broken down the concept of manifestation into four parts:

PART A – First you must understand universal energy and lore (law)[1];

PART B – Second you should cultivate the ability to 'receive' energy;

PART C – Third requires creative visualisation and alpha[2] state flow;

PART D – Last, to supercharge results, try the power of group energy to manifest.

PART A – Understanding universal energy and lore (law)

Let me premise this section with 'please use this information for good and not for evil', as what you will learn here is powerful stuff. Mess with karma* and it will mess with you. I am going to share some key universal concepts about energy and law (lore) and they are not pulled out of 'The Secret'[3] movie or hyped Hollywood versions of magic meditations. Rather, these ideas stem from indigenous tribes who, despite living vast distances away from one another and some in different eras, seem to share the same common wisdom and beliefs about how universal energy works. These notions are also being backed up by latest consciousness science; finally science catches up to what tribal shamans have known all along. Understanding these ideas will help explain why manifestation works and how we can use it correctly and authentically to thrive in our life and business.

i) The Holographic Universe*; Everything is Energy

Do you really understand that you are a 'fractal' (part) of the world (the universal hologram) and that what you imagine and focus on, is likely to magnetise back to you?

Fractal = a fragment of the whole which has the same data or character as the whole.

Universal Hologram = the entire whole (universal) world or matrix as it appears to us with all of its code, information and structure.

Therefore if **we** are a fractal of the universal hologram = then **we** hold ALL of life's knowledge and infrastructure and intelligence within our cells, our body and our very being. We are a miniature version of the world around us.

What are we made of?

Although humans may appear solid, we are actually just vibrating in a particular way that gives us the physical appearance of being solid dense beings. We (humans) are in fact brilliant energy beings made up of sound, geometry and mathematics (amongst many other things), just like the universe and the galaxy around us. Every human is a fractal (smaller part) of the hologram (the energy field of the universe). Everything in our body (or self) holds all of the information or codes that the greater universe holds. If you analyse the information in your cells, they will hold all of your ancestral memories of the previous generations before you.[4] They will also hold information about the nature and structure of the universe.

Nassim Haramein is a quantum scientist that has shown our world around us is 99.99999% space and that only 0.000001% is solid matter. Even our protons (the small measure within our cells) have the same mass as a cubic cm of outer space, which is technically empty matter. [5]

It seems we have the same information and structure within our cells as do outer space. His theory is that we, as humans, come into and out of reality through an energy field so quickly that it only appears we are solid three dimensional beings. We are really just beings of energy vibrating in a pattern that gives us solid form.

Considering we are a fractal of this greater world or hologram, we need to really think about what this structure is made up of. If it is 99% space, what does that mean in terms of manifesting material things into our life?

I will refer frequently to this universal hologram as the matrix. It is best if you think of the matrix like a series of blue energy grid lines that connect everything together and hold all thoughts, memories, code, geometry and sound. These invisible blue threads are intelligent and continually weaving together a three dimensional world around us through a series of energy formations called a torus energy field and through a geometric pattern or structure called the star tetrahedron. Some of those things we can see with our physical eyes (houses, mountains, people, animals, trees etc.) and some things we cannot see like radio waves, emotions and thoughts).

Gregg Braden is renowned as a pioneer in bridging science, spirituality, and the real world. Following a successful career as a computer geologist for Phillips Petroleum during the 1970s energy crisis, he worked as a senior computer systems designer with Martin Marietta Defence Systems during the final years of the Cold War. In 1991, he became the first technical operations manager for Cisco Systems. He has now spent the last 20 years looking at the world of quantum science* (what is the tiniest measurable unit of matter) and heart coherence (heart and mind in harmony).

Braden's work follows on from the discoveries made in 1944 from quantum scientist, Max Planck – who discovered that the world was essentially a 'Matrix', a source field of energy and light and that there was no measurable or solid matter at the root of physical structure (human and other). Further experiments theorise that this 'Matrix' connects everything to each other.

In addition, further studies in quantum physics have delivered a new branch of quantum science around ancestral memories and it is termed 'epigenetics'*. If your Great Grandfather went to war, somewhere in your cells – you will hold memories of that war as you are an ancestor. These may not affect you day-to-day unless triggered, but they do exist. These memories are one of those examples in the matrix that we cannot see with our eyes. Leading cellular biologist Dr Bruce Lipton in his book *The Biology of Belief*[6] explores how our cells are more controlled by energy states (you as a fractal of the universe) and environment than by your hard wired physical DNA. He has now proven that our physical state is primarily governed by the energy/memory locked in our cells and our thoughts and beliefs that drive us every day. We can have good programs switched on or negative ones. Ultimately, when we narrow us down to the tiniest parts of the cell, we are NOT solid beings, and these energetic frequencies within our being can affect us, emotionally and physically. Even the smallest part of us that we can measure (called a quark) is still just vibrating energy and the further you look under the microscope, it keeps coming up as 'empty of matter'.

I have thrown a lot of science and theory at you, so what does this have to do with manifesting goals or good business outcomes?

In the matrix, like attracts like. It is one big mirror. What you project outwards is what you experience reflected back to you.

Think about energy vibration in terms of magnets. If you vibrate at a certain level, then you will attract something of that same magnetic frequency back to you. If you are feeling heavy and tired, then what sort of goals are you going to magnetise? Your cells need to be vibrating at the right frequency that will mirror back to you the frequency of a goal you want. It would seem mismatched for someone stressed and burnt out (constantly giving out energy) to magnetise abundance or a goal that requires something positive.

If you want to experience something happy and abundant, you will need to cultivate that energetic feeling within.

If you are not getting what you want, ask this question:

What is blocking your goals on the energetic side of things? How strong and centered is your personal energy?

When you find the key to unlocking or opening up **your personal** energy to a better and more positive vibration, all goals and desires in life become easier. Remember the energy you send out to the matrix brings back to you a vibrational match. Our day to day state does affect our everyday life experience in the matrix or source field that we live in.

Universal Law

In regards to your energy vibration and the matrix around you, there are some rules that are useful to know so that you can play the game of abundance. The indigenous tribes knew this law/lore well and paid it much respect. And when I say indigenous, I am referring to the Indigenous Australians (Aboriginals), Aztecs, Peruvians, Mexicans, Native American Indians, African shamans and more. These laws/lores are important to navigate your way in this life (this matrix). Not knowing them is working against energy itself. A little bit like the law of gravity, whether you know about it or not – the simple fact is that if you step off a cliff you will indeed fall to the bottom. Likewise, whether you know these laws or not, they still play out in the matrix around you regardless of whether you are aware of them.

What are some of the laws that we know of?

1. **Law of creation:** Your spirit (life force) is the most powerful tool you have – like a miniature sun within you. We discussed before that your cells are the equivalent structure to a cubic cm of universal space. You have the power to create your own reality.
   Business application = Back the power of yourself to deliver what you need. You have the ability to manifest without fail if you keep your energy in flow. You do indeed have infinite energy within you, so respecting it and accessing it is intelligent.

2. **Law of sovereignty:** Don't pray to anything outside of yourself as this gives your power away and you may be subject to that outside influence.
   Business application = Don't envy someone else (guru) or want to be them and not yourself. Don't entangle yourself

in a destructive or draining relationship (person, business, entity) where you are negatively affected by the other. Don't give your power away to your boss. Remain free and in charge of your own destiny.

3. **Law of space:** He who enters the game of another is subject to the rules of that game.
   Business application = You are less in your power when entering the physical offices of another or entering a partnership that was set up after or without your input/ stamp. Create your own rules and space to work from, or if you cannot, keep the intention of your own boundaries when interacting with others.

4. **Law of agreement:** If any two parties agree, so shall it be so.
   Business application = An agreement (handshake, verbal or contract) is a serious intention and energetically binds you to that agreement. You need to be mindful as to what you really want and commit to. Consider everything carefully and don't be reckless with what you commit to.

5. **Law of intention:** When you want something, ask your Spirit to bring it to you.
   Business application = The more serious your focus and clarity on your goals, the easier they will appear. Want to super-charge it? Get group energy on board.
   Remember that it is just as easy to attract negative experiences into your life if your focus is on fear, so stay mindful of letting go of fear as you may attract the very things that scares you the most. The matrix has no judgement and it will simply match your vibration or thoughts; good or bad.

6. **Law of karma:** He who negatively projects on to another, shall receive this psychic projection back upon himself.
   Business application = Don't mess with someone else's free will (when trying to achieve something) or you will face the consequences at a later time. Basically don't play dirty to get your goals as every action has an opposing reaction to the same magnitude.

So, that means if we understand how this matrix works and the laws within it, then we can work **with it** to bring about the flow that we want. We have everything we need within our own energy, so our mission is to learn the rules so that we can play and win (win, meaning within our own race and destiny, not competing). That which you don't know or are not prepared for, is the cause of any failure. Some businesses call it risk assessment or R&D (research and development). Learn about the rules of this amazing holographic universe so you are playing with an even chance to master it and get what you want along the way.

ii) Everything is Alive

Your body, your mind, your thoughts, your plants, your pets, your house, your business, your artwork and more. Everything has its own energy and its own existence in the world. Your marriage or business partnership has its own purpose and its own energy or spirit. In Australia, every business needs to hold an ABN. Businesses or companies are called an 'entity' as they are their own creation or legal structure. Therefore, the creation of this 'ABN of entity' indeed acts like an entity in that it has its own spirit and only knows its own creation. Was it created out of love, fear, financial hardship or rush?

This is an indigenous concept and I can see clearly how it operates in the business world. Let's use an example of how a simple belief can become alive and hold its own consciousness.

One day I go into work expecting to get a promotion for all of my hard work. For two years now I have worked overtime and gone above and beyond. Then, when it comes to the big announcement day, my lazy and incompetent colleague gets the promotion instead of me. All of that hard work I put in and no pay off! What can happen here?

1. I develop a 'thought' that says 'No matter how hard you work, you never get ahead' in your career. Or maybe 'I'm not good enough, I have to work harder'.
2. If you allow that thought to stew in your mind and start nagging you or taking over your happiness, it can start to grow into a 'thought form' whereby it develops its own energetic imprint. You now start to create an internal

'belief' that this is what happens to you in relation to work promotions. This belief can actually start delivering you that very outcome as you unintentionally magnetise it towards you.

3. Soon you start to experience more incidences of feeling like you are working hard and being let down or not rewarded for your hard work. Perhaps it is at home or in your friendship circles. More than likely it happens at work. As this thought form starts to 'feed' itself, so does this 'thought form' take on an energy of its own – becoming a 'life form'. It only knows its creation so it repeats itself again and again, mirroring the same experience.

4. This 'life form' now does not want to die. Its very existence relies on experiencing that same condition of being under-valued and it will fight hard to stay alive. Energy is alive and now your thought, that became a belief, that became a life form will run the show and attract similar life scenarios; hence the law of attraction. A life form only knows its own creation.

Have a think about your business challenges (or life); does anything come to mind that is a repeating pattern or event? Pay rises, relationship conflicts, personal addictions, learning issues, body issues and more. Some life patterns are so deep- seated that they feel overwhelming. This could be an internal 'life form' or 'entity' that you feel you often cannot control. Energetically it can magnetise and neurologically it cements. And that's how our challenges can grow bigger than us. These negative life experiences can cement in and overtake us. They need to be released in order to change.

Q. What negative thought forms relating to your working life might you have developed over time? Examples are:-

Money is hard to make;

People are always trying to screw me over;

I cannot trust anyone that works with or for me;

I have to work long and hard to be successful and make loads of money;

I am technologically challenged.

List yours

_____

_____

_____

Experiments on Energy

There are many experiments completed on the effects and impacts of energy consciousness in cells which shows they are, on some level, alive and reactive to our thoughts. Even our cells have their own conscious thought.

This shows us how our energy can be affected and how it reacts to meditation, media and movies. What we say, do and see in our lives impacts on the vibration of our energy, down to a cellular level.

One such case got my attention early on and it involves an experiment conducted on soldiers in the US military. The idea was to prove that certain emotions and feelings can create a physical cellular reaction in the bodies of military personnel. In the study, military men were shown a series of violent video clips and images. Afterwards, their cheek cells were scraped to see how their cells reacted to the violent clips. All cells collected showed an elevated physical response (aggravation) which revealed how their emotional response to visual stimuli can adversely affect the physical health of a soldier.

To take the study further, the test was done again but this time the soldiers cheeks cells were pre-scraped (before exposing the men to the violent media clips) and placed in isolation in a Petri dish next door. The study shows that even though the cells were outside (not connected) to the body at the time, when the violent media was shown to soldiers, their cells still tested positive to aggravation. This shows clearly that our cells are alive with their own consciousness and are deeply connected to our emotional and mental state of mind (even if removed from the body). Once again, they repeated the experiment but decided to drive the pre-scraped cells over 50 miles away from the soldiers' location. The idea was to see if the distance severed the energy connection between the cheek cells and the thoughts of the soldiers. After showing the soldiers the violent media again, they tested the reaction on these cells located 50 miles away, and found them still strongly reacting to the emotional responses of the men.[7]

Doesn't that blow your mind? That even the cells *outside of your physical body several miles away* are still linked to your thoughts and feelings. Imagine the intensity of the cells *inside* of your body still connected by tissue when you feel stress, fear, agitation or more? What do you think they do when you get stressed at work? Or, on a more positive note, what could the cells do if you exposed them to happy, high energy thoughts? Imagine getting all of your cells to sing a happy song and feel connected through teamwork? Want a happy outcome to your goal – get your cells in the right cultural mood to deliver, because angry cells aren't useful to any goal. Can you imagine what angry cells mirror back to you from the universe?

Understanding the science behind energy can arm us with the right tools to help us manifest. You can see how important it is to nourish your energy and to ensure you have a strong strategy for how to boost it, refill it and work in flow with it. Which is kind of what this whole book is based upon.

iii) Everything is Connected

We just showed that your mind, body and spirit are potentially all connected based on the US military experiment. But what about the world or matrix? Considering we are all just energy and life forms, technically we are all connected by energy waves in some way. Our thoughts can send out energy signals and we can pick up on people's energy signals (that's sort of like ESP - when someone you are thinking of suddenly calls you). You can ripple out intentions into universal energy waves and they will bounce back if you wait for them (based on the laws of the matrix). There is no actual physical space or time between you and your goal, it is more about alignment and vibration. Are you blocking the vibration or signal or are you creating a free flowing energy source to it? Are you sending the right emotions and thoughts into the cell so that it attracts the things that you want. It's tricky to get what you want if you are tuned into the wrong radio station.

In his books and documentaries, Braden explains the direct connection between the 'Matrix' (universal hologram) and human beings. His theory is that we 'as a fractal or part of the world' can indeed affect the world.

Braden and others talk about the 'GOES' satellites that sit in the skies of both the Southern and Northern hemisphere and their role is to measure the magnetic fields of the earth and send back those electro-magnetic* readings every 30 mins. These readings normally fit into a certain range considered 'normal'. However, these satellite readings spiked massively on Sept 11, 2001 - 15 minutes after the first plane hit the twin towers building. It seems to supports the theory that our emotions and energy can indeed affect the universal magnetic field readings as measured by these satellites.[8]

Studies done by the HeartMath Institute[9] reveal that human emotions can affect the electro-magnetic energy of our heart which then can affect the world energy around us. In Braden's example above, it seems the group energy of human emotion may be able to extend far beyond just our bodies and immediate environment and reach up to satellites thousands of miles above the surface.

For more information on the heart check out Braden's You Tube videos "Our Electro-Magnetic Heart Affects Our Reality".[10]

So our energy can affect the world around us, and the world can, in return, affect our energy. A two-way system it seems.

That means we can affect the matrix as we are part of it and connected to it. And the universe affects us back feeding in the general vibe of the universal mind. The next time the anniversary of September 11 rolls around, tune in and see how heavy it feels. As the world (especially the US) starts to grieve that day, you can feel the mood of the energy around start to drop. That is because the matrix is picking up on grief and fear of the anniversary of that fateful day and reflecting that back through those invisible grid lines around us that we cannot see.

And that is as simple as it gets. What radio station are you tuned into? The 'happy abundant' one, the 'stress head' or the 'poor me' one? Harnessing the source field or matrix around us to get in flow with energy, to set our intentions and create the right vibration to bring the goal back is not magic, albeit it feels that. It is quantum science. Learning how to master it and enjoy it should be a lifetime study.

That is the summary of the science and energy side of things; now let's have a look at how we must learn to receive and therefore harness energy.

PART B – Cultivate the ability to 'receive'

This concept is extremely simple to explain but difficult to do for many of us. It is even harder for busy worker bees and people who have energy, drive and talents.

Cultivating the art of receiving energy is necessary and quite a fundamental principle of manifestation.

Chapter 1, Mastering Yin and Yang, outlined this concept. Basically you can have Energy coming IN or Energy going OUT.

Yin = energy IN

Yang = energy OUT

We need to be in the mode of Yin (energy in) to truly receive our goals. That means we must learn to be creative, meditative, reflective, inwardly attentive and so forth. But let's take it one step further.

We can speed this up ten-fold if we practice these basic steps of receiving:

1. **Accept** – that means accepting support from others, compliments, help and any kind of gift coming inwards;
2. **Ask** – that means we must practice speaking up and requesting what we need from those around us (family, friends, work, community and more);

3. **Nurture** – we must allow others and the universe to take us in with kind loving hands and care for us when we are rundown, need help or a rest;

4. **Say No** – we must not over-give our own resources or supply. We need a good sense of self care to say 'no' to the things or people that are depleting us, so we send out the message that we are valuable and come first.

These four things are very hard to do, and here's why.

If you are a hard-working manager or business owner, you have constant demands on your energy and time, supporting lots of people and you get stuck in a very 'giving' role. It can be hard to sit back and allow yourself support.

If you happen to be also supporting a family, then you have another tribe of people to financially support. This starts to create a one-way flow and you get out of practice from literally receiving energy. That does not mean you don't manifest at all. It just means you need to drive and push and sometimes force things. That is a much harder road to follow and things are much easier should you practice the above stuff.

If you are a mother (or father) too, then the natural instincts of giving out to your cubs will also create a vortex of giving out energy. Whether working or not, there is a natural tendency to support and feed the little people, leaving not much room for your own needs.

As I mentioned, the concept is very simple to interpret and makes obvious sense. However – it is hard to practice in our busy life.

If you don't stop and replenish enough, that is a sign or signal to the universe that you don't want to receive anything – whether that be goals, gifts, support, money, love and more.

Don't make the mistake of doing everything yourself and don't always be the 'Go To' person. Say 'NO' sometimes and place some focus on balancing the give versus receive state.

There is not much more to understand here as it is more about practice, so if you need to work on it, our exercises later on will give you a good starting point. Here is a direct example of how quickly the universe responds when you get into the flow of receiving.

The Power of Receiving to Create New Life

I don't broadly advertise it, but part of my healing work involves fertility treatments for women struggling to fall pregnant, often after several attempts or trauma such as miscarriages, failed IVF and so forth. They have normally tried acupuncture, herbs and a series of other alternative treatments before they wind up on my healing table.

One of the KEY ingredients I advise every fertility client is that they need to re-establish a 'receiving' energy flow into their body. With life being so busy in our current world, many women (and men) just cannot seem to slow down and fall into that wonderful 'Yin' mode we spoke about. For a baby to birth into world, there needs to be space and room to arrive. I give my clients tasks that include saying 'no' to demands on their time, asking for more support, doing a meditation/visualisation that I tape for them and learning the art of receiving.

After years and thousands of dollars spent on fertility treatments (IVF and alternative), 80% of these beautiful people fall pregnant within a few sessions (over three months or so). What is the secret? I truly believe that switching their energy flow from give and more give – to receive, support, ask and slow-down is the absolute key to it. They just need the permission to do it and I am convincing enough for them to follow through. My treatment with them is just another aspect of receiving and getting the body into flow.

Let's review what we have discussed.

Firstly, we understand the world is energy, that it is alive and that it is connected and we can impact on this energy field or matrix.

Plus, we know the importance of getting into 'receive mode' so that we can harness the flow of energy back toward us positively.

Now, we can start to work with the concept of creative visualisation to hone in on exactly *what we do want* to receive so we can supercharge our MANIFESTATION.

This is now the focus part of manifesting and that requires us to master the technique of visualisation ...

PART C: The Power of Creative Visualisation

If you aren't meditating or using visualisation (both utilise focus) as a tool to power up your working success and manifest, then you literally are short-changing yourself. The power of intention and vision creates the way for reality to emerge (using the holographic field). If you think it up, you can do it. If you dream it, it can come into existence. Creative visualisation is like meditation and lucid dreaming combined.

It's a funny little world we live in, don't you think? How has it come to be that we are a planet spinning and rotating through space around a giant star we call the sun, that is also rotating through space and time? Yet we have the illusion of being still. There are universal rules and lores (laws) that govern our space here on Earth. Gravity is one of them. The law of attraction is another. Simple as that.

When you want something in your life, you do have the power to intend it so. The power of the mind (thinking energy point) combined with your Heart (emotional energy point) is a powerful engine of creation. Let's think of it in relation to the three Minds.

Mind #1 – The Conscious Mind – sets a goal or intention. Feed it your dream ideas and it can get excited about what may come. This is the easiest part.

Q. What is a core goal of yours? Write it here ... get excited and bring it to life.

_____

_____

_____

Mind #2 – The Sub-Conscious Mind – thinks in pictures. Feed it visual images, tangible suggestions and clear signals. This is the bit where you put some effort in and repetition is the key.

Q. What images would you use (i.e. what would you see happening in your life) to show this goal has come into existence? Write them here.

_____

_____

_____

Mind #3 – The Super-Conscious Mind – works with deep heart feelings, the torus[10] field of the heart (we discuss the torus field later) and the holographic source field of energy around you. Connect to your inner spirit, find meaning in your goals and watch the changes around you.

Q. What feelings would you have if this goal had already happened and you had it right now? Think joy, happiness, calm, love, excitement, gratitude etc. These feelings excite and switch on the cells within you, generating a bigger energetic amplitude.

_____

_____

_____

Science is now proving that visualising what you want (with both visual images and feelings) has a powerful ability to bring that thing into your energy field via the matrix. Back to Gregg Braden, who is both a scientist and spiritualist and who conducts energy experiments on manifesting through intended visualisation. Check out the scientific tests Braden has completed on manifesting using the heart on You Tube, called *"The* Power of Visualisation"[12].

In a nutshell, he proves through scientific experiments that when the heart connects to a feeling of happiness or excitement around a goal, it sends a signal through to the cells of the body which then communicate with each other and change their energetic state to one of excitement or happy energy. Then, once these cells are charged/excited – they then affect the matrix around the body by sending out that pulse or signal beyond our physical self - seeking that same energy source to return back to it. The magnet affect means that it seeks a similar experience or the goal you are thinking/ feeling about - and pulls it towards you. Similar to how thought forms attract the same repeating situation, the feeling/intention that you ripple outwards, will seek its matching counterpart. So, connecting to your heart energy can literally ripple back your goal to you if you repeat this experiment regularly. Doesn't that excite the hell out of you?

Lesson: excite your cells and get them on board with your desires and you will attract your goal over time.

How to Master Creative Visualisation (to manifest and more)

First things first. You are going to have to get familiar with meditation. If you have not already, then get prepared to do so. Here's a step-by-step guide to visualise for manifesting.

1. Let's first establish what wave patterns your brain should be in:

There are four key mind states as shown below. The theory is that true mindfulness or meditation brings us into what is called an 'alpha' wave* state. Our brain patterns slow to a pace where our cognitive functions increase and different parts of the brain light up. In other words, we get smarter and can manifest better when in alpha.

The main levels of brain function states include:

(Hertz (hz) = unit of frequency, equal to one cycle per second.

Beta (14 – 40Hz) - our day to day busy minds; logical, linear and task-oriented. While Beta brain waves are important for effective functioning throughout the day, they also can translate into stress, anxiety and restlessness. Not good for focus or manifesting.

Alpha (7.5 – 14Hz) - an increased state of awareness; ability to think more creatively, visually and intuitively (a slowing/ smoothing of brainwaves). It is the gateway to your subconscious mind and lies at the base of your conscious awareness. The voice of Alpha is your intuition, which becomes clearer and more profound the closer you get to 7.5Hz. Great for manifesting.

Theta (4 – 7.5Hz) – a deep, deep meditative state that feels a little sleep-like (in fact it is those stages just before you drop off and upon awakening). Many deep messages come through here and your awareness is still present and open to another level of cognitive brilliance. Expect vivid visualisations, great inspiration, profound creativity and exceptional insight. Unlike your other brain waves, the elusive voice of Theta is a silent voice. I myself have been in theta states for 45 + minutes and supposedly 20 mins of it can represent 4+ hours of sleep. It does deliver. Awesome for manifesting.

Delta (0.5 – 4Hz) – the slowest of the frequencies, delta is like a deep, dreamless sleep or an exceptionally deep & transcendental meditation state where awareness is fully detached. It is often considered the gateway to the Spirit or the universal mind and the collective unconscious, where information received is otherwise unavailable at the conscious level. Deep sleep is important for the healing process – as it's linked with regeneration. Not having enough deep sleep is detrimental to your health in more ways than one. This brain pattern makes it hard to control the manifestation process as you are in a very deep, sleep-like state.

So, in summary we think better, increase creativity, decision-making skills and innovation when we are in a mindful state. **Alpha for day-to-day is desirable** and **theta for those super-charged ideation moments** where you truly do need a state of transcendence. Of course if you are seriously burned out, try getting to delta more often. That takes time and commitment but is super regenerative.

So, the first goal is to learn how to reach basic alpha brain waves and that relies on some sort of meditative practice. So stop faffing around and nail this critical tool. (I would word this differently?) So many people whine about not being able to meditate. If you put some effort into it, it's actually a natural skill we all have. A bit like running, it hurts at first but then you get used to it.

2. Learn the art of guided visualisation.

I think you might as well combine #1 & #2 together. That's what I did and I reckon it is so much easier to learn meditation if you have a guided story to follow. Busy minds find it hard to follow that Buddhist style of 'just follow your breath'. I grew up on guided landscapes to meditate and I consider myself pretty advanced in meditation. They assist your imagination and improve your meditation skills quickly and richly.

What is guided visualisation? It's a script (I like it with music) to follow to stay focused on the story. I enjoy natural landscapes and elements of air, fire, earth and water. Once you are able to follow the story all the way through, you are mastering visualisation and meditation together (the art of manifesting). Meditation is simply a present focused state where everything slows down and you grow calm and insightful. It's a right brain (Yin) thing as opposed to a linear logical left brain (Yang) state.

I recorded a whole album full of guided meditations for busy business people. It's called Zen Business and you can get a copy to practice with here. http://zenfulbusiness.com.au/product/zen-business-online/

3. Connect that visualisation into the Heart centre.

There is a great energetic torus field that surrounds the heart that is quite incredible. I go more into this in the final chapter on Heart Entrainment. This torus field cycles energy through the body and listens to signals coming from the heart. So a critical part of your manifestation technique is to ensure you connect deeply with the **emotions and feelings** of what the goal means to you (on a heart level). This may require some of you to form a better dialogue with your body. A beautiful client of mine struggles to feel into her body and connect or talk to it. Admittedly, she has a lot of injuries which are painful and therefore connecting and listening to the body is not pleasant. However, the key to changing any current state is to learn to feel deeply into the body and especially the heart.

We spoke earlier about meaning and the value of being truly connected to something. Giving the heart emotional meaning is the key to heightened energy flow.

You can easily talk to your body and listen to its signals and signs on a daily basis. If you are pretty good at that, then tapping into the feelings of excitement and joy around a work goal and how it would feel to have that in your life should be relatively easy. Once you connect what the mind wants with your heart feelings, you enhance that powerful torus field so it can place your order into the universe. If you stay in your third eye/mind only, then you are missing half the potency. Kind of like having a mocktail instead of a cocktail. There is no kicker in it!

One more trick for the heart. Your goal must be meaningful and connected to you, otherwise your heart won't truly feel the emotions behind the energy. For example, your goal cannot just be about money, there must be the reason BEHIND why you want the money that is truly exciting. For example, if you want money, get clear on why such as investing in a new business or product, giving yourself a good rest or holiday or contributing to a cause or study. We discussed in Chapter 2 the value of your Blueprint. If your goal supports your purpose, then it will be even easier. If it pulls you away from it, it's probably going to be an uphill battle. Don't seek for that which does not fulfil your destiny. Trust me, when its right for you – your manifestations will happen overnight. I have proof of that myself.

4. Practice daily or consistently.

Your subconscious mind (the autopilot brain) is also partly responsible for goal manifestation so you had better get some good habits going. You want to keep your heart open to your visual exercise and also your brain well trained as to what you wish for. Things can happen quickly or can take longer, depending on your subconscious being on board or not. Keeping the subconscious mind happy and preoccupied with what you are seeking is part of it. Give it pictures and it can play along with you. Work out any blocks and attempt to release them. Future chapters discuss how you can remove these limiting blocks and free up your manifestation energy should it be thwarted. As we know, the source field can be free flowing or blocked depending on your energetic state, so learning the art of unblocking yourself is as important as sending your message out. Think about the radio signal example. The message can be broadcast, but if there is static or interference on the line, it can be blocked from getting through. This chapter is all about getting the signal sent, we can deal with interference in a later chapter.

Once you have learned to creatively visualise and reach alpha state easily – I have a quick and easy meditation that will supercharge your manifesting efforts.

It's a six minute brief meditation that talks you through both visualising (mind) and connects to feelings (heart) of your goal. Play it regularly and see what happens. Of course, I encourage you to do your own practice but this is a great start. www.zenfulbusiness.com.au/creative-visualisation

Your mission? Learn the art of guided meditations first so you can quickly get to that inner place of stillness. Remember there is no shortcut to meditating. I suggest you get my Zen Business album first or another meditation album as discussed above so that you can get yourself into a comfortable rhythm. Aside from manifestation work, meditation will truly heal your inner soul. Side effects are stress relief, bliss, stillness, releasing conflict and more. There's no downside to meditation.

So, a summary of your meditation development:

1. Phase 1
   You must have a goal in mind that is connected to your heart and you feel excited about.
2. Phase 2
   Master short guided meditations – be able to hold a 15 min story (focused) which generally means you have reached alpha state.
3. Phase 3
   Connect your heart (feelings) and mind (mental picture) to form a connected and deep alpha meditation – that means you can 'see' and 'feel' it happening as though it already exists in your life.

Best way forward is to start dabbling with meditation and focus and see how you go. Set small easy goals and practice manifesting them. That would mean that you probably shouldn't start with world domination ... just yet! Open up to receiving and get the flow of energy coming to you.

PART D – Power of group energy to manifest

It is one thing to try individual manifestation for a particular work goal, but what happens when a group of people get behind a meditation (visualisation) to bring about a joint goal? Well, that experiment has been done with success. Transcendental Meditation (repeating and meditating on a mantra or desired statement over and over) in the US was trialled to see if it could reduce crime in a particular city that had some big issues around criminal activity. A group of people meditated at a particular time each night (all with the same mantra) with the intention of crime statistics dropping in that local area. See the results for yourself below – a massive drop in crime on the graph shows the power of intention, and the changes that can be made, when energy is directed in a group environment to the source field.[13]

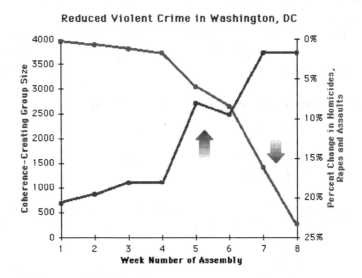

Reduced Violent Crime in Washington, DC

What does this mean for you, your team or your business?

Why not supercharge your team efforts by employing this simple protocol?

202

Step 1. Set Objectives and Vision for what your team or project needs to achieve; it might be a soft measure like an effect on culture or it could be a hard measure like a deadline or specific outcome.

Step 2. Ensure you get 'buy in' from everyone in the team (or at least the stakeholders) so that the concept holds the group energy and commitment (remember our discussion on the law of intention and everything is alive). You want to get the pure group commitment to it and ensure everyone is on board and nobody is thwarting the outcome.

Step 3. Shorten the outcome to an easy-to-read paragraph or mantra that covers the intention. Then list some of the positive feelings/emotions that you will all feel once this objective is met, e.g. proud, excited, grateful, happy, energised, connected and so forth.

Step 4. Take the time every week to get together (whether in same location or distant), and spend ten minutes visualising and feeling this objective as if it has already happened and practice feeling those excited and happy feelings about it. If you cannot do it all together, then at least the group finds their own time during the week to do that short focus.

This will be like super-charging your results. I imagine not only will it speed up but the outcome will be bigger and better if the group energy is behind it.

Watch out for SHADOWS (next chapter) that might come up to thwart your goals from manifesting. These exist in the deep recesses of your brain, so if they hold power – they can work against you. Which is why it is important to deal with blocks and any kind of stuck 'thought forms' or energy. They can really get in the way of your purpose and manifesting specific goals you really want in life.

Your mission? Learn the rules of the game and start playing it with all of your heart. Understand the matrix. Lean to harness your energy. Add some savvy creative visualising/meditation and go for it. Even more ... try a group effort to supercharge your dreams.

Beginner

You are unlikely to have the whole meditation thing sorted. You may have dabbled a bit in the idea but never quite got the hang of it. Perhaps you have not tried at all, as you don't quite see how your busy mind could cope with sitting still. Perhaps you even have your own physical/sporting-based mindfulness activities that you feel do the job to rest your busy brain?

You probably haven't thought too much about energy, the universe and how you exist in the world. You certainly don't look to any indigenous cultures to learn the wisdom they might have to offer.

You might have read about the law of attraction, about visualising to create more success in your life, but cannot quite scientifically accept the viability of this. Your mindset is that to make things happen and to bring opportunities, you need to make this happen yourself through strong actions and planning. Well that is half of the equation and you know it. There is some kind of magic you don't fully understand that forms the remaining part of the equation. It's non-rational and you have felt that flow and ease for moments of time when you know you are in some kind of magic synchronicity with the universe. You might be a) afraid of it b) don't fully understand it or c) think it's a load of hogwash. Think again and try going out on a limb a bit - as you might surprise yourself.

Graduate

You have practiced some form of meditation and likely have been to a class or tried some headspace[14] meditation tracks at some time. You accept and understand the value and validity of meditation and may (or may not) have linked this to manifesting goals. You probably get excited by the idea of manifesting and doing some kind of ritual to sew your dreams out into the fabric of the universe, the hologram, and see it returned to you in ways you never imagined.

You may be a seasoned meditator or at least are trying to be. Your will is there, and intellectually you get the process of what to do. Maybe you need some tweaks into how you can connect the mind and the heart to strengthen the energy behind manifesting. It is likely that you have not developed the daily habits and true inner knowing that it takes to manifest every day and to do this with near instant results. People who have not yet fully mastered manifestation have not learned the valuable daily task of ASKING. This final step needs to be fully embraced. You ask and stop getting caught up with the HOW it will happen. You will probably never be able to imagine the creative ways in which the universe will provide your goal/s. You understand the holographic universe on some level but have not fully mastered its magic quite yet. Let go of how your dreams manifest (thereby creating stress around logical outcomes) and you will see the results.

Master

To be a master in meditation and manifestation is truly a powerful state. Well done. You don't need to be a millionaire to prove you have mastered this skill, you just need to be aware that what you have and what you need is indeed just a simple act of ASKING and holding a focused energetic vision – without anything blocking that flow coming toward you.

You probably have your purpose quite sorted and therefore your meditation energy is supported by your heart's joy. You know on a cellular level the bliss and tranquillity that comes from being in an alpha state more often. You find yourself more calm and centred with life's challenges, as you know that you manifest everything (good and bad) in your life and to change matters, you simply need to correct and amend your energetic focus on what you are bringing in. You never feel you are a victim of bad circumstance because you take 100% accountability for your life goals and manifestations.

You work with the principles of universal lore and when something is not working, you know it's a block you created in the matrix. You set about working out what it is and disentangle yourself from it.

You have a regular practice of meditation going and invest in your own ceremonies to bring additional energy forth. People usually sense a master of meditation because there is a certain calm behind their eyes that feels so safe and knowing. You understand how quickly you can manifest when you focus your energy and keep it flowing. People probably consider you 'lucky' because good things happen to you frequently. However, you know differently as you have actually been working at this manifestation and meditation thing for a while now. It's a simple concept but not always easy to create habits around. You feel that happy glow of mastering a big part of life's great mystery.

References Chapter 9

1. http://www.holographickinetics.com/#!laws-of-lore/cyce
2. http://www.sciencedaily.com/terms/alpha_wave.htm
3. http://www.thesecret.tv/
4. Lipton, Dr Bruce *The Biology of Belief* (United States, Hay House, 2008)
5. Haramein, Nassim *Black Whole* Documentary (United States, Gaiam, 2011)
6. Lipton, Dr Bruce *The Biology of Belief* Chapter 2 (United States, Hay House, 2008)
7. Talbot, Michael *The Holographic Universe* (Great Britain, Harper Collins, 1991)
8. Braden, Gregg *Fractal Time: The Secret of 2012 and a New World Age* (California, Hay House, 2009)
9. www.heartmath.org
10. www.youtube.com "Our Electro-Magnetic Heart Affects Our Reality", Gregg Braden
11. https://www.heartmath.org/gci/resources/downloads/the-energetic-heart-gci-edition/
12. www.youtube.com, "The Power of Visualisation", Gregg Braden
13. http://istpp.org/crime_prevention/
14. Headspace; a phone app for meditations

10

Shadow Integration

Quote: *"Your task is not to seek for love, but merely to seek and find all the barriers within yourself that you have built against it"* Rumi

Key Learning: Don't try to avoid the things you don't like about yourself (these are your shadows). Instead integrate these 'shadow' parts (love them) and learn to work with them.

Key words: Light. Shadow. Reflection. West facing. Ego. Duality. Integration. Karma. Accountability. Growth. Acceptance. Openness. Self-development.

A Native American tale told many times around the Sacred Fire

An old Grandfather said to his grandson, who came to him with anger at a friend who had done him an injustice ...

"Let me tell you a story. I too, at times, have felt great hate for those who have taken so much, with no sorrow for what they do. But hate wears you down, and does not hurt your enemy. It's like taking poison and wishing your enemy would die."

"I have struggled with these feelings many times. It is as if there are two wolves inside me; one is good and does no harm. He lives in harmony with all around him and does not take offense when no offence was intended. He will only fight when it is right to do so, and in the right way.

But ... the other wolf ... ah! The littlest thing will send him into a fit of temper. He fights everyone, all of the time, for no reason. He cannot think because his anger and hate are so great. It is helpless anger, for his anger will change nothing."

"Sometimes it is hard to live with these two wolves inside me, for both of them try to dominate my spirit."

The boy looked intently into his Grandfather's eyes and asked, "Which one wins, Grandfather?"

The Grandfather smiled and quietly said, "The one I feed."

I love this story because it is timeless. Which wolf do you feed every day? The wolf that is mindful, harmonious and conscious? Or the wolf that lives from a busy, competitive and judgemental framework?

What is a shadow and why is it important in business?

A shadow is an aspect of yourself that you don't like, suppress, are ashamed of or try to hide from the public. It could be part of your personality you don't like or an old memory of an event that you cannot let go of or make sense of. Shadows get their name because they follow you around (like a shadow) until you face it and resolve it. The more you deny it, the bigger it grows.

It's probably the most important thing you will ever learn for your own growth ... and when applied to business blocks (whether that be blocks around goals, challenging relationships or abundance issues), shadow work is the most profound way to get quick and dirty change.

And whilst I am totally into mindfulness and being centred, I like the concept of 'quick' when it comes to resolving blocks. What I don't like is ignorance of the issue or having to repeat the same annoying lesson again and again, which happens when you don't deal with shadows. Also – if your shadows are affecting other people in your life (partners, lovers, children, colleagues, staff etc.), then it is quite reckless to ignore them and not take responsibility for reflecting and integrating them. Notice I use the word integration? The idea behind a shadow is that if you try to bury them, deny them, isolate them or get rid of them – they grow in size and become monster shadows. By embracing them or integrating them into you – they reduce their negative impact.

So where do shadows live? Firstly, take a look at this iceberg image...

The tip of the iceberg poking out of the water is like the Conscious Mind* – the part of you that is aware and can dream, set goals and logically order things. The submerged part of the iceberg (the much larger part) is your Subconscious* Mind. That part of you that is hidden or shadowy, the autopilot, the repeating scripts and the deep parts of yourself formed from early childhood right up until now.

Example: One common shadow for entrepreneurs is 'workaholism'. That is the inability to slow down and stop 'doing' stuff. Workaholics think that non output tasks like wasting time down at the beach or getting lost in creative thought is luxurious and wasteful or decadent. This shadow can drive a burnout over time that is hard to recover from.

This hidden part of yourself (subconscious) contains your baggage as well as your good habits so learn to love it too. The part of you that showers daily, brushes your teeth and drives yourself to work lives here. It helps your heart pump blood and your lungs to breathe. However, the baggage or gritty bits that it houses, can create havoc in your life. If you consider your key career or life blocks, here is where you will find the key to unlock that undesirable behaviour, challenge or issue you face. Remember too that sometimes your greatest gifts (that inner drive to achieve excellence) can also be your greatest shadow (workaholism).

The word 'shadow' is a well-used term in the spiritual world to represent your blocks, your challenges and those parts of the self or ego that we try to push away, are ashamed of or keep hidden. Shadows usually relate to personal characteristics or emotions we harbour, but can also be events (often traumatic ones) and people (those we fear or hate). A shadow is something 'unresolved' hence it has power over you – making you feel a certain way without being able to control it. Or it drives habits that we cannot control. They can be subtle too and creep up on you. How do we know we have become a workaholic until our personal health and relationships are strained?

Where do shadows come from?

I won't go into detail too much here, but there are three main ways 'shadows' form.

1. **Epigenetics**: passed on from your parent and ancestors through cellular memory. Epi means 'above', so epi-genetics is 'above the gene'. That means beyond the DNA is a certain energy or cell memory that can hold past trauma or blocks. We discussed earlier that if your Grandfather went to war, somewhere in your cells and genes will be stored that trauma. Whether it interferes with your life depends on whether it is triggered.
2. **Experiences**: in this life time we experience events and emotions that can get locked into our psyche. They can start as 'thought forms', grow into 'life forms' and turn into a living things. Like attracts like and if you look at the Aboriginal dreamtime understanding of 'lore' (law), they say that your dreamtime is your personal story. What story do you have and own that you feed? The same issues thwarting you

again and again are thoughts or energy stuck in cycles of time that grow into their own life form and can really create havoc for you.

3. **Spirit/Blueprint:** regardless of whether you believe in past life experiences, you are born into a body with a spark of life, a soul or electricity (whatever your spiritual beliefs). This spark or Spirit animating your body also has its own life force and path – both positive and negative.

If a shadow is a trauma for you, it will most likely dominate your working life to the point where your plans get seriously disrupted. Very intense repeating patterns should be given the appropriate care and you should seek out a session to repair this.

A good example of a shadow 'thought form' that has developed energy of its own behaviour is impatience. That can manifest as an ugly irritated monster when it grows too big within you. It will become imprinted and will seek to survive, therefore attracting situations to manifest. More reasons for you to be impatient. Although you are responsible for it, it can be running the show without your consent! Tricky to remove unless you work through your shadow. Willpower alone probably will not move it …

Other examples of shadow behaviour are control issues, ego-tripping, confidence issues, feeling like a victim, cash flow leakage, conflicted relationships, anger and more.

A shadow 'event' could be a really nasty experience in business like going bankrupt and losing your business or having a major fallout with a work colleague. It could be an embarrassing drunken Christmas party where you had a work-related affair or you lost control of your tongue and told a co-worker what you really thought of them. At one of the advertising agencies I worked, one of the employees lost control of his shadow and punched his boss in the face. Another one of my advertising colleagues punched her client in the face at a work function because he dumped her after a torrid affair!

A shadow challenge could be feeling like you always get passed over for promotions or are paranoid about competitors or feeling

Debbie Pask

insecure about your skills or personal image. Failed sales results, a bad year in business or so on.

The way to heal your shadow is to bring it into the 'light' – that being to integrate it back into yourself (you are like a mini sun, hence the light) and accept it/love it as part of yourself. This means you must spend some time reflecting on what the shadow is so that you know what you need to integrate. It is not that you are 'broken' per se – but more that you are split within (duality), and this crack needs to be glued so that it does not widen and split you in two. People with BIG cracks can manifest serious mental stress and create struggle for themselves in life and work.

The key to shadow integration is to be KIND to yourself. We are all trying to create a successful working life are we not? If you see a shadow arising, don't see it as a weakness but rather as a way to grow and to become more aligned and healed.

Let me be clear here. It is reckless not to look at and resolve your shadows if they are impacting on your business or career.

Why? Because you are here to evolve and grow as a spirit and person. Your shadows belong to you, yet they are not the whole you. You are responsible for them, yet they are not bigger than the sum of you. You are born with the skills and aptitude to heal them and they are there to be your greatest teacher. Your biggest shadow is your greatest gift.

So learn to form a deep love and respect for them so that your working life and personal life grow richer every day. I am not saying you should make it your life work to review shadows. That's a dark road. But when you are blocked or challenged with something, then it is the time to do shadow work. It might be once a week or once a year. Everyone is different. If you deal with the biggies first, you will find that later on the shadows become lighter and less intense, so a much easier load to cope with.

If we don't deal with our emotional shadows, then we often wind up compensating in some way that can affect our health negatively. Here are some common ways we compensate:

We drink – to drown out our emotions;
We smoke – to suppress our emotions;
We eat – to stuff down our emotions;
We do drugs – to escape our emotions.

I remember a beautiful client of mine that had a really hard time struggling to get over the fact that his big business went bankrupt. It was such a part of his identity that he used to drink copious amounts of alcohol every night to drown out the grief. (I cannot imagine functioning every day with that level of alcohol in my body.) His main shadow here was ego - not being able to accept the loss of his business. Regardless of the reasons for how his business failed, he felt naked without a successful and money-making business behind him. It was such a large part of his identity that it became bigger and more valuable than his health and his sanity. Instead of getting on with his life and working through this challenge, for quite a long time, that shadow continued to grow and take over the beautiful, happy and generous person that he knew himself to be.

The big question is, how do you heal a shadow (big or small) and what types of shadows might you have? Let's start with a list of what some typical shadows look like? They are different for everyone of course depending on your karmic journey in this life, your childhood and environment and what lessons you need to learn to fulfil your purpose. I have tried to relate these to business shadows, but to be honest we cannot separate the person from the business, so I suggest you don't either.

Here are some examples below of people's shadows …

Fear of not being good enough	Controlling	Power tripping/ Ego identification
Reckless financial management	Workaholism (overdriving)	Lack of motivation (procrastination)
Feeling unintelligent	Depression	Judgement (self and others)
Impatience/ Irritation	Anxious/Fidgety	Fearful (in general)

Anger	Envy/Benchmarking	Lack of confidence
That I'm only good if I achieve/ work for it	Competitive	Fear of failure

Any of these feel familiar? Shadows can really hide within you. For example, people who have a strong workaholic drive often have a hidden shadow in that they feel they are not 'good enough' as is and feel that by achieving continually they are valuable. They often are not okay just to BE. I still occasionally struggle with the concept of just 'being' as opposed to going out there and outputting ideas and generating content, sales, courses and all kinds of work-related things.

I have worked through some big shadows in my life and am still working through some. Key ones for me are impatience, judgement and fear of being controlled. I would say I have a good grasp on most of these issues, but they certainly test me on occasions.

It is interesting to note that impatience and control are very similar. Impatience is about controlling the timing of when something will happen. It implies a lack of trust that you will get what you need or want and therefore you try to reach the outcome faster. It is also tied into overdriving. I need to have it now because I have no time to spare before I need to achieve my next task! Having zero time to wait and be mindful in the moment does awful damage to the nervous system; it switches on our fight, flight or freeze system and over a prolonged period of time creates adrenal fatigue.

Pretty much every 'over driver' I know has some degree of adrenal exhaustion – symptoms being tiredness, needing coffee as a prop, aching in calf muscles, digestion issues, 3 pm slump at work, sleep issues, feeling tired and foggy upon awakening in the morning, sugar cravings, headaches, irritability and more.

I remember having adrenal fatigue in my late 20s and remember barely being able to get out of bed even after a long sleep. On slow walks on the beach I would feel my legs ache – as if they couldn't get moving, which is a sign of adrenals. Making management meetings at 8 am was very hard for me, and that was part of the reason I resigned from my board role and started my own consulting practice. I just couldn't get out of bed anymore.

If you have attempted to be conscious and self-aware in your life, you probably have a good grasp on what your shadows are. If not, then it's time to get real with yourself.

Take some time below to write down your major shadows – what patterns or challenges most block you in your career or life? Let's start with two or three of them. Just observe what they are for now:

1.

2.

3.

How to work on shadows?

The successful and intelligent entrepreneur will want to integrate these cracks and will be invested in this healing process. Many indigenous cultures use dance and song to help shift shadows. It's a right brain process and can happen very quickly especially as there are memories in their DNA/cells from their past ancestors which activate this type of healing very quickly. It is like there is an instant recognition of the dance or song that gets activated. But in our western culture, I believe we need some mindful/mental reflection and what I call 'flipping' in our brain to be able to love and integrate our shadow.

Of course I welcome you to go out and do a shadow dance with fire and some drumming music, but I can tell you from experience, your neighbours will think you're doing some kind of sacrifice ceremony! I ran a workshop in my front yard where I was living in Sydney one evening for shadow release work. It is a tradition to work with the element of fire to purify and transform anything darker within us, so I created a lovely fire in a brazier and ordered these fantastic little cardboard mini coffins (very symbolic of letting go) so that workshop attendees could write all of their shadows down and stuff them into the coffin – contemplate them and then throw them into the fire to release the negative energy. These traditions are powerful and you can really feel it in your bones when you do it. Needless to say, the neighbours in surrounding units could only see us all standing around a fire at night, with miniature sized coffins (the length of a small baby!), with loud drumming music playing and throwing them into the fire. They looked at me strangely from that day on.

Note: for really serious shadows that are violent or destructive, I recommend you seek help from a third party, someone who is experienced in altering your dreamtime (personal story). One of the most effective modalities I have seen for removing BIG shadow stuff is Holographic Kinetics – a form of Aboriginal Dreamtime healing. Be prepared for an intense session though.

The Shadow Flip exercise

To flip our shadows we need to look at the lighter (positive) side of them and reveal why we have them and how they translate to gifts/ skills for us. This may be a tricky exercise for some people, but it is seriously useful. The reason it's challenging is because it often requires an external person to reflect back to you the answers you need. Our shadows are so merged with us that we often cannot identify them easily (they hide), let alone flip them upside down to see their gifts. It is like shining a big spot light on yourself to see your warts.

In my online study program, called The Conscious Self – I have a whole module dedicated to shadow work that really hones in on what is going on. Everyone has some degree of shadow playing out in their life, whether it is more work-oriented or in personal relationships. It can be tricky to self-reflect on your shadows, so perhaps ask someone you trust to help out if you get stuck. The easiest what to do this is to ask someone how they see you become stuck in life and what behaviours play out. Then ask them how this trait or quality also serves you in a good way. With every challenge comes a gift.

You will see in the diagram below, a grid with a dividing line in the middle. On the left side you write down your shadow/s (issues) and on the right hand side of the line, you will be attempting to write down how those shadows have a positive impact (gift) on your life.

What gift you might say? Yes – every shadow has a gift once you view the challenge correctly. The key here is to be AWARE of the dividing line (the fence) and stay on the positive side of it. How? By being aware of your shadow and naming it, you are already halfway there. That's called 'witnessing'. You are able to objectively view your shadow. You automatically pull it out of hiding. Once that is done, you can start to monitor your behaviour and find the right balance of how to use that shadow in its 'gift' state – not the negative. Loving that aspect of yourself and appreciating it in its delicate balance of curse vs gift is truly accepting it and embracing it back to you. Once you embrace this imperfection, the beauty of it surfaces and the light will always overpower the dark (shadow).

Here are a couple of examples …

SHADOW	GIFT
Impatience	Helps me to achieve and to drive projects. Find solutions quickly – quick thinker, good in crisis. Find efficient ways to revolve things – speed. Things in my life don't go unresolved. Good voice for change.
Fear of not being good enough	Have spent my life mastering things and learning to improve my skills and achievements. Don't judge others and more focused internally on development. More accepting of others – acknowledges skills.
Too Controlling	Have mastered the art of projecting all scenarios in the mind as to what possible outcomes might occur. Good leader in times of high pressure. Accountable and Responsible – trying to push for good outcome. Ambitious and motivated – action-oriented.

Your Shadow?	FLIP?	

Write down one shadow that you want to flip. Choose one from your top three listed above. Then have a go at flipping it.

If I can learn to see how this shadow works as a gift, I can step into the lighter aspect of that shadow and use it effectively. If I stop getting annoyed that I have this trait, I can see the good in it and then it stays positive. Do I still struggle with impatience? Yes – occasionally when I am over tired. Generally though, it's really not such an issue anymore for me and I certainly enjoy that aspect of myself. In addition, when I do feel the negativity of impatience, I can see it really quickly now and I can see that I might be overdriving to feel that way. It's about being reflective and self -aware. My impatience tends to arise when I am too 'in my head' and busy.

Impatience therefore becomes a warning bell for my life getting too busy. If I see the early signs, I try and make changes before it snowballs.

So that means I need to be mindful of two things:

1) How my shadow is used in the positive (lighter or 'flipped') state?

2) Being a witness to when it starts to become darker; observing behaviour and not allowing it to take over me.

The shadow lives in the ego primarily and doesn't want to die. It has a life force so remember to be gentle with yourself and if you slip up – don't berate yourself. Your mind will put up a fight at first so just be ready and get prepared to practice the witness mindset.

Another way you can work on shadows is via the subconscious mind. If you think about the brain – it has a conscious rational brain and a subconscious autopilot brain. The autopilot brain runs most of your daily functions and scripts so it is critical to make changes on this level especially as it tends to process 40 billion bits of info every day and is considered to be running the show.

What happens when a BIG shadow presents itself?

Every so often in life (and it's happened to me around three times) a big chunky shadow surfaces. These knock you out a bit and will generally be forced upon you if you are not paying attention to the hints you receive months earlier! Big shadows may require you to enter the Void*. See the model below that explains the Void. This can apply to your personal life and business life. Aren't they the same really? I mean, we don't just suddenly become a different person when we enter the world of business. I always hated that phrase in business when someone would say, it's not personal, its business. Crap - it's always personal because we are people, human.

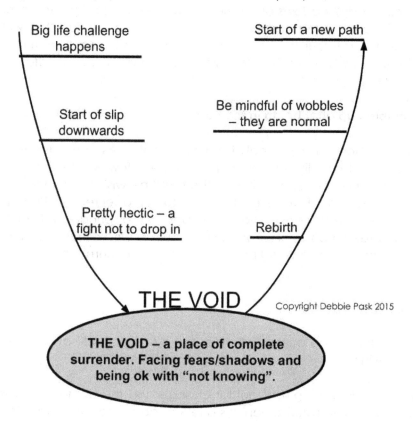

Big life challenge happens

Start of a new path

Start of slip downwards

Be mindful of wobbles – they are normal

Pretty hectic – a fight not to drop in

Rebirth

THE VOID

Copyright Debbie Pask 2015

THE VOID – a place of complete surrender. Facing fears/shadows and being ok with "not knowing".

Falling into the Void

The conscious and logical aspect of you will want to problem solve and 'fix' a problem without accessing your true deep inner self. The slope downwards to losing an old part of yourself and really healing your crises/big life hurdle is actually harder than actually sitting in the Void. As you grip on to the side walls, fear starts projecting scenarios in your mind. The void itself is actually quite calm, the pressure of trying to cope lifted and you sit there for however long you need to 'rebirth'.

This does not mean you GIVE UP. It's not an excuse, rather a deep personal reflection. Giving up has nothing to do with the Void!

Sitting in the Void

Facing fears/shadows and being ok with 'not knowing'. Not trying to 'fix' anything or control outcomes. The idea is to just 'be' with yourself and your challenge. To reflect and fall into a shaman's* death (letting go of the old part of you – habits, identity etc. not needed).

Climbing up after being in the Void

The journey back up feels fresh and lighter. As you have reset aspects of your life or self, there may be a few wobbles on and off until the new part settles in. There will be wisdom gained and lessons learned that are evolving you for a bigger reason. Perhaps it is part of your life direction or purpose, or to springboard you to better relationships or people. Enjoy the upward climb and don't rush. The idea of moving forward is not force or hurry – but dreams and willingness.

So, the Void hey?

I love this place called the Void, but it's ridiculously awful when you're in it.

It is literally the biggest tool for change and the biggest catalyst for business transformation. It's a letting go process, staring a fear directly in the face and choosing to accept where you are at and that you 'don't know the way out'.

Magical things happen from the void but at the time it feels rotten …

Some examples of the Void include:

- career crisis;
- redundancy;
- bankruptcy;
- business partnerships dissolving (or major meltdown);
- significant business screw-up;
- health challenge – dire state of physical health;
- market crisis (in your industry sector.

The Void will usually happen to help your 'train' return to the train tracks after being off course for some time. If you are wildly off course, the Void will occur and it will feel devastating at the time.

What exactly is the Void?

There are many definitions and adaptations in eastern philosophy of what the Void really means. I use this concept in my coaching practice regularly and refer to it as a place of unknown or uncertainty. It is an empty space where anything is possible and there is no logical solution or process to follow. It feels foreign and strange because you cannot grasp it and the key lesson of the Void is to accept the uncertainty and enjoy the emptiness until a fertile new opportunity presents itself to enrich our life.

AIM: Sit in the Void (let go) until you can integrate the shadow behind the Void. When you understand that the fear behind the Void falls into two categories:

1) Fear of the unknown (that's a control issue); or
2) Fear of judgement from self or others (that's a self-love issue.)

you can learn to respect what lessons are coming up and heal the shadow internally so it does not happen again. Unresolved shadows will rear their ugly head again and again until we deal with them.

So what are the steps to recovery?

1. Follow the West steps on the Medicine Wheel (once over the initial fall;)
2. Practice mindfulness and sitting in 'not knowing';
3. Use the idea of wicked problem solving – one organic step at a time;
4. Allow yourself to be supported and accept that you don't have all of the answers;
5. Once you feel strong enough and you understand the evolvement you need, slowly get back in the driving seat ...

Remember this great quote..."It's none of your business what other people think about you".

One last mention quickly on shadow stuff. Only read this if you are open to a bit of spirituality or 'woo' as it is often called.

I work a lot with people's Astrology natal charts as it acts like a mini blueprint of your life. Whether you believe in it or not, there is a really interesting planet called Chiron in the chart. Chiron is believed to be a representation of our greatest shadow or wound that we have in this life time. I have never seen this formula fail to highlight a person's major challenge or shadow. It is very accurate and can open up new ways of working through these challenges. It consistently mirrors that person's issues or shadow. Where Chiron sits (houses 1- 12) and what sign he is in (Libra, Aries, Cancer etc.) always makes sense in relation to that person. There is a theory that when Chiron returns to the same place in the sky when you were born (that's roughly a 50 year cycle), you need to have cleaned up this big shadow/wound or you can get sick or much challenged. I see a lot of people approaching 50 years old (starts at 48) who get the physical signs starting of illness if they haven't addressed the 'Chiron Wound'.

Something certainly to think about.

Beginner

You have not looked too much into your own personal demons and find it hard to delve into the emotional past. It is likely that you work around your challenges and set up your life to counteract any conflicts that arise to force you to confront those parts of yourself. For example, you might avoid public speaking or presenting due to those deep-seated fears of judgement.

You might find it hard to face criticism and when you bump heads with others, you might look at blaming that person or external circumstances for the conflict. You are either just way too busy to spend the time investigating and growing from life lessons or perhaps you are too rigid and stuck in old ways of thinking to bring them to light.

You likely have some desire to work through these blocks and your intelligent self knows that by clearing them, you will have richer working experience. Perhaps you just don't know where to start the journey and are looking for ways in. Alternatively there are some of us out there living in absolute ignorant bliss of their shadows! Many beginners just think they need to control their behaviour or feelings which actually just make it worse. Suppressing, denying or judging our behaviour feed the life force behind it.

Graduate

You understand your personal challenges and seek ways to address these in your life as you know what benefits it will bring. But understanding them and mastering them is a different ball game altogether.

You may have dabbled in various self-development or reflection exercises and might even see a coach or counsellor to discuss your shadows. You have a mini quest going now to master these parts of yourself and you are keen to see how far you can take it. You could even start the journey of change (or certainly be aware of it) but not quite get there.

Your outlook is optimistic and you see most difficult situations as grounds for learning and self-growth; looking for the lesson and how you can evolve along the way. Your shadows can be a bit heavy and get you down occasionally, but mostly you spring back up as you have some tools (always growing) to cope along the way. You have probably resolved your big obvious shadows and are making your way through the layers to fine-tune things. You regularly pick up books like this one to learn more about your inner journey.

Master

You are a seeker of shadows and thoroughly enjoy the analysis, dissection and healing that takes place when you really sit with your personal shadows. You understand that life can sometimes be a bit of an emotional rollercoaster ride, but know that if you sit quietly and accept what comes your way; things have a way of resolving.

Your working life is humming along well as not too many heavy issues weigh you down. You have learned to have a deep care and respect for your inner self – both the good bits and also the bits you are challenged by. Therefore you tend to attract other people to you that match your higher vibration and energy. You approach business issues or challenges intuitively and always learn and grow from difficulty.

Being aware of the power of the mind and subconscious, you are finding more and more ways to practice mindfulness and meditation as you see the powerful benefits of clarity, peace and flow. There does not seem to be anything in the way of you becoming the best you can be. There is a feeling of lightness and freedom around you, accessible whenever you need it. You are human of course, so when those shadows do crop up, you know exactly what to do with them. You love VOID moments because you see them as true gifts. However the likelihood of a VOID situation is slim because you normally see them on the horizon way before they blow you up!

11

HEART Entrainment

Quote: "To be successful you have to have your Heart in your business and your business in your Heart". Sir Thomas Watson Jnr

Key Learning: Your Heart is 5000x more electromagnetic than the brain. Science now proves that when you energise the Heart, you become smarter. Your Heart is a second, and more superior, brain. It is our best asset in business.

Key words: Love. Peace. Compassion. Feelings. Release. Joy. Lightness. Power. Connectedness. Contribution. Restoration. Flow.

I have left this model until last because all of the previous chapters have pointed us toward a unique and powerful energy that exists within us, and this energy lives in the Heart. With the latest Heart-monitoring devices and the emergence of Heartmath.org, science is now backing up how wonderfully powerful this organ really is.

How many brains do you have?

It is said that we have three intelligent and central brains within us:

Our Mind – the cognitive aspect of us (inspires us);

Our Heart – the feeling and connected aspect of us (gives us joy);
Our Gut – the instinctive aspect of us (nourishes us).

We process <u>thoughts</u> through our mind.
We process <u>emotions</u> through our Heart.
We process <u>instincts</u> (gut instinct) through our stomach/gut.

These three parts to us are all useful and provide a valuable resource, which is why if we don't look after all three (mindfulness for the mind, joy for the Heart and good digestion for the gut) – we can get very, very out of flow.

Which one/s are you neglecting? Which one is in the best condition? Rate them here out of 10. (1 being low/poor, 10 being high/well.) |

MIND

HEART

GUT

I could spend days talking about the gut brain or the mind brain, but this chapter is about the Heart brain, because out of the three, it is the master. If you want to seriously know how to take care of your gut, read Don Chisolm's book *Have you got the guts to be healthy?*[1] His advice will change your health in a serious way. If you want to start mastering the mental chatter, then read Michael A Singer's *Untethered Soul*[2] to start you off.

Your Heart brain is intrinsic to your energy flow and intelligence - the ability to be in tune with the right decisions (the Heart is intuitive) and to access your greatest (yes greatest) creative flow imaginable. What comes from the Heart, in my experience, is more intelligent and will touch more people in business than anything else.

Want the science to prove the power of the Heart?

The awesome organisation called the HeartMath Institute (<u>www.Heartmath.org</u>) has spent the time, money and research into experiments and research of the Heart. Here are a few snippets you will love and you can also jump on to their site and read the thick and juicy number of papers published.

STARTING FACTS

#1. Your Heart is 5000x more electromagnetic than the brain. It sends a lot more signals to the body/brain than the brain does itself.

#2. Your Heart is 60 -100x greater in amplitude than the electrics of brain; meaning it produces far more electrical pulses than the brain does.

When we talk about electro-magnetic energy of the earth, it relates to electrical and magnetic energy. The Heart has both of these energies too, so it makes sense that the Heart and the earth could communicate in some way, right?

#3. Your Heart communicates with the brain/body in four ways:

i.   Neurological communication (nervous system);
ii.   Biophysical communication (pulse waves);
iii. Biochemical communication (hormones);
iv.   Energetic communication (electromagnetic fields).

You can see from the above that it is not just on an 'energy vibration' level that the Heart operates, but also is responsible for biophysical communication. That is pretty amazing, that the Heart's energy has a physical effect on your body. Makes you wonder what state your Heart might be in if you are tired, sick or depressed?

Here is a picture of that electro-magnetic energy field coming from the Heart. It is called a Torus* (electro-magnetic) field and it seems to flow out of the Heart and cycle back up into the body. If you are particularly interested in looking at the science behind the torus field energy, check out the amazing work of quantum scientist Nassim Haramein.

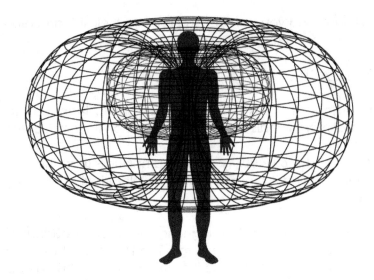

What does this mean for business? Well, let's review the models presented so far. The Heart is kind of central to all of them.

For 'Yin/Yang Balance': the 'Yin' state is the inner self, the creative and Heart self that makes more dynamic decisions and pulls magic out of the void;

For 'Becoming Conscious': it represents the true awakening and freedom of your Heart once you reach the top layers;

For our 'Blueprint': the Heart is what underpins your calling and purpose, what wounds the Heart and what ignites the Heart are opposite polarities and once joined together produce your career brilliance;

For 'Leverage': it means that we leave behind our Heart's legacy;

For "Soul Colleagues': it is about connecting your Hearts together for collaboration;

For 'Get In Touch With Naughty': it brings out the true joy and inner child of the Heart, something that everyone needs to stay light and connected;

For 'Mindful Moments': it's about letting the Heart be very still and present to soak up the joy and experience in life;

For 'Intuitive Problem Solving': it allows the intelligence of the Heart to drive important decisions for your best outcome;

For 'The Art of Manifesting': the Heart is required to send out the electro-magnetic pulses to the universal hologram to place your order; and

For 'Shadow work': we are delving deep into the Heart and releasing old wounds that get in the way of expressing the Heart's power source.

And lastly we come to the Heart itself. As it is so intrinsic to all of these business models above, your job is to have the best romance with it and to cultivate a strong, happy, energised Heart. That in itself, will give you bliss. By the way, the emotion of 'bliss' (according to David R Hawkins in his book, *Power vs Force*[3]) sends the Heart's electro-magnetic energy through the roof. The emotion of bliss is a huge energiser of the Heart's energy field. We discuss some examples below of how different emotions affect the Heart and brain rhythm.

Let's talk about three areas in your working life whereby the Heart can make a difference:

  A. Your Heart Entrainment – to make you smarter at work;
  B. Heart Entrainment with others – to make business (communications, negotiations, change management and sales etc.) easier; and
  C. Heart Entrainment with career/business – to ensure the 'spirit' of your business or career is aligned to you as a human being.

A. Your Heart Entrainment

What is entrainment? It is to fall into flow or rhythm with something. To modify or teach something to flow along to the same pulse or rhythm.

So when we have Heart and brain entrainment, it means that our Heart has spoken to our mind/brain and they are synchronised into a flow together. The studies show that when we achieve heart and brain entrainment, we become cognitively smarter. We think more clearly and more effectively. We are therefore aiming for 'coherence' between these two organs.

Coherence is the language and dialogue between the Heart and brain. It means they are communicating. So when we entrain Heart and brain, we get 'Heart Rhythm Coherence''. This beautiful dialogue is a powerful state.

In states of high Heart Rhythm Coherence, individuals demonstrate significant improvements in cognitive performance. The Heart and brain are actually in a dynamic, ongoing two-way relationship. That means that if your Heart (feelings/spirit) are in synch with your mind (thoughts/cognition) then you become smarter and you will communicate better - your value, your message, your presentation, your coaching and your words or pitch to other people. If you think back to a time when you heard a great speech, did it seem like it was coming straight from the Heart? It probably was.

Let's see what that means for us?

The HeartMath Institute did a study on 'Heart Rhythm Coherence Feedback – 'frustration vs appreciation'. They measured the Heart energy in response to feeling specific emotions. They wanted to see the difference the impact would have on the Heart if the mind conjured up thoughts of frustration versus if the mind conjured up thoughts of appreciation.

The results are almost instantaneous. The frustration emotion took the Heart into jerky inconsistent Heart rate measurements that were uneven and dipped high and low on the scale. The emotion of appreciation however immediately ironed out the Heart rate to be a beautiful continuous flow, never dipping too high or low. It looked the way you would *want* your Heart rate to be – even, flowing and calm.

This is a direct quote from HeartMath.org:

"The Heart is the most powerful generator of electromagnetic energy in the human body, producing the largest rhythmic electromagnetic field of any of the body's organs. The Heart's electrical field is about **60 times greater in amplitude than the electrical activity generated by the brain.** *This field,* **measured in the form of an electrocardiogram (ECG),** *can be detected anywhere on the surface of the body. Furthermore, the* **magnetic field produced by the Heart is more than 5,000 times greater in strength than the field generated by the brain,** *and can be detected a number of feet away from the body, in all directions, using SQUID-based magnetometers. Prompted by our findings that the* **cardiac field is modulated by different emotional states."** *HEARTMATH.ORG* **(I bolded the relevant sections to stand out.)**

HeartMath Key findings: As people learn to sustain Heart-focused positive feeling states, the brain can be brought into entrainment with the Heart. Coherence occurs. Connecting to the positive emotions in the Heart creates a flow and allows an open channel to the mind, supercharging your ability to think creatively and dialogue effectively.

What this means is that if you get in touch with joy and get connected to your purpose/passions in business, your Heart will do the electrical work for you and make you smarter!

We need to let go of what is NOT Resonant with us ... and move towards what is. What is not resonant within us creates negative emotions. This is not just about the actual career we choose, albeit that is the most powerful impact, but also the level of enjoyment and fun and passion we experience day-to-day in our working life. If a task, an event or a person is creating tension within us, our performance lowers and weakens. Our manifesting ability slows and our Heart health declines.

When middle aged men die of a Heart attack, often the autopsy will show that the pericardium around the Heart (that is the envelope of tissue that holds the Heart gently in the chest) has tightened and hardened, squeezing the Heart literally until death. Energetically it is like the Heart has had all of its joy and fun squeezed out and it has become so disconnected that it suffocates, hence the Heart attack. I wonder if these older men have hardened up in business and forgotten to connect to the joy and innocence of their career. Maybe their work has taken over their ability to connect deeply to their Heart?

An easy practice to do to keep your Heart clear is this: when a negative thought or feeling occurs at work about someone or something, take a moment to recognise it and then choose to immediately let it go. Michael A. Singer talks about this in his book *The Untethered Soul*. We need to do this consciously and tell the Heart which feelings we want to let go or keep. He says that you can literally take a deep breath in and blow out this negative emotion (out the back of your Heart centre). Instead of allowing it time to incubate and glue with you, where it festers and grows bigger, choose to release it quickly. Keep your Heart clear and it will help to keep your mind clear. You are always in control of how you feel and what you decide to fester on or let go. Keep your Heart clear so that you keep your mind clear.

QUESTIONS to ANSWER

1. What aspects of your working life are 'out of synch' or joyless and hence draining your Heart energy? E.g. colleagues, your work tasks, the ethics of company, a partner/supplier or your office space?

_____

_____

_____

2. Are you working in your passion and joy day-to-day? If not, why is this not a priority? If you are in your joy, how can you fine-tune it to the next level?

_____

_____

_____

B. Heart Entrainment With Others

So, you might master your own Heart entrainment, but what about with other people? We touched on this briefly in our chapter on Soul Colleagues.

The last two studies summarised in this section explore interactions that take place between one person's Heart and another's brain when two people touch or are in proximity. This research elucidates the intriguing finding that the electromagnetic signals generated by the Heart have the capacity to affect others around us. Our data indicates that one person's Heart signal can affect another's brainwaves, and that Heart-brain synchronization can occur between two people when they interact.

Within us there is a silent pulse of perfect rhythm ... individual and unique ... yet connecting us to the universe, a wave of sorts. Resonance is where two wave forms of similar FREQUENCY lock into phase with each other (Heart and mind is key).

This is called Rhythm entrainment or Sympathetic vibration and it increases the amplitude of the waves collectively. As you can see in this image below, every wave has a length and amplitude. When two waves lock into the same length and amplitude, they are in the state of entrainment.

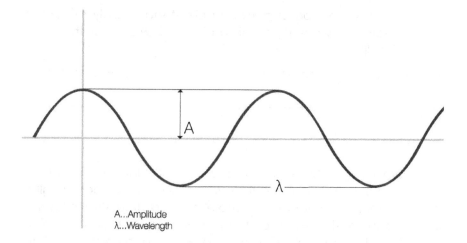

A...Amplitude
λ...Wavelength

All speech has rhythm, so communication is like dance, if people are engaged - and then entrained – the message will get through.

Others will decide if they want to resonate with you, or away from your message. Don't tell people what they want to hear as the resonance will simply be inauthentic and you weaken yourself and the connection with them over time as you cannot fulfil your promise. If you talk with an open Heart (connected to your passion), people will make up their own mind. This is a sustainable relationship.

Now, who's going to tell me that communicating based on marketing intelligence is better than old fashioned 'being in LOVE' with what you do? If you don't love or KNOW your purpose in business or your career role – the power of electromagnetic energy is probably not aiding your cause ... What a bummer.

QUESTIONS to ANSWER

1. Does your marketing message or resume originate from or connect with your deep underlying Heart purpose?

_____

_____

2. Who is the type of person or client that is likely to have a matching wave type with you? E.g. How do they think and feel like you?

_____

_____

An easy way to achieve coherence with a business colleague or client is to find a shared platform to connect on; a shared value or shared life experience. A simple conversation that allows a deep heart sharing (such as the love for nature hiking or going through a tricky situation) can deliver the beginning of Heart Rhythm Coherence through this connection. Once established the proceeding conversation becomes more fluid and aligned. That is why sharing your own personal life story often paves the way for good relationships and understanding.

C. Heart Entrainment Within Your Own Business or Career

Most people understand and agree (as does quantum science) with the concept that you have a Soul or Spirit. It's a living energy field within your body and both Body and Soul need to be vital and nourished to fire on all cylinders. Another way of naming this Spirit that is less religious or confronting is to refer to the resting place of the Spirit – aka The HEART!

Similarly a Business has a Heart or Spirit. We briefly discussed this in the manifestation chapter and universal lore. Your business Spirit (should have been) birthed out of a passion of your own personal Heart. It is a living entity – an extension of you such as a creative project or a child. It even has a birth date (business registration date). When you have a clear connection between the Spirit/Heart of the business and Your Heart/Life purpose, magic happens. There is nothing more in flow and more abundant when you achieve that 100% translation between you and the business.

A fascinating case study on a business handed down through the family

This case study shows us a real life example of how the Spirit of a business can be negatively affected when handed over to the next generation of family. We all know that many family businesses pass between father and son, mother and daughter etc. This is a common practice, however knowing that a business has its own energy (entity or Spirit), how do you think a business feels about being passed off to a relative or even a third party?

In this case study, we had a family building business being handed over from father to son. The business had been very successful and was in good condition upon handover. However soon after, the business started having cash flow problems and business slacked off. In addition, a few accidents happened to workers and also the new owners - materials collapsing causing injury and so forth.

The new owners contacted us to get some insight into these challenges. After doing what we call a surrogate session on the 'Spirit' of the business through the owners – the business told us that it felt abandoned by the original (father) owner and that it did not feel the handover was thorough and respectful enough. This business was unaware of the new owner's intentions. Where was the Heart entrainment and care? Therefore the energy of the business was scattered and messy, creating issues and accidents. After working on this issue with the Spirit of the business and repairing it, the new owners found that business picked up again and no more accidents occurred. This may sound a bit 'woo' to you, but if you think about it, the business has its own name and energy and respecting that and taking time to work on why things are not going well can save you a bunch of headaches!

Q. Are you properly Heart entrained and connected to the Spirit of your business?

I think it is important to understand how the career you have or the business you own can fulfil your deep personal purpose. This conscious knowing (purpose) amplifies the 'why' behind why you do what you do. There is nothing more infectious than a business owner who knows their Heart purpose and radiates it in business. When they speak, people become Heart entrained as we discussed above - meaning 'connected and linked' – hence making a much better and deeper client relationship. You don't need to 'sell' things, as your Heart does it at a much deeper energetic level. Our intuition can sniff out authentic passion in others.

Most people neglect one or the other or don't integrate the two aspects (life and business purpose) properly – hence the business or career becomes weakened, challenged and poorly nourished. Anyone living in this current world needs to accept that being a fabulous business person is not enough. You need to be conscious (awakened to the effect of energy in the world) and aware of a deeper Heart purpose that you are here for and driven by.

This 'knowing' will take you FAR beyond anything you can imagine. No, I'm not going to get all religious or overtly spiritual on you! It just means that you have a unique blueprint (like fingerprints) in this life and nobody can replicate your creativity and skills. Finding out what this unique purpose and passion is important as it will lay the foundations for an exciting career, it will drive you to build brilliant ideas and products PLUS it will magnify and accelerate your business success tenfold.

People are not looking for a shiny or overtly professional front face – they are looking for the real depth behind why you do what you do and why your business or role authentically cares about its own products or services.

If you have a glitch in your current role, career or business, then take the time to heal those wounds and reset the energy of the business or career. There are loads of ways to go about this; the first step requires that you value and respect the energy behind it and work out a way to connect to it.

You can work in your business or career in so many ways. Here are a few:

Meditate on it or with it in mind;

Work out the deeper meaning of why you do this business or role;

Have a personal healing or coaching session to amend any cracks (as per the example above);

Do your own reflection work or have a birthday or ceremony for your business – remember it's alive!

QUESTIONS to ANSWER

1. What is your relationship like with your business or career? Where are the weaker spots and where do you shine together? What could be improved?

_____

_____

_____

2. In what ways could you be better entrained with your business or working life? Where could you respect it more and show more love and commitment? This might even be in your language – how much you whinge about business …

Finally – when we are truly evolved in the Heart we arrive at …

Contribution

I heard an interesting TED talk by an architect designer called Stefan Sagmeister.[4] A lot of what he said about working life made sense to me. Here's what he said about the levels of work:

A 'job' is all about making $.

A 'career' is about advancement and learning.

And a 'calling' is about a deep Heart-centred creative pull.

Great summary I think. But he failed to list the last and grandest one … that beyond our calling and beyond deepening our own creativity, there is another agenda that is called 'Contribution'.

Contribution is about doing something that affects far more than just us and our own insular world. It is a greater purpose that requires our full Heart energy – after all, our Heart's electro-magnetic energy does expand out a long way past ourselves, so doesn't it makes total sense that if we were given such a powerful machine, that we must use if for what nature intended?

In his TED talk, Stefan talks about how he went to Bali and observed all of the neglected dogs there. He turned what is a sad story of animal neglect into funny t-shirts with pictures of dogs on them. That may very well be creative and it might be funny to him, not so funny to me. Anyone who has travelled to Bali has seen the grave situation of the homeless dogs and the terrible condition their health is.

What could he have done at a higher level of contribution? Sure, he could create the t-shirts as he did (that's a creative pull), but what about donating a % of the sale of those t-shirts to a dog rehabilitation clinic or desexing services or relocation/adoption services. Now that's a serious and awesome legacy and contribution to make. Be creative and be compassionate at the same time ... because we can be. We have that luxury in our privileged position.

I believe that we are all hardwired to give of service and contribute our gift, and once we reach a certain level of consciousness, we feel drawn to doing precisely that. Thinking about the 'group' is so much more powerful than the individual. Many of my work colleagues already are on this path and feel excited by their calling to contribute beyond their own ambitions.

That feeling is fantastic. I won't spend too much time here, but truly Heart-centred business people cannot help but feel a pull toward contribution. Anthony Robbins speaks about this, as does Deepak Chopra and a host of business leaders. Regardless of spirituality, they mention a calling towards a higher level of service that brings happiness that we cannot truly know until we go there.

I don't think we all need to do it in the same way. That isn't the point and it would make the world boring if we all copied the same formula. Sure, some people go and build orphanages in 3rd world countries and some people retrain young women to build a new career after being caught up in the sex slave industry. Some rescue animals and others look at healing the earth. For yourself, think about how your contribution matches your soul purpose and your natural passions. Ultimately we are all driven to give back if we tap into our Heart 100%. In numerology and other studies, it is said that contribution or service often kicks in fully at around ages 52 – 54. Regardless of age, you will find this occurring when you connect to the power of your Heart.

Who Gives a Crap[5] is a great example of an earth-friendly and humanitarian business that donates 50% of profits to WaterAid, to build toilets for underdeveloped countries that don't have them and hence are prone to disease and other hygiene-related dangers. These guys have a sustainable business (selling recycled toilet paper) that makes money and also gives back to humanity. What superstars they are! Creative, entrepreneurial and contributive.

QUESTION to ANSWER

Where do you feel drawn to make a difference in the world? What change would you like to see in your lifetime and how can you be a part of it? How might it (or can it) relate to your passions and work?

Beginner

You probably don't know much about the Heart beyond the fact that it pumps blood in your body and is critical to survival. You are probably aware of the emotions and connection to Heart health, but have not fully connected the dots or understood the deep importance of it. Perhaps you don't have time to do this or believe you don't have the time.

Your business life can vary between happy and stressful and you might have just accepted your job or business as a way to make money and thrive in the world. You hear people talking about life purpose and either think it is a load of baloney or unreachable, perhaps even a luxury. After all, you have money to make and family to look after or something similar.

You may have developed an interest in learning more or are underway on a journey of discovery but know deep down that you certainly have not mastered the answers to the Heart ... yet.

Graduate

You are probably clear (or halfway there) on how important it is to connect your emotions and love to your business life. You have a solid idea of what makes you happy and you are designing your work to do more of that and less of other draining things.

You appreciate the intuitive nature of relationships and value the 'energetic' building blocks that underpin any good communication and relationship management. People usually get drawn to your vibration as they can see and feel the magnetism you have for your work and want to be a part of it. Most days you are plugged in and firing on all four cylinders as you have a good Heart and mind entrainment, which energises you long after anyone else finishes.

You may not fully understand the life force behind the business or career yet and may not understand the full integration of YOUR Heart, the BUSINESS Heart and OTHER PEOPLE's Hearts. Once you form the sacred trinity, wow you will rock!

Debbie Pask

Master

What a delight you are to be around. Your Heart is flowing with business love and you are in your passion and purpose 100%. You have probably mastered the beautiful communication of language (marketing), vibration (physical abundance) and connection (to business and clients). You easily attract opportunities and clients or projects because the universe is in flow with both your soul and the soul of your career or business. Collaborations are abundant. That doesn't mean that you are earning a million bucks yet, although it is certainly possible if that be your goal.

You have either started or given some thought as to what legacy you want to leave behind in the world. Whether an individual project or part of a community project, there is a deep desire to birth something meaningful, whether business-related or not. It might be a money-making venture or not. It simply needs to bring you intrinsic joy.

Getting to Master level indicates that you have found any blocks and barriers (well most of them) to your Heart's joy and let them go. Your shadow stuff would be quite integrated. You probably feel quite free and mindful. You understand the rhythms of yourself in relationship to this world and others better than most. Your Heart health is strong and energised and you work at a higher level of vibration, having mastered those Maslow consciousness layers fairly well - whether you are conscious of them or not. Of course, not everything is a fairy tale in life, but living from the Heart space means you pop back easily after a knock or challenge.

Considering people will be drawn to this magnetic energy, why not give them a kick in the right direction by asking them 'What are they doing to find their Hearts purpose and joy?'

References Chapter 11

1. Chisolm, Don, *Have you got the guts to be healthy* (Australia, Book Pal)
2. Singer, Michael A, *Untethered Soul* (CA, New Harbinger Publications, 2007)

242

3. Hawkins, David R., *Power vs Force* (United States, Hay House, 1995)
4. Stefan Sagmeister, TED talk https://www.ted.com/talks/ stefan_sagmeister_the_power_of_time_off?language=en
5. http://au.whogivesacrap.org

12

Rate Your Performance

Want to feel like you have a master plan to get any lower scoring models on track? For the A type personalities especially, you will enjoy this list making exercise.

Think of the next chapter 12 and chapter 14 like an organic workbook. It is your own personal journal or workbook that you need to keep accountable to. This chapter will ask you to summarise your ratings of student, graduate or master for each of the 11 models. Once you have a feel for where you sit across all of them, then chapter 14 will give you some ideas and strategies for improving and mastering that particular model.

If you want further suggestions, you can jump on to my website (a specific URL is provided for each model) and learn more about how to fine-tune your efforts.

So, your next task is to complete the one page overview below of where you think you are at with each model and you will see an easy visual diagram of your progress across all models.

Shade in the box/es up to the level where you feel you have reached. E.g. If you are 'Graduate' in Yin/Yang balance, then colour/shade or tick in the first two boxes – both Student and Graduate.

If you feel you have not even reached 'Student' level in a category, then leave all three boxes blank. You have a lot to do in that area! If you believe you have mastered something, by all means tick/shade the three boxes.

Model	Student	Graduate	Master
Yin/Yang			
Becoming Conscious			
Blueprint			
Leverage			
Soul Colleagues			
Get in Touch With Naughty			
Mindful Moments			
Intuitive Problem Solving			
The Art of Manifestation			
Shadow Work			
Heart Entrainment			

Have a review of your overall levels. Where are the big gaps and unshaded boxes?

Which models are mastered?

Turn to chapter 14 and see the relevant page for exercises and tips in the model or category/ies that you most need work on, so that you can move to mastery level if that is what you are seeking. There is no right or wrong in your answers or efforts. Some models may not be as important to you or your career. If it resonates with you to work on a specific model and feels right, then use your intuition and pay more attention there. The overall objective is to give you access to more energy and more flow in your working life.

13

Becoming Zenful

Bringing it all together

What insights have you had about yourself?

After rating your scores in the previous chapter, answering questions and digesting the models presented, I expect that you will have some new insights into your working life – such as what you might be a natural wizard at or what areas you see yourself as failing in. The idea is not to judge or benchmark against others, but to look for ways of balancing your work life or seeing a new perspective you had not thought about before.

My intention for this book is to give you a process to work through and questions to reflect upon as opposed to just downloading theories. I hope the 11 models presented have created some organic thought as to how you personally can flow and perform at your best in your career.

And what do I really mean by performing at your best? My definition of being the best that you can be is feeling connected, energised and balanced in your approach to work. That you can maintain a state of mindfulness and flow at work and therefore in life. The next chapter will give you a host of exercises and practices to do (for each model) that will bring you closer to this sense of flow and presence. Hopefully this book becomes a handy reference manual that gets old and dirty (dare I say crusty?) as you refer back to it again and again - an old friend that you call upon to make changes or fine-tune your approach to your career success.

However, there is something that absolutely underpins everything needed to create change and growth. I call it 'Mental Mastery': the commitment to personal development, the ability to observe your thoughts and/or actions and the awareness to cultivate a daily practice of mastering your mind and your consciousness. If we want to grow our 'Zenfulness' muscle and cultivate these models, we need to give it consistent effort so we can grow a healthy habit. We know the 'what' to do, we know the 'how' to do it based on the exercises presented, but our biggest risk is not making the time to do it. To give it thought, reflection and space. You don't need to hurry everything and have mastered the 11 models in one month. In fact, that is probably a ticket to overload and burnout. *I am so busy trying to become mindful and in flow that I have an adrenal blowout!* Not a useful approach.

I encourage you to choose a couple of areas to focus on and work organically at a pace that is happy and authentic for you. Training your mind to commit to this daily, weekly or fortnightly is the hurdle to overcome. That is mental mastery. Step back and see things from a higher perspective. Practice the art of observing. In the animal kingdom, eagles are known to have a higher vision. They can see a bird's-eye view and make strategic decisions for food and survival. We must also be able to step back and be 'on' our working life and not always 'in' it. We need to make some effort to stay aware and be mindful. I have coined my own term for this kind of mental mastery: I call it the 'Zenful Self'. When we have a 'Zenful Self' we can cultivate a 'Zenful Business' life. This means we are on track, we reflect regularly, we think about the bigger picture and we work more in our super-conscious state to create alchemy (the art of turning lead into gold).

My wish for you is to have alchemy in your daily life, to thrive and to make a difference. After all, haven't you ever pondered the question of 'Why was I born into this life, at this time, in this country and to these parents and working in this career?'

I ask this question all the time and that is what keeps me connected, in flow and performing at my best. If you step back and make some of these energetic changes to your working life, everything you do becomes so much easier and Zenful.

Enjoy finding your inner Zen.

Debbie Pask

Practical Exercises

Your work starts here. Read through these practical strategies and ideas to master the models that you seek the most improvement in. I have kept the ideas simple and uncluttered (only two suggestions per model) so that you have a starting place. However if you want more inspiration, check out the web links for each model to find further strategies to take you deeper into your practice. I have many more ideas and tools to share that literally won't squeeze into this book.

Model 1: Yin and Yang Exercises

Observation

Look at people around you and notice who is more Yang oriented (structured and active) and who is more Yin (creative and intuitive) oriented at work? Take time to really observe how they operate and where they could improve in regards to balance. What great qualities does the Yin person have that you could adopt? What great qualities does the Yang person have?

Does anyone you work with have a good balance of both that could be a role model for you?

Next, start observing your own efforts and try to create a better balance. Do you need to be more Yin or more Yang at work? Try some more mindfulness activities if you are too Yang or organise your diary and routine better if you are too Yin. By noticing your own balance of the two states, you will automatically start to adjust.

Relationships Balance

Choose a relationship in your life that you feel might be out of balance. It could be with your partner, children, friends or a work colleague. You can choose a couple of different people to do this experiment with.

Think about how this relationship might be out of balance in Yin and Yang terms. For example:

i) Are you giving too much to the relationship (effort, actions, emotional comfort, and control) and not being supported back? That means you are too Yang and not receiving the Yin energy back to help nourish and fill you up.

OR

ii) Are you taking too much and not giving enough back? Perhaps you rely on a person too much and have created an unhealthy dependency? That means you are too Yin and not active enough in your own self (giving and achieving).

List some of the <u>actions</u> and <u>communications</u> you could employee to balance the scales a bit. For example, you might start asking for what you need more so you practice receiving. Or perhaps you may start initiating more actions to feed the relationship and seek some freedom if you are too dependent.

Watch the other person's reactions to this new behaviour. Some people will love it and some might feel threatened as they are used to either being in control or needing you to prop them up.

Watch your own reactions and energy. You should notice a positive change when the balance starts to occur. If you are very Yang you will start to feel nourished and restored by learning to receive better. If you are very Yin, you will grow your power and confidence by taking actions into your own hands.

The key for both exercises above is to observe and start changing habits to be more balanced. Don't judge your past actions; just be mindful of moving to a better balance where you are able to feel both nourished and powerful.

For more inspiration on Model 1, visit <u>www.zenfulbusinessbook.com/ yinyang</u>

Model 2: Becoming Conscious

Values

Think deeply about what your personal VALUES are. These are not just a list of 'nice to have' values such as honesty or integrity. These are your intrinsic qualities (deal-breakers) that drive your inner spirit. If you clash with your own values, your energy drains away very quickly. In fact, you cannot really function well without them. For example, if freedom is one of your greatest values and yet you are constantly in controlling relationships, I consider that a major clash.

Choose no more than three to five values and think about why they are important to you. Mine are freedom, clarity, passion, mindfulness and nature.

Think about whether work is clashing with any of your values? What might you do about this? Turning your attention inwards and contemplating this is a conscious thought process.

Self Development Plan

Being conscious means that you are committed to developing yourself at a deeply personal level. Devise a plan to really start your self-enquiry journey. Work on the 'you' within. Here are some of my favourite books and study ideas you might want to think about to become more conscious and open in your day-to-day working life. Choose one that resonates with you and begin dabbling ...

Book: *Wisdom of the Enneagram* – Don Riso and Russ Hudson. It's a book and you can do a short course but it really gets into your head and helps you understand how you psychologically and energetically operate. Great personal insight. Great insight into how you work and how others work.

Book: *Anatomy of the Spirit* – Carolyn Myss. Want to link your emotional baggage to body pain? Read this transformational analysis of the mind and body loop and you will never see your body in the same way again.

Book/Study: The Artist's Way - Julia Cameron. Develop your creativity and watch your inner self emerge.

Book/Podcasts: The Untethered Soul - Michael A. Singer. A great book to master your thoughts and your 'inner critic'. You can listen to his podcasts too, but definitely read the book. Take your time.

Online Program/The Conscious Self – this is my own online study program. It consists of 12 modules (best of the best learnings) designed to strengthen your inner self and develop your spiritual and intuitive brain. Includes video lessons, audio meditations and reflection activities. www.rezinate.com.au/conscious-self

For more inspiration on Model 2, visit www.zenfulbusinessbook.com/conscious

Model 3: Your Blueprint

Chase After Your Passions

It is said that your passions are like breadcrumbs to finding the path of your soul purpose. Make it your mission to go and do all of the passionate things you love in life. They give you clues every day to what really makes you tick. If you are a little lost on your Blueprint, just relax, let go and start moving toward the hobbies and activities that make your heart sing. I recently found out that horse riding is the love of my life. Only took me 40 years! Don't stop searching.

You will find that your natural interests and hobbies in life become your work if you are in true alignment. So, what if you are a chief financial officer and love golfing on weekends. Get a CFO role for an international golfing resort. Or if you truly live and breathe it, explore becoming a golfing coach (even part-time). It won't feel like work if you love it.

The more you open your heart, the more you open up opportunities to live out your Blueprint. Follow the joy. **Make a list of all the activities that you TRULY love**. If you cannot think of anything, then delve deeper and think about what you loved to do as a kid. Don't try to create a work scenario out of it right away. Just start the hobby or passion. Of course, if you already have loads of hobbies, then please start looking to integrate one of them into your work.

Seek Career Mentoring and Coaching

But please don't go to a traditional career counsellor that just wants to match your current skill set to some boring structured job role. Find someone you resonate with and someone who has a creative mind to guide you. I am not everyone's cup of tea, but my passion is to help people find their life purpose and translate that into a useful career that is commercially viable. There are processes and techniques to guide you along the way. I have found career Astrology readings to be ground-breaking and deeply inspiring to assist in working out Blueprints for others. I use them myself and they never seem to fail in giving a deep and meaningful perspective. Considering our career is so important to us, seek help to course correct your path. They say that when Apollo 13 travelled to the moon, they were only on course 3% of the time. 97% of the time was course correction.

Start something and course correct as you go; it's an organic approach and very useful. Getting someone to help reflect your dreams back to you is useful.

For a quick and dirty exercise on this ... list your current skill set with your favourite hobby. When you blend them, you have a hybrid – e.g. if you have a sales background and love boating on the weekends, then become a sales director for a yachting company.

For more inspiration on Model 3, visit www.zenfulbusinessbook.com/blueprint

Model 4: Leverage

Take Some Time to Dream

The chapter on leverage probably felt like the most dry and practical in the book (well it did to me), however it is far from that. If we are going to stretch ourselves and dedicate time to a legacy that stretches beyond just ourselves, then it needs to have serious love and meaning to us. A meaningful project is driven by energy beyond the mind and has so much more power behind it than commercial value.

So, if you have not started something (or you have but are questioning it), try reflecting on these questions below to give your ideas and dreams more substance:

Q1. Whether it is work or personal life, what do people come to you for?

E.g. counselling, direction, support, technical advice, handyman stuff, financial advice, great network, health advice, ideas, inspiration, business intelligence, analytical mind, fun, adventure, joy or other? Think this one through carefully because, hidden in your day-to-day identity and how people see you, will be the key to unlocking your leverage.

Q2. What changes do you want to see in your life, industry or professional world? What has a deep meaning for you that would connect you to the ideation and creation of your leverage? Perhaps think about what bothers you in the world where you would like to see changed, transformed or resolved? What turns the lights on at home within you?

Collaborations and Connections

As we move toward a more conscious mindset, we have moved away from the 'individual mindset' to the 'group mindset'. Collaborating and finding like-minded people to work with is becoming more and more important. I have noticed this trend growing since we hit the year 2000 and even more so since 2010. Watching successful events and activities I have noticed that joint ventures and many minds working together are kicking butt over other ones that are individually run. The consciousness of the world is moving away from 'I compete' to 'we collaborate'.

Start connecting with others who have a similar vibrational mindset to you. You can contemplate who these types are and how they think and feel. If you come across them, make the effort to keep them in your circle, as they may just be the next person you collaborate with in your efforts to leave a legacy. Whether they support you or partner your idea, it is important to foster these good relationships and swap ideas for the greater group.

Your Mission? Find your first collaboration or group to start working with. Perhaps you simply start as a supporter first and connect to the people or organisation, as opposed to jumping straight into a formal venture. Don't pressure the outcome. Just start connecting in to something or someone to extend your influence and purpose.

For more inspiration on Model 4, visit www.zenfulbusinessbook.com/leverage

Model 5: Soul Colleagues

Find Your Tribe and Get Inspired!

There is nothing more effective to opening up your energy flow than other people who inspire you. The idea sharing is one thing, but there is also an invisible energy swap that occurs between people in similar tangents or vibration that can be very powerful. If you already work in an organisation that employs these kind of peers, that is very lucky. You get to see these people every day just by turning up to work. Be grateful for and enjoy this gift, making sure you plan ways to harness this energy through joint business projects or shared learnings. Outside work meetings? Shared lunches? Project initiatives to present up the ladder?

If you work for yourself or are not surrounded by a team of inspired awesome people, then I suggest you be proactive and join a group to connect. Where do like minded business people hang out? Is there a business network I can join? A local volunteer project I can be involved with that has meaning? Maybe a lunch every month with old work colleagues that keeps us feeling stronger as a unit? These guys will be people that you rely on to:

a) support any ideas and ventures you might have;
b) collaborate with when the timing is right; and
c) give you feedback on business.

Create a plan to have this regular connection: decide who is on the list and why, then make arrangements to see these people either individually or a group so that you stay connected to the flow of soul colleagues. I suggest you draw a circle diagram and start defining who fits into the inner circle of 'soul' friend and who sits on the second layer of general 'tribe'.

Let go of draining business connections

This is quite a fascinating activity because we often think we need to stay connected with people that we don't like for political reasons or reliance on something we might need. Obviously we don't need to do a community announcement stating that we are no longer friends with 'such and such'. Or call them and tell them they are now on your 'black' list! But what we can do is shortlist WHO in business drains our energy and work on releasing these guys from our regular contact. The universe hates a vacuum and once you clear dead wood out, it will make way for new energies and new business friends to enter.

Steps you can take:

1. Shortlist who in your working life is a drain on your energy, anyone that you don't resonate with. Try listing reasons why so you are super clear on what you don't want to attract and also so you can see why they push your buttons.
2. Make an intention to let them go and do an energy release on the person/s. Choose a symbolic ritual for this – cutting chords, writing their name on a letter and burning it etc. Remember that everything is energy and you need to deal with them on the energetic level first. I have a great meditation for letting go of people and conflict, which is track number 5 on my Zen Business meditation CD.
3. Once the intention is done, I suggest you decide how to physically distance yourself from them. This will come down to your personal communication style. Some people just withdraw and move away bit by bit. Others are more direct in their approach. Step #2 will make it easier regardless, it is just a case of how you can extract yourself from people holding you back. That may mean leaving a job if the whole culture is wrong for you, or shifting departments if that whole team is wrong for you. If it is an individual to let go of and you work with them, then you need to look at your issue with them on a deeper level to let go. Of course, if you run your own business, then let go and rehire with integrity and respect.

For more inspiration on Model 5, visit www.zenfulbusinessbook.com/soulcolleagues

Debbie Pask

Model 6: Get in Touch with Naughty

Plan Your Diary

This requires a bit of organisation to create some freedom and fun. If you are not used to injecting nourishment and downtime into your working hours, then the best option is to colour code your diary. Whether your diary is electronic or paper, I suggest that you plan each week ahead colour coded so you know that you get fun and healthy activities into your schedule. Here's what I do:

Orange – work meetings that cannot move.
Blue – work tasks that are flexible
Pink – for naughty or fun time (as outlined in chapter 6)
Green – for health and fitness (can be within work hours or not – mine is outside of work)

I always start my week mapping out pink and green activities first.

Get a Fun Buddy

This is a simple strategy. It is always better when you bring someone else naughty along for the ride. Work out a buddy (or a few) to connect with when arranging your fun (pink) time. I have buddies I horse ride with in my work day on Friday. I also like to involve a friend if I go to a movie or have a long lunch.

I think social connections make life rich and happy. Collaborate with another funster who can make a commitment to you to mix up your serious working week with some lightness and frivolity. I don't like the motto 'work hard and play hard'. I prefer the idea of 'work passionately and play consistently'.

For more inspiration on Model 6, visit www.zenfulbusinessbook.com/naughty

Model 7: Mindful Moments

Turn Your Goals into Values

Pick a big and important goal that you have set yourself. I suggest it is an ambitious one that really excites you. There is no problem in having this goal, however we don't want it to be some far off goal you have whereby until you get it, you are not connected into the joy or gratitude of it.

So, your mission is to think about the values or essence of what that goal would bring you; e.g. if your goal is to have a thriving and wealthy career or business that brings you in 500K per annum, then perhaps the value underlying the 500K here is freedom (of choice), or peace (security) or adventure (money to travel) or philanthropy (contribution).

So, my question to you is HOW you can (right now) experience the values of freedom, choice, security, peace, adventure and contribution. There are definitely ways you can have these values play out in your life today and once you do this you will love your big goal for sure, but you will love your life even more along the way.

Spend ten minutes a Day Doing Nothing

To be truly mindful we need to remember that just 'being' is never wasteful. This ten minutes per day is hard for anyone to do, regardless of how well trained you think you are. Spending ten minutes (preferably as your first morning ritual) per day staring at the ocean, nature or just sitting and reflecting with no outcome will probably be one of the most important things you master in terms of mindfulness.

Start with just allocating yourself that time and deciding to get comfortable with sitting and pondering. Your mind may wander; attempt to bring it back to an internal focus on you or something inspiring. It can certainly be like a lucid dream. The key parameters are to attempt to keep the focus on you – not work, other people or 'to do' lists.

There is not a fail or succeed outcome here. The only mission is to stick with it until you enjoy that ten minutes of silence you gift yourself. Once you become seasoned at this task, you can steal random ten minute segments anytime during the day and enjoy it. Make a date with yourself every day until you fall in love.

You know you have mastered this when those 10 minutes become the most precious gift in your day – as opposed to an anxious fidgety exercise whereby you count down the minutes to your next task.

For more inspiration on Model 7, visit www.zenfulbusinessbook.com/mindful

Model 8: Intuitive Problem Solving

Yes and No Question Exercise

This exercise helps you to tap into the power of your own body to deliver intelligent choices and actions. Mastering intuition takes time to develop, but this exercise can be practiced regularly to hone your efforts.

Sit down and take some deep breaths in. Start to feel your breath in your body and tune inwards so that you begin to separate yourself from the outside world. You will probably need a calm and quiet space to do this.

Start asking yourself for a 'yes' response in the body. Basically you say the word 'yes' in your mind (and feel good feelings) and see what part of your body activates. It may take some time but eventually you will feel a physical or energetic trigger somewhere that tells you that is 'yes". This is an ongoing project and you will strengthen this over time so don't expect to nail it on the first go. My physical sign for 'yes' is a rush of energy starting in my lower belly and shooting upwards.

Once you have a go at the 'yes' exercise – try the 'no' response. 'No' is saying that word silently in your mind and thinking about things you don't want, then tune in for the signal. Remember that it will take time and start observing in your life when you don't want something and see if you feel your body react a certain way. My 'no' signal is a jerking of my head backwards like my neck is being pulled.

Once you think you are getting it, get a friend to give you five statements that are TRUE and FALSE. You obviously don't know the answers to these statements. Test your 'yes' and 'no' responses to them and see what you come up with. Then ask your friend to verify your intuitive responses.

This body trigger response is similar to the kinesiology model of muscle testing; whereby your body will respond with yes and no answers that lie deep within the unconscious mind. Your body knows the truth often when our own mind cannot get out of the way.

Connect Your Body Into Your Emotions

This exercise helps you to understand and read the signals your body is sending you. Your gut instincts rely on you sensing what is going on in your physical body, so cultivating a better communication system is the key to being more intuitive.

Starting at a basic level, I suggest you try to 'feel' into the emotions stored behind any pain or physical issue in the body. A sprained ankle will hold an emotion behind the ache. A headache will have a stuck emotion creating stagnant energy flow. Any physical disturbance will have a resulting feeling, thought or emotion that coincides with what is happening in your life. Start by asking yourself (inner dialogue) why you have a pain or ache or problem in your body.

Sitting to reflect on that emotion or feeling will deliver you clues to why it manifested and will definitely open up your intuitive senses. Growing this and strengthening it will give you a huge advantage for intuitive problem solving. Use your body as a testing case study. Just like we need to exercise to grow fitter and stronger, so do we need to practice intuitive exercises to hone our 6th sense to the point where it supports us and excels our natural skills.

For more inspiration on Model 8, visit www.zenfulbusinessbook.com/intuitive

Model 9: The Art of Manifestation

Meditation - Do a Short Course

Learning to meditate and visualise (or even lucid dreaming) is important to your career simply for the matter of materialising more quickly the things you desire. Most people I know think that meditation is a boring and 'focus on nothing' practice. Quite the opposite, my preferred meditation is a creative focus and a serious visualisation practice. Finding a meditation class (offline or online) or a meditation guided album is useful for 90% of people who struggle finding the patience to start.

I like methods like 'The Silva Mind Control Method' by Jose Silva or simple guided meditations into landscapes such as my album 'Zen Business'.

Practice Receiving

It sounds very, very simple but it is one of the most powerful methods of manifesting. The universe works on 'energy in' and 'energy out'. Applying this practice in simple everyday life will strengthen and grow your ability to attract abundance, whatever that means for you.

START with small requests. If someone offers to help you or buy you a coffee or shout you lunch, just say yes straight away. Feel the energy of gratitude and appreciation. Ask and allow the universe to deliver more.

NEXT start asking specifically for things you want. They can be small requests from co-workers, partners or friends. Later on you may start asking for bigger things, a payrise or more business from people if you run your own show or are in sales.

PRACTICE daily for small simple things and monthly for larger requests. They might take time to manifest, so give the universal source field energy and room to pay out on your request. As soon as you begin to fear or doubt the viability of your request, the energy of manifestation slows or stops in response to this opposing feeling.

Ask energetically (state your intention and meditate on it) and physically (follow up with asking and get comfortable with receiving help that doesn't come from yourself). Driving outcomes is wonderful – but trying to control all of them is like running with one leg. Get smart and receive at least 50% of the time.

For more inspiration on Model 9, visit www.zenfulbusinessbook.com/manifesting

Model 10: Shadow Work

Define Your Limiting Beliefs at Work

Limiting beliefs can hold us back from feeling happy and confident at work. They can be very hidden too so most of us don't really know they exist, but feel the effects of what isn't working in our life. Have a go at soul searching and identifying some limiting beliefs you might have that you would like to undo ... examples are:

I am disorganised and never seem to get on top of my workload;
I am always bullied by my co-workers;
I don't trust people to truly help me manage or support my business or role;
I can never get on top of my workload;
I never make enough sales and people around me seem to do it easily;
I get nervous or stressed about presenting in front of others;
Why am I not making as much money as xx person?;
I am not growing my career or business as quickly as I would like;
I hate any type of criticism – from clients or co-workers;
Management never value me enough or I get passed over for promotions;
I am always pulling up the slack and get the raw end of the deal;
I am too stressed and don't have enough work/life balance;
I get angry with people that don't perform or see my way of thinking;
I am constantly underpaid;
You have to work really hard (or be stressed) to make good money *(I hate this one the most.)*

Obviously there are ways of working on limiting beliefs with various mind techniques such as Psych-K (Bruce Lipton is a big fan of this), NLP and a host of others. However, you might be surprised what your conscious mind can do given the focus and latest science on brain neuroplasticity*.

Once you list what you think your limiting beliefs are - simply pay attention in real life to see where they arise and surface at work. There is no pressure to kill these beliefs! Just watch them because attention alone is often what starts to create the shift. Whether you meet the right person to help you move past them or they unravel simply because you give it focused attention and your neural pathways respond. Maybe it attracts you to the right book to help you out. Don't rush to the outcome – just start observing.

List Someone Who Really Pushes Your Buttons

This is a challenging exercise and very simple:

1. Write down the name of someone who gets under your skin. Someone who has qualities you dislike and really explore and explain those qualities. Why don't you like that part of them and summarise it in a few words what is the most annoying. Got it off your chest? Right, now do step 2.
2. Now that you have listed that person's qualities, it is time to see **where in yourself** you see those same qualities. This can be quite confronting but very useful. Where are you fearful about displaying these qualities or judging yourself on? Anything that really pushes your buttons will show up on some level (or you fear they will show up) within yourself.

This exercise is a great way of identifying your own shadows and working on them. People will usually only push your buttons when there is a conflict within you.

For more inspiration on Model 10, visit www.zenfulbusinessbook.com/shadow

Model 11: Heart Entrainment

Nature Blessing

Sandra Ingerman in her book 'Awakening to the Spirit World talks about how we can communicate with nature via our heart centre. As we have discussed. The heart is a very intelligent source of energy with a power of its own. She discusses the idea that we can deliver a blessing to nature and in return, it delivers us back a kinetic energy blessing. It is kind of like an exchange or greeting that says 'I honour you'.

Next time you are out in nature, choose a flower or tree and without words, send a communication from your heart to say 'you are beautiful' and wait for the return gesture. You may think this sounds like a total hippy thing to do, but if you read any kind of research on plants, science has proven they respond to our energy. Read The Secret Life of Plants by Tompkins and Bird if you want more proof. Nature is alive and operates at a much lighter and clearer vibration, unhampered by the emotional complexities of the human brain. Swapping some energy with a tree is highly therapeutic for you; but probably not the tree!

This is a great start to entraining and connecting your heart to other living beings that have such a pure and safe energy response.

Eulogy – Write to Self

This is a powerful exercise to cut through any wasted notions of how you want to live your life. It helps define and focus your attention on what is truly important to you on a heart level.

When you have some peace and space, sit down and write out your own eulogy that you would want read out at your funeral. What would you want someone to say about you? What you did in life? How you lived your life? What kind of contribution and legacy you left? What you meant to friends and family and co-workers? What adventures you undertook and what values you held dearly?

This summary of your life gives you an end point and a very dynamic and clear picture for how you need to connect to your life and the meaning you want your work, your life, your health and your relationships to have.

Once you write this and take time to refine and digest, it needs to bring a tear to your eye and strong emotions in your heart. That is when you know you have heart and mind entrainment with your future plans. Think about how unstoppable you will be once you combine the power of your heart and mind together.

For more inspiration on Model 11, visit www.zenfulbusinessbook.com/heart

Bibliography

Riso, Don and Hudson, Russ, *Wisdom of the Enneagram* (UK, Pan, 1995)

Myss, Caroline, *Anatomy of the Spirit* (Australia, Bantam, 1997)

Cameron, Julia, *The Artist's Way (Canada, Sounds True, 2010)*

Tompkins, Peter and Bird, Christopher, *The Secret Life of Plants (United States, Harper & Row, 1973)*

Silva, Hose *The Silva Mind Control Method* (New York, Pocket Books, 1977)

Ingerman, Sandra and Wesselman, Hank *Awakening to the Spirit World* (Colorado, Sounds True, 2010)

Chisolm, Don, *Have you got the guts to be healthy? (Australia, Book Pal)*

Singer, Michael A, *Untethered Soul* (CA, New Harbinger Publications, 2007)

Hawkins, David R, *Power vs Force (US, Hay House 1995)*

Braden, Gregg, *The Spontaneous Healing of Belief,* (California, Hay House, 2008)

Lipton, Dr Bruce, *The Biology of Belief* (United States, Hay House, 2008)

Talbot, Michael, *The Holographic Universe,* (Great Britain, Harper Collins, 1991)

Harris, Russ, *The Happiness Trap* (Place?? Exisle Publising, 2013)

Debbie Pask

Ober, Clinton and Zucker, Martin, *Earthing; The Most Important Health Discovery Ever* (US, Basic Health Publications 2010).

Loehr, Jim and Schwartz, Tony, *Harvard Business Review: The Making of a Corporate Athlete 2001*

Novak,Jokovic, *Serve to Win*, Random House, 2013

Statham, Bill, *The Chemical Maze*, possibility.com 2001

Chisholm, Don, *Have you got the guts to be really healthy?* Bookpal

Sauer, Jost. *Higher and Higher; from drugs and destruction to health and happiness* Australia, Allen & Unwin, 2006)

Anodea, Judith, *Wheels of Life Minnesota 1987 Llewellyn Publications*

Printed in the United States
By Bookmasters